British Working-Class Fiction

Also available from Bloomsbury

The 1990s: A Decade of Contemporary British Fiction
edited by Nick Hubble, Philip Tew and Leigh Wilson

The 2000s: A Decade of Contemporary British Fiction
edited by Nick Bentley, Nick Hubble and Leigh Wilson

British Working-Class Fiction

Narratives of Refusal and the Struggle Against Work

Roberto del Valle Alcalá

Bloomsbury Academic
An imprint of Bloomsbury Publishing Plc

B L O O M S B U R Y
LONDON · OXFORD · NEW YORK · NEW DELHI · SYDNEY

Bloomsbury Academic
An imprint of Bloomsbury Publishing Plc

50 Bedford Square	1385 Broadway
London	New York
WC1B 3DP	NY 10018
UK	USA

www.bloomsbury.com

BLOOMSBURY and the Diana logo are trademarks of Bloomsbury Publishing Plc

First published 2016
Paperback edition first published 2017

© Roberto del Valle Alcalá, 2016

Roberto del Valle Alcalá has asserted his right under the Copyright, Designs and Patents Act, 1988, to be identified as Author of this work.

All rights reserved. No part of this publication may be reproduced or transmitted in any form or by any means, electronic or mechanical, including photocopying, recording, or any information storage or retrieval system, without prior permission in writing from the publishers.

No responsibility for loss caused to any individual or organization acting on or refraining from action as a result of the material in this publication can be accepted by Bloomsbury or the author.

British Library Cataloguing-in-Publication Data
A catalogue record for this book is available from the British Library.

ISBN: HB: 978-1-4742-7374-9
PB: 978-1-3500-4459-3
ePDF: 978-1-4742-7376-3
ePub: 978-1-4742-7375-6

Library of Congress Cataloging-in-Publication Data
A catalog record for this book is available from the Library of Congress.

Typeset by RefineCatch Limited, Bungay, Suffolk

Para Sol

We will say that THE *plane of immanence is, at the same time, that which must be thought and that which cannot be thought. It is the nonthought within thought. It is the base of all planes, immanent to every thinkable plane that does not succeed in thinking it. It is the most intimate and yet the absolute outside – an outside more distant than any external world because it is an inside deeper than any internal world.*
                          Gilles Deleuze and Félix Guattari, *What is Philosophy?*

[T]he thought of the outside is a thought of resistance.
                                            Gilles Deleuze, *Foucault*

Contents

Acknowledgements — viii

1 Introduction: British Working-Class Fiction and the Struggle Against Work — 1

2 Between Capitalist Subsumption and Proletarian Independence: Alan Sillitoe, David Storey and the Post-War Working Class — 11
  2.1 From consensus to antagonism, or, the post-war rebirth of subjectivity — 11
  2.2 From the factory to the social: Alan Sillitoe's proletarian subjects — 19
  2.3 Capitalist subjectivation in David Storey's *This Sporting Life* — 36

3 Reproductive Work and Proletarian Resistance in Transition: Nell Dunn and Pat Barker — 49
  3.1 Desire and the labour of subjectivity: On Nell Dunn's proletarian women — 49
  3.2 Reproduction in revolt: Pat Barker's *Union Street* — 63
  3.3 Prostitution, death and the subversion of life in *Blow Your House Down* — 76

4 Beyond Civil Society: Proletarian Exodus in James Kelman and Irvine Welsh — 87
  4.1 The collapse of measure: Postmodern abstraction and proletarian flight in James Kelman — 88
  4.2 Beyond civil society: On Irvine Welsh's *Skagboys* — 110

5 Work in Crisis: Precarious Subversions in Monica Ali and Joanna Kavenna — 133
  5.1 Untamed bodies, fleeing minds: Monica Ali's *In the Kitchen* — 135
  5.2 'Madness, the absence of work': On Joanna Kavenna's *Inglorious* — 157

6 Conclusion — 171

Bibliography — 179
Index — 187

Acknowledgements

My first debt is to the Department of English at Uppsala University, for allowing me the time and resources to develop this project. During my time here as a postdoctoral researcher I have encountered intellectual stimulus and personal encouragement second to none. I would particularly like to thank Robert Appelbaum for his unfailing support and generosity. Danuta Fjellestad, David Watson, Michael Boyden, Ashleigh Harris, Leonard Driscoll, Kristen Rau, Ryan Palmer, Stuart Robertson and all of the other regular participants at our work in progress seminars, offered valuable comments on various parts of the manuscript and provided me with an intellectual community when it was most needed.

Niamh, Tove, Gregory, Michael, Åke and Christer also made the non-academic part of Uppsala life feel more like home.

My colleagues at the Department of Modern Philology at the University of Alcalá allowed me a generous amount of research time during which this project began to take shape.

I am also grateful to the Spanish Association for English and American Studies (AEDEAN), and in particular its Critical Theory panel, for valuable feedback over the years.

At Bloomsbury Academic, I wish to thank its helpful staff, as well as the three referees who commented on the project, for their enthusiastic encouragement.

My parents, Vicente and Geni, and brother, Guillermo, cheered me on from afar, as did Pedro, Susana and Antonio. Jaime, Jara, Ana and Damián were among those who provided me with a sense of temporary freedom from work back in Spain. *Gracias a todos*.

And of course, none of this would have happened anyway had I not crossed paths, many years ago, with María Lozano and David Musselwhite.

Finally, Sol Juárez, resistant worker *extraordinaire*, supplied the infinite love without which this task would never have been accomplished. This book is for her.

*

Parts of Chapter 2 have appeared in *Genre* 48: 3, 2015, and parts of Chapter 3 in *Lit: Literature Interpretation Theory* 26: 3, 2015. I wish to thank the editors and publishers of these journals for permission to reprint, as well as their reviewers for important feedback.

1

Introduction

British Working-Class Fiction and the Struggle Against Work

Critical analyses of the literary representation of work under capitalism have been traditionally aligned, especially in Britain, with a socially transformative aspiration. The politically informed assumption that literature is directly involved in the construction and processing of shared social experience has led to the consolidation of a critical practice that finds, in the textually mediated treatment of exploitation, a fundamental resource for denunciation, contestation, and, ultimately, for the achievement of effective social change.[1] Marxism remains the principal master narrative informing this analytical practice, which makes thinking about the representation of work in literature virtually indissociable from the promotion of a class perspective. Reduced to a basic schematism, Marxism is nothing but the reordering of social relations

---

[1] It is reasonable to argue that the contemporary critical standard on labour and working-class writing in Britain was set by Raymond Williams. His suggestive analyses of the experiential formation of culture were linked, from the beginning, to a radical awareness of the materiality of capitalist productive relations and to an overtly militant drive towards the democratization and reconfiguration of culture itself (including literary writing) as a 'common' undertaking. Albeit variously modulated by its articulation with a range of theories, the left-culturalist imprint of the critical project initiated by Williams can be felt in a majority of contemporary accounts and studies of working-class literature in Britain. Williams' own major statements on this kind of writing can be found in, among others, *Culture and Society* (London: Hogarth Press, 1958), *Politics and Letters* (London: New Left Books, 1979), *Writing in Society* (London: Verso, 1983) and *Culture and Materialism* (London: Verso, 2005). Some examples of the enduring vitality of this critical perspective in contemporary analyses of working-class writing would include Gary Day, *Class* (London: Routledge, 2001), Ian Haywood, *Working-Class Fiction from Chartism to Trainspotting* (Tavistock: Northcote House, 1997), H. Gustav Klaus and Stephen Knight (eds), *British Industrial Fictions* (Cardiff: University of Wales Press, 2000), John Kirk, *The British Working Class in the Twentieth Century* (Cardiff: University of Wales Press, 2003) and *Class, Culture and Social Change: On the Trail of the Working Class* (Basingstoke: Palgrave, 2007), Morag Shiach, *Modernism, Labour and Selfhood in British Literature and Culture, 1890–1930* (Cambridge: Cambridge University Press, 2004) and Alan Sinfield, *Literature, Politics and Culture in Postwar Britain* (London: Continuum, 2007), among others.

around the divisive and antagonistic category of wage labour. This implies that work under capitalism is not a natural extension of human creative capacities, but the result of a social operation whereby the latter are transformed into a marketable commodity – labour power. For all the naturalizing efforts made by capitalist ideology, the formative scene of capitalist work is a violent one, premised on the forcible 'transubstantiation' of a nonspecific potential quality (the capacity to create) into a highly specific and appropriable quantity (labour power).[2]

It is nevertheless surprising that, despite the central position accorded by Marxist theory to this operation, a majority of Marxist-influenced analyses of the literary representation of work have tended to focus more on the derivative social aspects of the work relation. The emphasis on class as social context and cultural formation (rather than as the central figure of a power relation) characteristic of these strands of criticism has often prevented the clear visualization of the latent or explicit antagonisms underpinning capitalist society.[3] In this sense, a critical discourse avowedly committed to the radical questioning of capitalism often runs the risk of leaving the nucleus of the capitalist operation unquestioned. The aim of this book is to contest this tendency and to bring the antagonistic logic rehearsed by the Marxist analysis of work as a foundational problem of capitalist society (as a basic operation of power designed to shape society according to its value-creating interests) back to the central stage of literary critical concerns. My intention is not to displace the prevalent critical focus on class, but to place it in the semantic and political

---

[2] I should note at the outset that the distinction frequently made in philosophical discourse between 'work' and 'labour' is not relevant to the aims of this project. For Hannah Arendt, this distinction is based on an anthropological differentiation between two paradigmatic tasks of the human, the activity that preserves and reproduces life (and which the polysemy of the English word 'labour', with its reference to the strictly biological activity of giving birth, neatly underscores) on the one hand, and the artificial creation of objects on which the modern logic of production is based, on the other. In Arendt's analysis, both labour and work are opposed to action, on which properly political life is predicated. This distinction, although philosophically significant, is hardly useful in a critical context that seeks to analyse the specific shifts affecting capitalism since the post-war period, when – as we will see – the boundaries between objective and subjective production, between *homo faber* and *homo laborans*, all but disappear completely. See Hannah Arendt, *The Human Condition* (Chicago: University of Chicago Press, 1958).

[3] This is particularly true in the case of criticism produced over the last thirty years or so, in which a culturalist agenda sometimes narrowly concerned with the discursive proliferation of identities (sexual, racial and national, in addition to the strictly class-based ones) has detracted from a profound understanding of the materiality of productive relations in the context of an increasingly globalized – and as I will argue, *socialized* – economy.

context of the capitalist modulation of work as an enforced, and consequently antagonistic, relation. I will do this by following a relatively marginal lineage of Marxist theory that has arguably done more than most to advance the understanding of work under capitalism and to problematize its relation to class.

So-called Autonomist Marxism insists that the traditional vindication of labour by the working-class movement is symptomatic of its co-optation by a socially mature form of capitalism. The basic thrust of its argument suggests that the adoption of an identity linked to the enforced logic of capitalist work cannot possibly result in a truly revolutionary position. The exploitative regime imposed by capital upon human ability – in other words, the forcible operation that founds the class relation – can only be subverted if its central operator, work, becomes the target of every resistant move. Those cultural forms, including literary texts, that express a basic dissatisfaction with the normalized regime of exploitation through labour cannot be unproblematically subsumed within the latter's identity claims. For to offer a critical evaluation of the relative deprivation or subordination of a social form of life whose defining experience is work and not to directly confront work as a structural problem is to miss the material specificity of the analysed reality. Following the central emphases of Autonomist Marxist theory (and some of its post-Marxist epigones), I want to argue in this book that work is a broad analytical and ontological category that extends beyond its narrow definition as waged – and primarily industrial – labour. And in order to do so, I would like to emphasize the significance of my historical focus and the sense in which the theoretical references on which I will draw speak directly to the latter.

This book is first and foremost an engagement with fiction written in Britain since the 1950s, and thus a commentary on a particular series of fictional responses to the development of capitalism over the last sixty years. The outstanding features of this development – I will argue – can be easily mapped onto the conceptual grid proposed by thinkers, such as Mario Tronti and Antonio Negri, among others, who have read this history as simultaneously a history of the expansion of work in capitalist society and of the generation of resistant responses. We will see – as the specifics of this theory are explored in succeeding chapters – how the expansiveness of work in post-war and contemporary capitalism concerns not only the proliferation of activities that can be directly traced to the formative scene of capitalism as we have described it above (namely, the aforementioned 'transubstantiation' of human ability into labour power), but also the inclusion of other ambits of experience and social life which had not been traditionally regarded as work. Furthermore, we will see how this inclusive dynamic not only does not abolish class antagonism as its consequence, but indeed builds upon it, turning it into an equally ubiquitous and proliferating dimension of this phase of capitalist development.

If we accept that the historical logic of capitalist work undergoes a significant transformation in this period, we may also need to accept that the terms of definition and the strategies of representation of work rehearsed by the relevant literature are equally subject to change in relation to pre-existing modes and models. There is a sense in which this historical and aesthetic break would correspond to the canonical distinction between the modern and the postmodern. Although from a strictly formal point of view it is difficult to sustain this differentiating gesture, as working-class literary history has traditionally been complicated by a programmatic resistance to the more obvious forms of aesthetic modernism (resulting in an often backward reliance on more traditional paradigms of realism),[4] it can be argued that the status of its object of representation – work – warrants a distinction that also concerns its political effects. Thus, the heyday of proletarian writing, the 1920s and 1930s, saw an abundance of fictional productions concerned with the possibility of transcending capitalist labour, of attaining a revolutionary 'beyond' that would then resolve the structural injustice embodied in work, but also in its symmetrical (and thus equally capitalist) negation – unemployment.[5] In this sense, the more militant

---

[4] According to Williams, traditional working-class realism was often constrained by a debilitating regionalism: 'It is extremely sad to read proletarian novels which are totally authentic and have something of the breadth of interest of 19th-century bourgeois realism, yet to feel at the end that they are profoundly regional in the sense that the very forces which operate from outside on the formation and destiny of the class itself, which make for suffering and exploitation, cannot be represented within them', *Politics and Letters*, 267. See also, *Writing in Society*, 229–56. For a suggestive discussion of more experimental forms of working-class writing that effectively deviate from the realist paradigm, see Ken Worpole, *Dockers and Detectives* (London: Verso, 1983) and John Fordham, *James Hanley: Modernism and the Working Class* (Cardiff: University of Wales Press, 2001).

[5] This is perhaps the recognized generic staple of socialist realism in the Soviet mould, but also, more widely, of the prevalent definition of the proletariat (and its attendant forms of cultural expression) in the aftermath of the 1917 Revolution as the historical force called upon to *transcend* the capitalist

writing of this period rested on a clear specification of the social forms and circumstances of exploitation, which then enabled it to mobilize its own textuality as a weapon in the struggle. From this perspective, the contrast with post-war, especially post-1950s, writing about work is sharp. What increasingly becomes apparent in the later period is that the new social quality of work exhausts the possibility of transcendence. This is not to say that the revolution has been discarded as an aspiration (or even less, as we will see in the second chapter, that this is a 'post-ideological' era), but that the structural reorganization of post-war capitalism imposes work as an inescapable and proliferating milieu within which both exploitation and subversion (including, conceivably, those events of rupture that will merit the label 'revolutionary') will take place.

This would therefore suggest that older paradigms of historical modelling and interpretation, including those traditional forms of Hegelian Marxism premised on a dialectical logic of supersession/cancellation (*Aufhebung*) and teleology, should now give way to an immanent analytic of power without any transcendent getaways. What the historical and textual conditions of these literary interventions announce is an immediate imbrication of the forces in struggle. As the shifting nature of post-war labour becomes increasingly evident, and as the spaces of mediation through which the capitalist totality had hitherto been organized give way to new forms of exploitative immediacy and directly accessible abstraction, the social re-emerges as a saturated field of immanent relations in which capitalist exploitation no longer needs to hide behind ideological veils.

Post-1950s working fiction will thus exhibit a quality of immediacy. The dynamics of exploitation and resistance will appear inscribed within an ontological continuum without gaps, fissures, or hidden loopholes, in which the different subject positions will presuppose one another without exhausting

present. In Britain, this programmatic definition – although not strictly assimilable to the generic strictures of socialist realism – can be said to have been most fully realized in the novels of writers such as Lewis Grassic Gibbon, Harold Heslop and Lewis Jones. See David Bell, *Ardent Propaganda: Miners' Novels and Class Conflict 1929–1939* (Umeå: Umeå University, 1995), Andy Croft, *Red Letter Days: British Fiction in the 1930s* (London: Lawrence and Wishart, 1990) and Roberto del Valle Alcalá, 'Rising with One's Community: Socialist Theory and *Bildungsroman* in Lewis Jones', *Cultura, Lenguaje y Representación*, 7, 2009, 141–56. For a classic discussion of the proletarian novel in 1930s Britain, see Carole Snee, 'Working-Class Literature or Proletarian Writing?', in Jon Clark, Margot Heinemann, David Margolies and Carole Snee (eds), *Culture and Crisis in Britain in the 30s* (London: Lawrence and Wishart, 1979), 165–91.

their antagonistic nature. Indeed, whatever resistance we will encounter will be strictly immanent, strictly internal to the ontological plane or horizon of capital's unfolding. In other words, the 'beyond' – or better, the 'outside' that the struggle against work permanently points to – will have to be found, paradoxically, *within* the immediacy of capitalist relations, in a saturated social landscape. This suggests that, in this historical and textual context, the clash of opposites that characterizes the class struggle involves a dynamic link between exploitation and resistance, a starting position in which the two are united around and through the category of work. In other words, as work begins to command the entire horizon of social relations, as every space of mediation is abolished by the movement of capital, the antagonistic profile of the exploited becomes enhanced and radicalized. Proletarian subjectivity is thus paradoxically rediscovered, as it were, in the midst of capitalist sociality, developing into an increasingly non-compliant and indomitable figure. Conversely, the growth of what appears to be a definitive form of proletarian autonomy by no means arrests the process of capitalist expansion; on the contrary, it leads to a general increase of its valorizing and extractive power.

This dialectic without *Aufhebung* may seem like a dead-end. Propelled by a logic of immanent implication and reinforcement, it may appear as if the antagonistic relation between capital and the workers offers no real possibility of rupture, but rather a horizon of homeostatic fusion threatening an eventual neutralization of the struggle. However, the texts I will read all manage to circumvent this pitfall by pointing a 'subterranean' way forward, a pathway of 'absolute immanence', of immanence beyond immanence, as it were, that pushes the strategic deadlock of struggling subjectivities to its limit. The selection of primary texts in this book seeks to reflect a specific historical sequence leading from the disclosure of work as a concrete social relation projecting itself out of the factory (and into a plurality of institutional spaces), to its reconfiguration as so many instances and forms of diffuse, immaterial and biopolitical exploitation. Thus, the authors and texts studied below offer a particularly vocal and emphatic response to the transformations of capitalism and the new forms of social resistance that marked the passage from modernity to postmodernity. Far from being the only works (in this period and tradition) registering and engaging with these structural shifts, they are, nevertheless, in a privileged position to map this series of historical mutations.[6]

In the reconstruction of this historical sequence, we will see that the consolidation of postmodern capital's abstract tendencies, its radical dismantling of previous productive temporalities leads to a complete colonization of social life. From the commanding position of the Fordist factory in the productive universe of post-war capitalism, through its crisis in the 1960s and 1970s, to its relentless replacement by a diffuse and increasingly complex network of exploitative relationships across society ever since, all the texts examined in this book register a dramatic sequence of transformations in the logic of work and in the possibilities of its rejection by the working class. After an initial moment of proletarian self-valorization – of apparent 'independence' of the working class from its subordination to/through work – we will observe that the figure of the worker is fully co-opted, and sometimes violently suppressed, by capitalist subjectivity (that is, by the various subjective forms adopted by capital and its relational logic, including that of an adaptable, pro-systemic, working-class subjectivity). This, however, does not exhaust proletarian resistance, but rather determines a new ontological trajectory, a new modality of being for the latter. Thus, rather than revert to a fully-fledged subjective position – to a self-valorizing affirmation of autonomous subjectivity as the fulcrum of their resistant strategy against work – the working figures in these novels set out to undo their subjectivity and explore forms of being that may offer an escape route or line of flight from the compulsory logics of capitalist production (beginning with the production of capitalist subjectivity itself). Following a line of intensification, these oppositional subjects will therefore first grow in affirmative capacity, in potentiality and capacity to do, only to end up embracing a logic of negativity and 'impotentiality',[7] of radical passivity and capacity to *not do*, to abstain – either militantly or evasively, joyfully or traumatically – from the socially structured injunctions of capitalist work.

Echoing a number of theories about 'exodus' and 'flight', this book will chart the different routes followed by resistance in the context of post-war capitalism's

---

[6] I have therefore chosen texts and authors that can not only be considered 'canonical' examples of post-war working-class literature, but that effectively situate work, and the changing quality of capitalist relations, as their primary objects of representation.

[7] In the sense suggested by Giorgio Agamben. See, for example, *L'uso dei corpi: Homo Sacer, IV, 2* (Vicenza: Neri Pozza Editore, 2014), 88–96, as well as Chapter 4 below.

socialization. As already noted, it will pay special attention to the concept of subjectivity, its shifts and mutations in this historical process, as well as its possibilities and limitations. Ultimately, the problematic I will engage with in this book concerns the oppositional resources that can be found *within* (or perhaps *beneath*) the subject once the latter can only be constructed in a fully capitalist manner.

As already noted, the following chapters trace a precise historical sequence. Beginning with the opposition to the post-war discourses of consensus articulated by Alan Sillitoe in his working-class narratives of the late 1950s, I will examine the terms in which the antagonistic re-enactment of proletarian subjectivity could be envisaged in the midst of an accelerating process of capitalist socialization (complete with new consumerist trends and full employment). I will specifically focus on the limitations of the industrial perspective; that is, on the growing insufficiency, in this unfolding historical context, of identifying work with the factory, and struggle against the latter with industrial conflict. I will thus argue that the transition from *Saturday Night and Sunday Morning* to 'The Loneliness of the Long Distance Runner' signals a fundamental shift in the understanding of the organization and distribution of capitalist power in the so-called 'affluent society' of the 1950s and 1960s, as well as of actually existing forms of class resistance and opposition.

I will then consider the expansive and disarticulating effects of capitalist socialization in the context of David Storey's *This Sporting Life*. In what virtually reads as an inverted image of Sillitoe's explorations of proletarian empowerment, Storey's novel reconstructs the subject-like phenomenality of capital as it becomes detached from the forms of mediation associated with industrial labour (especially in its Fordist incarnation). A new logic of money will be uncovered here announcing a clean break with the traditional process of capitalist valorization. We will also see that the subjectivation of capital (that is, its entry into the battlefield of resurgent post-war antagonisms *as subject*) will lead to new levels of violence and encroachment upon the 'private' realms of life.

Chapter 3 will fully explore this latter point in the context of Nell Dunn's and Pat Barker's fictions about working-class women in the 1960s and 1970s. I will argue that the thematization of female desire and lived experience in these novels can no longer be written off as a secondary or complementary dimension of the representation of capitalist work in the post-war period. By shifting the focus from 'production' to 'reproduction' (that is, from the factory to a domestic space that is much more than mere background to the latter), the entire social cycle of value generation and accumulation is problematized, and the traditional association between the former and effective class struggle, questioned. As we will see, what Dunn and Barker posit is the centrality of life (understood as the desires, affects and corporeal aspects that make up the 'intimate' realm of the subject) to advanced capitalism, and, consequently, the *biopolitical* quality that any form of resistance conducted within this ambit will inevitably acquire from now on.

In turning to the formally experimental and demotic fictions of James Kelman and Irvine Welsh in Chapter 4, a parallel tendency in the development of post-war capitalism (which the early novels of Sillitoe and Storey were beginning to make out) will become fully apparent. The collapsing distinctions between work and non-work (and/or between production and reproduction) will be further seen as reinforcing the sense of a generalized abstraction in society, of a perceived correlation between the 'abstract' logic of money and the lived experience of the working subject. Moreover, the institutional sphere will be dramatically unmasked in these texts as a necessary extension of capital's extractive dynamics. The State will thus emerge as an integral element of exploitation seeking to reduce working-class forms of life either to mere appendices of a co-opted sociality or to equally subordinate, but even more dramatically exposed, expressions of 'bare life'.

Going against the grain of these oppressive incursions into the lived textures of work, we will encounter properly proletarian gestures of subversion and overcoming of the latter (in other words, genuine moments of refusal of work *and* of its institutional architecture) in a series of deviations or *détournements* from constituted subjectivity. I will thus analyse the resistant possibilities pulsing within a number of paradoxical and even traumatic forms of experience, including social marginality and madness. In the final chapter, I will argue that the recent context of economic crisis has given rise to fictional engagements with neoliberalism in which the subjective nature of capitalist growth and expansion is confronted with an internal boundary. Thus the old revolutionary aspiration to exit the sphere of capitalist labour is materialized as the endlessly proliferating subjectivities on which the latter rests become unworked or are rendered inoperative. In other words, the limit to capitalist appropriation, to the ubiquitous socialization of work in this period, lies within those same strategies that had first enabled its expansion. In this case, more than ever before, the revolution emerges as an immanent possibility.

2

Between Capitalist Subsumption and Proletarian Independence

Alan Sillitoe, David Storey and the Post-War Working Class

2.1 From consensus to antagonism, or, the post-war rebirth of subjectivity

British social and political discourse in the 1950s was quite adept at formulations that tended to efface the antagonisms of capitalist society. In one of its classic statements, Anthony Crosland's *The Future of Socialism*, the structural dissymmetry of the class relation was wishfully resolved through the invocation of an alleged transfer of economic power from the owners to the managers of the means of production. In the post-war period, Crosland argued, 'economic decisions in the basic sector have passed out of the hands of the capitalist class into the hands of a new and largely autonomous class of public industrial managers'.[1]

According to this view, the growth of management had resulted both in the public limitation of private capitalist power and in the reconfiguration of the State as an eminently technocratic – and hence, ideologically neutral – apparatus of governance. This structural development of post-war capitalism found its faithful programmatic reflection in the Labour and Conservative Parties' shared acceptance of a basic and unquestionable set of policy principles devised to root out the sources of economic uncertainty that had been prevalent in the 1930s. These principles, collectively known as the 'post-war consensus', had effectively made traditional definitions of socialism, based

---

[1] Anthony Crosland, *The Future of Socialism* (London: Constable, 2006), 12–13.

on the direct participation of the State in productive ownership, largely irrelevant.

This revisionist picture of the post-war period was further enhanced by the absence of overt class conflict, to such an extent that even the category of class itself was called into question. The classic conceptualization of this fading of class under the pressures of the new economic settlement was the so-called 'embourgeoisement' thesis. According to its proponents, the growing affluence of consistently better-paid workers had led (via their wholehearted embrace of emergent and increasingly entrenched patterns of consumption) to a tendential merger with the middle classes, which in turn announced a rightward drift in their politics.[2] Although this thesis was soon disproved by sociological observation – most notably, by the pioneering work of David Lockwood and John Goldthorpe[3] – the intuition that decreasing conflictuality entailed a dissolution of the class structure (and of its extant identity markers) persisted in a variety of political and intellectual discourses.[4]

The revisionist argument set out by Crosland and developed by various complementary formulations, such as the said embourgeoisement thesis, had inevitably come under leftist fire from an early date. In particular, New Left intellectuals like Raymond Williams warned against the dangers of projecting a falsified image of social egalitarianism based on abstract political calculations. Despite structural changes in the distribution of income, in macroeconomic policy, and in the dispensation of welfare, British society remained fractured – it was argued – along traditional class lines with respect to effective democratic participation. Political and cultural, as well as economic, institutions continued to express, in this supposedly consensual period, the inequalities and power hierarchies which had plagued earlier phases of Britain's history. According to Williams, it was necessary for socialists to address the 'whole way of life' of the nation and thus to reassert the priority of full democratic

---

[2] See John Westergaard, 'The Withering Away of Class: A Contemporary Myth', in *Towards Socialism* (London: Fontana/New Left Review, 1965).

[3] See John H. Goldthorpe, David Lockwood, Frank Bechhofer and Jennifer Platt, *The Affluent Worker in the Class Structure* (Cambridge: Cambridge University Press, 1969).

[4] Thus, the notion that affluence and consumerism fundamentally altered (much for the worse) the quality of working-class experience was deeply buried in the otherwise path-breaking analyses of Richard Hoggart's *The Uses of Literacy* (London: Chatto and Windus, 1957). As Francis Mulhern has noted, 'the story it tells is of decline already far gone and perhaps unarrestable', *Culture/Metaculture* (London: Routledge, 2000), 58.

participation in all the different areas of society. The aim was to found the emergent rationality of advanced industrialization on a progressive and integrative (rather than merely organic and backward) notion of 'community'.[5] Democratic integration – and with it, an intensified smoothing-over of class antagonisms – was thus the fundamental emphasis of early New Left politics in the late 1950s and early 1960s. As Williams symptomatically put it in *The Long Revolution*:

> In an industrial economy, social production will either be owned or controlled by the whole society, or by a part of it which then employs the rest. The decision between these alternatives is the critical decision about class, and if we are serious about ending the class system we must clear away the survivals, the irrelevancies, and the confusion of other kinds of distinction, until we see the hard economic center which finally sustains them. With that basic inequality isolated we could stop the irrelevant discussion of class, of which most of us are truly sick and tired, and let through the more interesting discussion of human differences, between real people and real communities living in their valuably various ways.[6]

The polarity of ownership/control, within which socialist debate in Britain oscillated in these years, was generally geared towards a real overcoming (either in the right-wing fiction of post-capitalism or in the leftist programme of socialist transformation) of the properly antagonistic profile of class struggle. The transition, whether actual or possible, revisionist or radical, could thus effectively relinquish the sticky ground of revolutionary change, and enter the gradualist terrain of a multiplicity of national 'roads to socialism'.[7]

It is against this problematical background of class def(l)ection that the early working-class fiction of Alan Sillitoe acquires its relevance. Despite the efforts of disparaging critical interpretations that tend to emphasize the alleged lack of political edge in these works,[8] narratives such as *Saturday Night and*

---

[5] Raymond Williams, *Culture and Society* (London: Hogarth Press, 1958).
[6] Raymond Williams, *The Long Revolution* (Harmondsworth: Penguin, 1965), 363.
[7] *The British Road to Socialism*, the 1951 programme of the Communist Party of Great Britain, was one of many post-war Communist programmatic statements that renounced the revolutionary orientation of its predecessors. See Noreen Branson, *History of the Communist Party of Great Britain 1941–1951* (London: Lawrence and Wishart, 1997), 232–9.
[8] See, for example, Ingrid von Rosenberg, 'Militancy, Anger and Resignation: Alternative Moods in the Working-Class Novel of the 1950s and early 1960s', in H. Gustav Klaus (ed.), *The Socialist Novel in Britain* (Brighton: Harvester Press, 1982).

Sunday Morning and 'The Loneliness of the Long-Distance Runner' offer a fresh perspective on the persistence of class antagonistic dynamics (of exploitation and resistance) in a supposedly post-classist society. Although often misleadingly conflated with the productions of writers like Kingsley Amis, John Wain, John Osborne or John Braine under the convenient, if rather vacuous, label 'Angry Young Men', Sillitoe's early work is not concerned with the perceived effects of the blurring of class lines: its subject matter is not the estrangement suffered by the upwardly mobile, but rather, critically, the foregrounding of antagonistic subjectivities in determinate class contexts. Its pattern is not one of mutation or refraction, but one of structural opposition and real confrontation. Thus, it is highly significant that in his first novel Sillitoe in no way circumvents the materiality of industrial work, or the centrality of the capitalist productive process. Even if consumption features prominently in the novel's portrayal of this life (and we will see exactly in what terms), production, that is to say, labour, is neither excluded nor minimized in the configuration of affluence. Arthur Seaton's universe is governed by the Nottingham bicycle factory where he works (and, more precisely, by his job as a capstan lathe operator), to the extent that the 'Saturday night and Sunday morning' of the title can only be understood in dialectical relation with it. As Peter Hitchcock has noted, Arthur 'does not live in spite of his work, he lives through it ... work is not merely tangential to living'.[9] This centrality is presented, for all the muffling effects of Keynesian macroeconomic policy and the Welfare State, as an undisguised dialectic without consensual *Aufhebung*: labour is still clearly recognized as struggle between capital and the worker.

In 'The Loneliness of the Long-Distance Runner', the persistence of conflictuality is projected beyond the factory without for that matter effacing the sharp contours of class. Rather, Sillitoe's portrayal of a young and bitterly rebellious Borstal inmate takes the collapse of the consensual illusion to an even higher level. The antagonistic but ongoing relationship between the young worker and the exploitative firm is here replaced by a wholesale rejection of society as the general incarnation of blind capitalist command. The tone of Smith's refusal, as we will see, starts from a recognition of labour's increasing

---

[9] Peter Hitchcock, *Working-Class Fiction in Theory and Practice: A Reading of Alan Sillitoe* (Ann Arbor, Michigan: UMI Press, 1989), 66.

subordination in the affluent society and proceeds to a practical declaration of independence and non-compliance with the coercive institutions of the capitalist class.

Thus, class represents, in the characterizations of both Arthur Seaton and Smith, a political, as much as social and economic, challenge to the containments and distortions introduced by both socialist gradualists and liberal revisionists. Its radical import is predicated on these texts' rejection of integration and harmonization as viable answers to the conjunctural changes undergone by the system. Instead of offering a reformist path, they point to a persistent rift, to a lasting separation which may effectively lead to self-worth without subordination. Sillitoe articulates in this sense a radical oppositional stance that exceeds the ideological and practical possibilities embodied in Labourism and trade unionism – but also in the post-revolutionary Communism of *The British Road to Socialism*.

The antagonistic 'truth' revealed, in their various ways, by both Arthur Seaton and Smith, is that the class struggle has surpassed the gradualist dynamics represented by the existing organizations of the Left, and consequently, the forms of collective action which they presuppose. Sillitoe's protagonists posit the need to rethink the experience of antagonism, to redraw the basic contours of the class struggle without the mystifying mediation of established institutional forms. The apparent individualism they express should then be seen as a direct response to the co-optation of collective agency by an ossified and ineffectual institutionality. This is not a retreat from mass politics, but an insistence that the fundamental lines of conflict need to be reassessed and revitalized if the notion of class is to retain its revolutionary valences. By following this approach (which, as Nick Bentley has suggested, underlines his links to French Existentialism), Sillitoe identifies 'the primary form of oppositional politics' from which a whole range of dominant programmes and hegemonic formulations (also, and especially, on the left) must be distinguished.[10]

---

[10] Nick Bentley, *Radical Fictions: the English Novel in the 1950s* (Oxford: Peter Lang, 2007), 202. For more on the connection between Sillitoe and French Existentialism, see William Hutchings, 'Proletarian Byronism: Alan Sillitoe and the Romantic Tradition', in Allan Chavkin (ed.), *English Romanticism and Modern Fiction* (New York: AMS Press, 1993), 35–47; Stanley S. Atherton, *Alan Sillitoe: A Critical Assessment* (London: W. H. Allen, 1979), 48–57; Anna R. Nardella 'The Existential Dilemmas of Alan Sillitoe's Working-Class Heroes', *Studies in the Novel*, 5 (1973), 469–82.

Thus, only after the veils of liberal and socialist complacency are torn, and after the possibility of a fresh antagonism (between the representatives of power and the exploited masses, however individualized and isolated they may find themselves) is discovered, will the possibility of working-class liberation emerge unchallenged:

> The poor know of only two classes in society. Their sociology is much simplified. There are *them* and *us*. Them are those who tell you what to do, who drive a car, use a different accent, are buying a house in another district, deal in cheques and not money, pay your wages, collect rent and telly dues, stop for you now and again at pedestrian crossings, can't look you in the eye, read the news on wireless or television, hand you the dole or national assistance money... Them are those who robbed you of your innocence, live on your backs, buy the house from over your head, eat you up, or tread you down.[11]

In this short fragment from an article published in an anarchist journal, Sillitoe condenses the argument of separation and working-class self-valorization on which he builds his early fiction. The workers, the poor (these terms slowly converge, despite 'affluence', on a unitary figure of the class), emerge as autonomous from the extraneous definitions of power by dint of their refusal to comply with its injunctions and seductions, through their more or less belligerent affirmation of a class-based singularity.

The fact that the oppositional 'us' is rendered in figures of primarily individualistic resistance in the fiction should not be regarded as a paradox or a contradiction, but as confirmation that the social fabric of working-class autonomy needs to be reconstituted in the face of so many defections and calls for assimilation. Both Arthur Seaton and Smith embody this urge to recommence class politics from scratch, for when the realm of the collective has been penetrated by complacency – they seem to argue – the rediscovery of individualized resistance opens the way for the class as a whole.[12] By this account, the reference to an overarching and predatory 'them' is ultimately

---

[11] Alan Sillitoe, 'Poor People', *Anarchy*, 38 (1964), 127.
[12] As John Kirk has noted: 'What *is* very interesting is the idea that workers used the notion of individuality and independence to articulate a sense of dignity, autonomy and pride and, in some cases, class awareness and association, something completely missed by theorists or proponents of individualism', *Class, Culture and Social Change* (Basingstoke: Palgrave, 2007), 93.

inclusive of all those institutional forms of radicalism – including the Communist Party – which have abandoned active refusal for gradual reform.

This notion of active refusal echoes one of the most radical attempts, in the 1960s and 1970s, to think through the enduring centrality of working-class antagonism and autonomy in the age of managed capitalism. Italian Operaist/ Workerist or Autonomist Marxism would find in the phrase 'the strategy of refusal' one of its main conceptual tools in its attempt to break the deadlock of reformism that had also plagued Italian Left politics since the onset of its own 'consensus' in 1945.[13] Workerist theorists started from a radical analysis of the period's economic and political transformations, which they did not read as an 'objective' development of capitalism's inner laws, but as a subjective effort, on the part of capital, to control and govern the increasingly autonomous self-affirmations of the working class. As Mario Tronti argued in the classic text of Operaismo, *Operai e Capitale* (Workers and Capital), capitalism had reached a high level of socialization in its attempt to control the inherent autonomy of the working class. Orthodox Marxism made a fundamental error in conceiving of capitalist transformations as independent from working-class resistance, for it was, rather, the historical centrality of the latter that determined the former's increasing expansiveness. Thus, the apparent equalization of post-war society under new principles of macroeconomic and social governance was in fact the result of capital's internalization of a number of social functions and dimensions which, in the earlier phase of *laissez-faire*, had lain outside its jurisdiction. The socialization of capital did not suppose the disappearance of capitalism but rather, the *subsumption* of society within it.[14] This, rather than abolishing exploitation, entailed a generalization of its mechanisms across a broad range of social ambits and functions, to the extent that nothing now lay outside the process of capitalist valorization. In this context, the factory acquired a new relevance as the vantage point from which subsumed society

---

[13] Steven Wright, *Storming Heaven: Class Composition and Struggle in Italian Autonomist Marxism* (London: Pluto Press, 2002), 6–31.

[14] The concept of subsumption is one of the theoretical cornerstones of the Workerist/Autonomist tradition. Originally found in Marx's text 'Results of the Immediate Process of Production', it contains a twofold division: formal subsumption versus real subsumption. Briefly, the former refers to the stage in which capital controls, without materially determining, the different forms of production operative in society (to the effect that capitalist and pre-capitalist forms coexist), while the latter alludes to that phase of capitalist maturity in which capital directly determines every single productive process and relation. See Karl Marx, *Capital, volume 1*, trans. Ben Fowkes (Harmondsworth: Penguin, 1990), 1019–38.

could be countenanced and contested. For within its walls, and against an increasingly diffuse dynamic of commodity circulation and consumption, the working class encountered a concentrated and direct form of exploitation. The daily struggle against the machine, against the foreman, and against time management on the assembly line provided a translucent instance of class antagonism and resistance to the capitalist tendency to transform 'living labour' (that is, working-class subjective autonomy) into 'dead labour' (that is, into an 'objective' and abstract quantity of labour belonging to capital itself).[15]

In what follows, I will chart Sillitoe's presentation of industrial production as the central locus of confrontation between 'them' and 'us' in *Saturday Night and Sunday Morning*. The factory, as in the classic Operaist account, contrasts in this novel with the affluent society as it foregrounds the oppositional endurance of working-class subjectivity. The constitutive dissymmetry revealed by the confrontation between living labour (as working class) and dead labour (as capital) frames the antagonistic dynamic and offers a breakthrough beyond the sterile sociological definitions of the period. In labour, in production, the working-class subject emerges as potentially free and autonomous from the narratives of embourgeoisement and capitalist incorporation, and hence, from the ideological temptations of a bland reformism.

It will be further argued that the vantage point offered by the factory, although important in drawing the main lines of working-class self-valorization under generalized conditions of capitalist subsumption, eventually fails to deliver a solid (and sustained) basis for the articulation of working-class refusal. The growing contradictions between the temporalities of production and reproduction – that is, between the time of 'life' and the time of work in the factory – lead to an eventual breakdown of the imagined subjective autonomy. Thus, while the dynamic of labour furnishes the worker with numerous expressions and attitudes of conscious independence, the rhythms of life outside the factory expose an increasingly vulnerable side. The internalized

---

[15] As Mario Tronti argues, in a way that to some extent contradicts his own analysis elsewhere in *Operai e Capitale* (as we will see below): 'Even if factory and society were to become perfectly integrated at the economic level, they would nevertheless forever continue to be in contradiction at a political level. One of the highest and most developed points of the class struggle will be precisely the frontal clash between the *factory, as working class* and *society, as capital*', 'The Strategy of Refusal', in Sylvère Lotringer and Christian Marazzi (eds), *Autonomia: Post-Political Politics* (Los Angeles, Semiotext(e), 2007), 28; *Operai e Capitale* (Roma: DeriveApprodi, 2013), 236.

conflict between the factory and society (which in this case is presented within a single subjective figure) makes it necessary for the project of working-class refusal to find new channels and material settings. The passage from *Saturday Night and Sunday Morning* to 'The Loneliness of the Long-Distance Runner' will mark, as we will see, Sillitoe's recognition of the aforementioned contradictions and a new tentative direction in the imagination of working-class autonomy.

The second part of the chapter will consider an alternative line of fictional engagement with capital's subsumption of society, one in which the *separatist* subjectivity of the proletariat is displaced and potentially abolished by a subjective absolute embodied in capital itself. David Storey's novel *This Sporting Life* offers a fine contrast to the political exercise sketched out by Sillitoe, as well as a revealing announcement of the expansive tendencies of capitalist development that we will examine in succeeding chapters.

2.2 From the factory to the social: Alan Sillitoe's proletarian subjects

Arthur Seaton's refusal in *Saturday Night and Sunday Morning* is framed, enabled and even produced by the factory, insofar as his life beyond its walls becomes increasingly vulnerable and exposed to the social domination and control exerted by capital. It is, precisely, the confrontational nature of labour, the oppressive quality of factory-work (complete with its revolting smells and insalubrious conditions), that grants him the possibility of regaining his distance from capitalist sociality, of reclaiming his individuality from the fully subsumed 'candy-floss world' of the 1950s.[16] Even if Monday should be described as 'Black Monday', as Arthur observes early on in the novel,[17] it should also be recognized as the day when the periodic mystifications of affluence give way to the harsh realities of immediate exploitation. The bitter encounter cannot be cushioned or mellowed. Its staging is crude and inevitable, and the worker recognizes it for what it is:

[16] Hoggart, *Uses*.
[17] Alan Sillitoe, *Saturday Night and Sunday Morning* (London: Flamingo, 1994), 24.

> Arthur walked into a huge corridor, searching an inside pocket for his clocking-in card and noticing, as on every morning since he was fifteen – except for a two-year break in the army – the factory smell of oil-suds, machinery, and shaved steel that surrounded you with an air in which pimples grew and prospered on your face and shoulders, that would have turned you into one big pimple if you did not spend half an hour over the scullery sink every night getting rid of the biggest bastards.[18]

Arrival in the factory brings with it a sensorial assault on the worker's body – a physical encroachment which cannot but rupture the ideological illusion of social democratic revisionism's 'distribution of economic power'.[19] For all its managerial pretence, capitalism makes itself known to the worker violently and corporeally. The mystifying effect that its socialization casts over the rest of society cannot reach here, on this pestilential factory corridor, the vivid consciousness of the worker: 'What a life, he thought. Hard work and good wages, and a smell all day that turns your guts.'[20] Filled with highly automated machinery, the factory appears as a radically hostile environment in which the alien will of the capitalist makes itself objective and concrete. The 'terror' of Monday morning is thus, despite the promise of high wages and full employment, the concretization of a technical universe which is neither managed by the workers nor aligned with their interests. The labour routine therefore expresses from the start an unequal encounter between the worker and capital, one in which the former is constrained to 'tame' the latter's objective manifestation in the machine:

> He pressed the starter button, and his motor came to life with a gentle thump. Looking around, it did not seem, despite the infernal noise of hurrying machinery, that anyone was working with particular speed. He smiled to himself and picked up a glittering steel cylinder from the top box of a pile beside him, and fixed it into the spindle. He jettisoned his cigarette into the sud-pan, drew back the capstan, and swung the turret on to its broadest drill. Two minutes passed while he contemplated the precise position of tools and cylinder; finally he spat on to both hands and rubbed them together, then switched on the sud-tap from the movable brass pipe, pressed a button that

---

[18] Ibid., 29.
[19] Crosland, *Future*, 6–21.
[20] Sillitoe, *Saturday*, 30.

set the spindle running, and ran in the drill to a neat chamfer. Monday morning had lost its terror.[21]

The terror of capitalist labour is here counteracted by the worker's efforts to resist his technical subordination to the machine, by his deliberate manoeuvring of fixed capital. As Hitchcock writes: 'Arthur's smile is an indication that he knows he works the machine and not the other way around, and that these moments of contemplation are resistance rituals (like absenteeism and pilfering) that clearly define Arthur's interests in opposition to those who believe they control him.'[22] Arthur's relationship with the machine, and hence his position with respect to capital's control over labour, is thus more complex than one of simple 'alienation'.[23] As Operaismo had suggested from the outset, the capitalist imposition of technology, of an increasingly developed technical rationality (in machinery, organization, etc.) upon the labour process, was not the result of an 'objective' development, but rather the concrete expression of capital's subjective exertions to control living labour. Thus, the 'alienation' induced by machinery, and more generally by the factory, is better understood as a dynamic movement, as a subjective struggle over command, rather than as a passive objectification.[24] Arthur is not objectified by the machine: he is ruled over, exploited and controlled by capital's material expression in technology. The machine, capital's 'fixed' expression in the labour relation,[25] *fights* Arthur in its pursuit of domination, in the process of exploitation, forcing the latter to fight back. As Hitchcock rightly observes, there is no passive acquiescence in his relation with the capstan lathe, just the tactical manoeuvring which presents his subjectivity as not – yet – fully defeated, fully incorporated, fully *alienated*.

---

[21] Ibid., 30–1.
[22] Hitchcock, *Working-Class*, 66.
[23] See Kathleen Bell, 'Arthur Seaton and the Machine: A New Reading of Alan Sillitoe's *Saturday Night and Sunday Morning*', in H. Gustav Klaus and Stephen Knight (eds), *British Industrial Fictions* (Cardiff: University of Wales Press, 2000), and John Sawkins, *The Long Apprenticeship: Alienation in the Early Work of Alan Sillitoe* (Oxford: Peter Lang, 2001).
[24] As Raniero Panzieri wrote in the first issue of *Quaderni Rossi*, the legendary Marxist periodical in which the early Workerists would serve their apprenticeship: 'It is obvious that simply to ratify rationalization processes (taken as the totality of productive techniques evolved within the framework of capitalism) is to forget that it is precisely capitalist "despotism" which takes the form of technological rationality . . . Not "rationality", but *control*, not technical programming, but a plan for power of the associated producers, can ensure an adequate relation to the global techno-economic processes', in Phil Slater (ed.), *Outlines of a Critique of Technology* (London: Ink Links, 1980), 54–5.
[25] As Marx writes: '*Machinery* appears, then, as the most adequate form of *fixed capital*', *Grundrisse*, trans. Martin Nicolaus (Harmondsworth: Penguin, 1993), 694.

Alienation is an intentional process in the factory to which the worker responds actively and consciously.

One of the most telling aspects of his resistant strategy concerns the use of time while working the machine. In the factory, labour is subordinated (in that it is made equivalent) to an abstract quantity or measure of time which abolishes its quality, its specificity and content: subsumed labour is, in effect, abstracted working time. The equivalence between labour and time is thus neither a natural nor an objective expression of productive rationality, but, as Negri puts it, an *'effect of coercion'*,[26] a subjective articulation of capital's command over the worker and the productive process. However, if by relying on the effort-saving dimension of industrial automation, the worker were somehow to withdraw from the temporal relation coercively imposed by capital, managing to compress or even dissolve the quantity of time appropriated by capital in the subsumed form of labour, it could be argued that capitalist command over the productive process would then lose its dominative efficacy, and that the autonomous subjectivity of the worker would be reasserted. This is precisely the way Arthur Seaton approaches the 'alienating' experience of factory work. The latter is consciously transformed by the worker into 'actions without thought',

> so that all through the day you filled your mind with vivid and more agreeable pictures than those round about. It was an easier job than driving a lorry for instance where you had to have your wits about you ... and you remembered the corporal in the army who said what a marvel it was the things you thought of when you were on the lavatory, which was the only time you ever had to think. But now whole days could be given up to wool-gathering. Hour after hour quickly disappeared when once you started thinking, and before you knew where you were a flashing light from the foreman's office signalled ten o'clock.[27]

The alienating/objectifying power of the machine is here 'hijacked' by the worker in a conscious operation of self-valorizing inversion. His daydreaming is not a sign of functional subordination to the objectified productive process, but a form of self-distancing, of antagonistic withdrawal from its control. If the living

---

[26] Antonio Negri, *Time for Revolution*, trans. Matteo Mandarini (London: Continuum, 2003), 28.
[27] Sillitoe, *Saturday*, 32–3.

quality of the worker is abstracted in a mere quantity of labour-time, if the labour process is reduced to the machine's confiscation of the worker's life in a highly impersonal and objective dynamic, then the latter's wilful separation from this mechanical abstraction is nothing but an expression of non-compliance and refusal. By alienating himself from the alienated processes of subsumed labour (that is, of machine/capital-controlled labour), the worker re-emerges as an unincorporated, resistant subject. Later in the novel, Arthur will explicitly allude to the subversive potential of his 'wool-gathering', noting that it represents a moment of failure for 'Them' in their attempt to dominate his class through the subsumption of labour: '[T]his lathe is my everlasting pal because it gets me thinking, and that's their big mistake because I know I'm not the only one. One day they'll bark and we won't run into a pen like sheep.'[28] In these and other passages, the formal presentation of the worker's thoughts in such an unmediated, direct manner (through narrative techniques that should be properly described as modernist) serves, as Nick Bentley has suggested, 'to counteract the externalized representation of the manual factory worker'.[29] In other words, the immanent rendition of the worker's subjectivity reinforces, at the level of narrative form, the effect of separation produced by his conscious refusal.

Arthur's antagonistic consciousness extends, beyond the immediate dialectic of subsumption expressed in the machine, into the domain of the wage, where a raging battle over rates and rhythms is fought out daily against capital. As Antonio Negri has argued at length, the dialectic of the wage conceals and obfuscates the vitality of labour power, the independence of working-class subjectivity with respect to the objective process of production. The wage represents capital's attempt to fixate and neutralize this movement of vital autonomy, to reduce it to a measurable quantity:

> [I]n the form of the wage [labor power] shows only the mystified aspect of its existence, this fixity that capital demands in order to measure it. But once we go beyond this necessity that capital imposes, we can see in the wage, beyond the wage, the palpitation of living labor in all its social reality, with all the power of its antagonism.[30]

---

[28] Ibid., 202.
[29] Bentley, *Radical*, 207.
[30] Antonio Negri, *Marx Beyond Marx: Lessons on the* Grundrisse, trans. Harry Cleaver, Michael Ryan and Maurizio Viano (New York: Autonomedia, 1991), 132.

In this sense, Sillitoe's foregrounding of the wage relation in the factory offers a radical development of the worker's resistant strategy. Beyond his routinized and internalized struggle against the machine, the wage marks an occasion for open class conflict:

> Though no strong cause for open belligerence existed as in the bad days talked about, it persisted for more subtle reasons that could hardly be understood but were nevertheless felt, and Friday afternoon was a time when different species met beneath white flags, with wage-packets as mediators, when those who worked in the factory were handed proof of their worth, which had increased considerably in market value since the above-mentioned cat-and-dog ideas had with reason taken root.[31]

All illusions about a possible neutralization of conflict are here shattered by the affirmation of an insurmountable, structural antagonism. In the factory, living labour confronts the wage through a radically antagonistic recognition of the latter's significance as precarious mediation and attempted imposition of an objective measure over its value. The fact that this, considered exclusively as exchange value, has increased with respect to the interwar years cannot lead to an assimilationist conclusion (to an acceptance of capital's law), but rather to an *autonomist* one. This conclusion increases the worker's awareness of his self-worth, of his qualitative difference from capital; for, in this context, 'capital is forced to see itself as relation, as proportion, as a rule imposed on a separation'.[32] Once the ontological difference between capital and living labour is established, once the mystified notion of consensus is dispelled, the path for working-class autonomy, understood as the negation, as the outflanking of capitalist rationality, is irreversibly opened. The proletarian subject returns from its presumed post-war lethargy through a vital affirmation of antagonistic intelligence and autonomous reason, as anti-capitalist productivity. In the context of *Saturday Night and Sunday Morning*, this process of separation or autonomization is not to be read as a *fait accompli*, but as a tendential manoeuvre of liberation from capitalist command, from the regulated subsumption of labour within fixed capital. The most significant expression of this operation is to be found in Arthur's unrelenting struggle against

---

[31] Sillitoe, *Saturday*, 61–2.
[32] Negri, *Marx*, 133.

the surveillance exerted by the rate-checker, the capitalists' shop-floor representative, and the workers' 'public enemy number one':

> [T]he rate-checker sometimes came and watched you work, so that if he saw you knock up a hundred in less than an hour Robboe would come and tell you one fine morning that your rate had been dropped by sixpence or a bob. So when you felt the shadow of the rate-checker breathing down your neck you knew what to do if you had any brains at all: make every move more complicated, though not slow because that was cutting your throat, and do everything deliberately yet with a crafty show of speed.[33]

Here, living labour's struggle against the wage comes across as a telling subversion of dead labour's mechanical rhythms; it is articulated as slow-down and as crafty performance of the productive routine. This petty ruse reconstructs produced value as an independent variable, as a subjective negation of capitalist appropriation. By tampering with the measuring function of capital (that is, in this case, with the rate-checker's 'rational' quantification of the value produced by Arthur), labour emerges as separation, as negation of profit, and hence as self-valorization. Here, however momentarily: 'There is no more profit because labor productivity is no longer translated into capital. There is no more capitalist rationality.'[34]

Thus, in *Saturday Night and Sunday Morning*, the factory emerges as the natural site of struggle against capital's domination. Within its walls, the postwar illusion of the 'end of ideology' gives way to a dynamic actualization of the class struggle and to an increasingly radical affirmation of working-class autonomy.[35] The enhanced consciousness and potential autonomy attained by Arthur in the factory nevertheless contrast (increasingly, as the novel develops) with his confusion and vulnerability outside. Thus, in the apparently comfortable universe of Saturday night and Sunday morning (the 'glad time' – as the novel puts it – of pleasure and recreation or, more technically, of

---

[33] Sillitoe, *Saturday*, 31–2.
[34] Negri, *Marx*, 150. According to Marx, 'profit is ... a transformed form of surplus-value, a form in which its origin and the secret of its existence are veiled and obliterated. In point of fact, profit is the form of appearance of surplus-value ... In surplus-value, the relationship between capital and labour is laid bare. In the relationship between capital and profit ... *capital appears as a relationship to itself*, a relationship in which it is distinguished, as an original sum of value, from another new value that it posits', quoted in Antonio Negri, *Books for Burning: Between Civil War and Democracy in 1970s Italy* (London: Verso, 2005), 70.
[35] Daniel Bell, *The End of Ideology: On the Exhaustion of Political Ideas in the Fifties* (New York: Free Press, 1965).

'reproduction'), the tough, anarchic worker regularly morphs into an irresponsible pleasure-seeker whose antagonistic outlook is replaced by a mystified sense of juvenile independence. Sillitoe builds a dramatic contrast between Arthur's militant determination in the factory not to 'let anybody grind me down',[36] and the emptiness of his recurrent insistence outside that he 'couldn't care less'.[37] One of the most significant episodes in this respect concerns his ongoing affair with Brenda, the wife of his fellow worker Jack. This relationship provides a crucial element of narrative continuity outside the factory, presenting Arthur as a hedonist, but as a rather egotistical and confused one at that. When, after a long stretch of unprotected sexual encounters between the two, Brenda finally tells him that she is pregnant, his reaction is one of denial and insecurity. In the abortion scene that follows, in which Brenda attempts, with the help of her friend Em'ler, to 'bring it off' by having a hot bath while drinking gin, Arthur is shown at his weakest – a pale image of his antagonistic, factory self:

> Never again, he kept saying to himself, never again. I'd rather cut my throat. He felt drunk, though he had taken no more than a sip of the gin. Sometimes he was part of the scene, sitting among the two women, warmed by the fire, choked by the steaming bath; then he was looking down on it, like watching the telly with no part in what he was seeing. He was only real inside himself.[38]

Disorientation alternates in this passage with an apparently deep sense of regret at having 'let such a thing happen'.[39] None of this, however, marks a turning point in his subjective development; nor does it lead to a consequential extension of his 'principles' to the personal/social domain of reproduction (that is, to the domain of life outside the factory). Instead of signalling a crisis, this episode is brushed off, leading to a mindless continuation of his hedonistic routine of pleasure-seeking. Thus, upon leaving Brenda's house, just in time to avoid running into her husband Jack, Arthur heads straight for the nearest pub where he will drink away his worries and – rather bathetically – start a new affair with Brenda's sister Winnie.[40]

---

[36] Sillitoe, *Saturday*, 40.
[37] Ibid., 93.
[38] Ibid., 88.
[39] Ibid., 88.
[40] As Nick Bentley has pointed out, Sillitoe's relegation of women amounts to their presentation 'as representatives of the system of control rather than as an equivalent subjugated group', *Radical*,

In his frivolous and rather chauvinistic interactions with women, as well as in his partiality for pubs and drink, Arthur emerges as the near-stereotypical representation of male working-class subjectivity, as a psychological staple of political neutralization. His vacuous hedonism is cast as the dramatic negation of the antagonistic consciousness displayed within the factory, as the paradoxical inversion of the latter's possibilities. In the remaining part of this section, we will attempt to explicate this contradiction by delving deeper into the Operaist concept of subsumption.

As Tronti explains in 'The Factory and Society' (included in the first section of *Operai e Capitale*), the primary function of the wage, especially in the context of managed/affluent capitalism, is to confuse the distinction between necessary and surplus labour, that is, between the part of the working day required for the reproduction of the labour force (the non-work part of the working day) and the part specifically devoted to the production of surplus value. By refusing to acknowledge this distinction, capital presents the wage as full payment for an abstract and totalizing amount of 'labour', which is now made to stand for the entirety of the working day. As we have seen, the labour to which the wage refers is not a separate, independent variable (it is not a subjective 'power' of the labour force), but a projection of capital itself – a constituent part of variable capital. This abstract category implies an extension of the productive process beyond the factory, a generalization of capital's law of valorization beyond the immediate ambit of production of surplus labour. As the distinction between the necessary time of working-class life and the surplus time of factory work is effaced, and as the process of capitalist valorization is increasingly presented, via the wage, as pervading the whole of society, the factory begins to lose its central position in the general configuration

---

225. In the words of Nigel Gray: 'Arthur is against all authority – except the authority of men over women', quoted in *Radical*, 225. I would suggest that this failure to articulate the 'equivalence' between the exploited position of men and that of women is to be read in terms of the subsumed state in which post-war working-class life finds itself. In this sense, the chauvinistic assumptions made by Arthur in relation to the realm of 'social reproduction' (which is here presented as little more than a locus of frivolous pleasure-seeking) only reinforce – and confirm – capital's hold on society, and thus attest to the vulnerabilities which his exclusive concern with the factory (his resistance against the foreman and management) exposes. Thus, by failing to recognize exploitation in reproduction, as well as in production, the male worker contributes to the consolidation of capital's dominion over his and his fellow, if unwaged, female workers' lives. For, under conditions of subsumption, as Silvia Federici has noted, 'the circuit of capitalist production ... began and was centered above all in the kitchen, the bedroom, the home – insofar as these were the centers for the production of labor-power – and from there it moved on to the factory', Silvia Federici, *Revolution at Point Zero: Housework, Reproduction, and Feminist Struggle* (New York: PM Press, 2012), 7–8.

of capitalist production. In order to understand the complex nature of the latter, we will now need to follow its development through circulation and consumption, for, in these, the production of surplus value acquires 'new determinations'.[41] The initial hierarchy of surplus value (which had seen the factory and the exchange between labour power and capital govern the process) is now subverted and mystified in a diffuse generality of valorization that puts circulation and consumption on the same level as industrial production: 'At this point, all parts of capital appear equally as sources of surplus value and thus also as the source of profit.'[42] The capitalist subsumption of society thus effectively refers to the process whereby capital presents an ever-increasing number of social functions and relations as directly *productive* of surplus value/profit. Capitalist production emerges in this sense as a 'generic social relation'[43] no longer restricted to one particular ambit: '[W]hen the whole of society is reduced to a factory, the latter – as such – seems to *disappear*.'[44]

Tronti's radical analysis in 'The Factory and Society' may seem to contradict his privileging of the factory as the locus of anti-capitalist resistance in 'The Strategy of Refusal' (alluded to above). However, this account is not invoked here to deny the validity and ongoing relevance of industrial conflict, but to frame and explain the limitations of the worker's tactics of opposition and autonomization in a context of capitalist expansion which is increasingly deprived of a solid and centralized material basis. In this sense, Sillitoe's novel is an insightful rehearsal of the contradictions and shortcomings of a working-class dynamic of *separation* from capital which takes the factory as the exclusive focus of the antagonism, leaving the social area typically associated with 'reproduction' fatefully exposed to capitalist penetration and erosion. In this sense, the transformation of the wage into an apparently neutral relation (especially when observed from the perspective of consumption and affluence) is nothing but a cover-up for capital's subjective co-optation of the living realm of the working class. Through the wage, and through the rhizomatic expansion of production operated by capital at the levels of circulation and consumption,

---

[41] Tronti, *Operai*, 40.
[42] Ibid., 40.
[43] Ibid., 46.
[44] Ibid., 49.

the non-work part of the working life (the part dedicated to reproduction) is reconfigured as the primary battlefield of capitalist subsumption – or, in other words, of capital's assault on working-class autonomy.

With the passage from *Saturday Night and Sunday Morning* to 'The Loneliness of the Long-Distance Runner', Sillitoe assumes the limitations and contradictions of the factory perspective and calls for a radicalization of the strategy of refusal pioneered by Arthur Seaton. In the later piece, Sillitoe will test the Operaist hypothesis that working-class autonomy can only be attained outside the labour relation. In 'The Factory and Society', Tronti noted that the old mistake made by Marxism had been to conceive of the industrial working class as external to capital, thus missing the dramatic consequences of subsumption. By imagining itself *outside* of capital, while effectively operating within a category of labour determined by it (and mediated by the wage), workers had often exposed themselves to the insidious penetration of capitalist dynamics. Under such conditions, Tronti argued, the working class could only liberate itself by finding its place within capital: '[T]he working class must materially discover itself as *part* of capital, if it then wants to oppose the *whole* of capital to itself.'[45] The first step is thus to identify itself as labour, and then to squarely reject the latter as the primary expression of capital as a whole. By refusing labour – that is, by refusing itself – the subsumed working class breaks free from capitalist domination.

However, the mystifications introduced by the wage and its rhizomatic penetration of workers' lives (through new levels of purchasing power and styles of consumption) makes the imperative to refuse work, and thus to break with capital, an objective that cannot be attained without taking aim at society as a whole. Against Operaismo's initial privileging of the factory as the strategic vantage point from which a mass revolutionary response could be articulated, Sillitoe advances a position which these Marxist theorists would only adopt in the 1970s as capitalism underwent a radical process of restructuration. Antonio Negri suggests that the 'factoryist' perspective advocated by the classic analyses of Tronti and others in the 1960s failed to make the truly social dimension of its theory operative in practice.[46] The high levels of massification of labour of

---

[45] Ibid., 52.
[46] Antonio Negri, *Revolution Retrieved: Writings on Marx, Keynes, Capitalist Crisis and New Social Subjects (1967–83)* (London: Red Notes, 1988), 105.

the 1950s pointed both to the generalization of a Fordist regime at the level of the wage (complete with an extension of State responsibilities in relation to social insurance and welfare) and to an increasing integration, as we have seen, between the areas of labour and reproduction, of work and life. Yet as this latter feature was increasingly comprehended and turned to its advantage by organized capital, the tactical emphasis on resistance at the assembly line became ever more powerless.[47] Under such conditions, only the effectively *separatist* figuration of marginal yet profoundly antagonistic subjects (of hitherto underrated yet significantly 'proletarianized strata of society') would warrant a conceivable breakthrough.[48] As the socialization of capital made labour increasingly diffuse and rhizomatic, sending its shockwaves in the form of capitalist valorization and the wage throughout the entire social body, only the literal outsider, the real outcast, now offered a possibility of refusal which would effectively escape the appropriative and dominative cycle of affluence. The 'them' versus 'us' dialectic was to be actualized in marginality and exclusion from society, in effective opposition to the State, and hence in a real and lasting image of the *refusal* of work and its civilization.

Sillitoe's critical change of setting in 'The Loneliness of the Long-Distance Runner' marks a fundamental clarification of the antagonistic tendency traversing post-war society. If the factory had projected, via the wage, a complex and confusing dynamic of subjective incorporation from which the working-class individual found it increasingly difficult to extricate himself, the Borstal institution now represented a far more unambiguous context in which the dialectic of domination and resistance was to be greatly clarified. This shift did not suppose a replacement of the production-based outlook of the confrontation, but rather generalized the directly exploitative nature of capitalist society beyond the hubs of industry. The subsumption of society under capital entailed, as we have seen, an extension of capitalist mechanisms beyond the literal factory to the more diffuse, and less immediately recognizable, social factory. In this context, the State played a fundamental role in assuring

---

[47] 'Fordism recuperated social motivations and made them functional to the Taylorist organization of work – it posed them as the prime and fundamental terrain of command in the factory. Gradually, the labour market and the fabric of relations between production and reproduction was becoming an operative field ... for the capitalist theory of factory command', ibid., 104.

[48] Ibid., 105.

the discipline of the social body with respect to the amplified cycle of production–circulation–consumption.

The blurry divisions between production and reproduction, between the extraction of surplus value and the 'domestication' of the labour force, now collapse and are replaced by a continuum of discipline in which the State assumes the directive role and function of capitalist command. In this context, the State is no longer an external structure superimposed on capital, but a political formalization or adaptation of the capitalist mechanisms of exploitation and domination. As Tronti observes, 'the process of unification of capitalist society ... does not tolerate the existence of a political terrain which may be independent, even in a purely formal fashion, from the network of social relations'.[49] Thus, in a context of growing socialization of the exploitative mechanisms of capital, the old disciplinary functions of the State acquire a new quality as specific functions of capitalist domination and self-valorization against the formulated autonomy of the working-class subject.

Unlike Arthur, Smith emerges in the factory-dominated landscape of post-war Britain as a marginal and outsider – a young delinquent who has broken with the mediating logic of subsumed work and the wage. His external position with respect to the commanding heights of industrial production does not, however, blur his class profile or deaden his antagonistic consciousness. On the contrary, his marginality epitomizes a heightened sense of autonomy from the integrated and increasingly rhizomatic system of capitalist production and valorization. What we find in the exclusion of the proletarian antagonist from the immediate system of industrial production is a liberation of his subjectivity from the blind-spots of incorporation to which the factory worker is still exposed. In this sense, Smith is a more complete and finished articulation of working-class independence, a more definite construction of the dynamics of separation adumbrated by Arthur Seaton. From the start, his ironic declarative style indicates the irreconcilable nature of the class antagonism in society, and his strategic position within it as a proletarian outsider. There is no easy introduction to this working-class universe, no 'candy floss' or 'glad time', but just the sharp-edged awareness of a systemic rift between the exploiters and the exploited, from which only sustained and obstinate resistance can ensue:

---

[49] Tronti, *Operai*, 48.

> As soon as I got to Borstal they made me a long-distance cross-country runner. I suppose they thought I was just the build for it because I was long and skinny for my age (and still am) and in any case I didn't mind it much, to tell you the truth, because running had always been made much of in our family, especially running away from the police.[50]

Running is presented as the sign of an irreconcilable difference, as a non-transcendable function of separation between the classes. 'Them', the class of exploiters, are identified as representatives and functionaries of the State whose presence in the narrative is directly and concretely coercive. The indirectness of exploitation (through the medium of labour, of fixed and variable capital) experienced by Arthur Seaton in the factory is here replaced by an immediacy of oppression, a disciplinary encroachment of the capitalist State (and the 'civil society' within which it is integrated), which now assumes the primary functions of command. Far from entailing a managerial dissolution of class differences, the socialized State of the 1950s represents a political deployment of the factory relation of domination, a further enclosure of living labour in society.

Smith is sent to Borstal after stealing money from a baker's shop, whereupon he is singled out as the institution's star long-distance runner and set to participate in the upcoming national Borstal competition. However, this athletic assignment harbours no ambiguity: far from representing a benevolent form of liberation from the ordinary discipline of the factory or the prison, it marks a new horizon of exploitation. Thus, even the free potentialities of the sportsman are preyed upon and expropriated by an ever expanding – and increasingly socialized – capitalist machine.[51] Even if exploitation dons here the appearance of a mutually beneficial trade-off between the warring classes, the bitter nature of the conflict is kept fully in sight by Smith. His vindication of marginality and delinquency is thus an uncompromising affirmation of class difference and independence from the paternalistic blackmail offered by his enemies:

> And when the governor kept saying how 'we' wanted you to do this, and 'we' wanted you to do that, I kept looking round for the other blokes, wondering

---

[50] Alan Sillitoe, *The Loneliness of the Long Distance Runner* (London: Flamingo, 1994), 7.
[51] William Hutchings, 'The Work of Play: Anger and the Expropriated Athletes of Alan Sillitoe and David Storey', *MFS Modern Fiction Studies*, 33: 1 (1987), 35–47.

how many of them there was. Of course, I knew there were thousands of them, but as far as I knew only one was in the room. And there *are* thousands of them, all over the poxeaten country, in shops, offices, railway stations, cars, houses, pubs – In-law blokes like you and them, all on the watch for Out-law blokes like me and us – and waiting to 'phone for the coppers as soon as we make a false move. And it'll always be there, I'll tell you that now, because I haven't finished making all my false moves yet, and I dare say I won't until I kick the bucket. If the In-laws are hoping to stop me making false moves they're wasting their time.[52]

The sharp division of society between 'them' and 'us', between 'In-law blokes like you and them' and 'Out-law blokes like me and us', situates the working-class individual on a free, external margin of living labour, in a social territory that no ideological or disciplinary operation can domesticate or internalize. Class consciousness becomes, in Negri's words, a 'moment of intensive rooting within my own separateness'. To be an Out-law, to be a working-class antagonist means, essentially, to be an 'other', to 'belong to the *other workers' movement*'.[53] Working-class subjectivity, as expressed by the logic of separation illustrated by the young Borstal outsider, negates both the collaborationist dissolution of conflict and the teleological movement of a predetermined class concept. Its substance, its materiality lies – rather – in the differential nature of proletarian life, of proletarian being: an ontological irreducibility which, through its very presence, negates the subordinate existence imposed by capitalist power: 'It is only by recognizing myself as other, only by insisting on the radical totality of my difference, that I have the possibility and the hope of renewal.'[54] This ontologically creative otherness is soon recognized by the proletarian outsider as a vital source, as a fresh constitution of life outside the constrictive perimeter of power-sanctioned existence. To be a working-class other is, for Smith, proof enough of his being alive:

I know when [the governor] talks to me and I look into his army mug that I'm alive and he's dead. He's as dead as a doornail ... At the moment it's dead blokes like him as have a whip-hand over blokes like me, and I'm almost dead sure it'll always be like that, but even so, by Christ, I'd rather be like

---

[52] Sillitoe, *Loneliness*, 10.
[53] Negri, *Books*, 237.
[54] Ibid., 237.

> I am – always on the run and breaking into shops for a packet of fags and a jar of jam – than have the whip-hand over somebody else and be dead from the toe nails up ... As I run ... I think more on the little speech the governor made when I first came. Honesty. Be honest ... It's like saying: Be dead, like me, and then you'll have no more pain of leaving your nice slummy house for Borstal or prison. Be honest and settle down in a cosy six pounds a week job. Well, even with all this long-distance running I haven't yet been able to decide what he means by this, although I'm just about beginning to – and I don't like what it means.[55]

The divide expressed by this passage, in which Smith considers the nature of the Borstal governor's discourse, is unsurpassable. The incarcerated working-class subject builds his autonomy on a foundational difference that cannot be negated or co-opted by any measure of paternalism. If there is no shared meaning of life, of the 'honest' life, there can be, in the end, no compromise or collaboration between the classes. Hence, the only possible outcome of the antagonism can be violent destruction of the oppressor:

> I think my honesty is the only sort in the world, and he thinks his is the only sort in the world as well. That's why this dirty great walled-up and fenced-up manor house in the middle of nowhere has been used to coop-up blokes like me. And if I had the whip-hand I wouldn't even bother to build a place like this to put all the cops, governors, posh whores, penpushers, army officers, Members of Parliament in; no, I'd stick them up against a wall and let them have it, like they'd have done with blokes like us years ago, that is, if they'd ever known what it means to be honest, which they don't and never will so help me God Almighty.[56]

Smith's destructive rage had already been prefigured by Arthur's violent outbursts against the political caste of the post-war settlement, and against the British State's Cold War drift.[57] In a similar vein, Smith declares his independence from the class interests represented by the latter: 'They can drop all the atom

---

[55] Sillitoe, *Loneliness*, 14–15.
[56] Ibid., 15.
[57] Most characteristically, perhaps, in the following passage: 'They were angling for another war now, with the Russians this time. But they did go as far as to promise that it would be a short one, a few big flashes and it would all be over. What a lark! We'd be fighting side by side with the Germans that had been bombing us in the last war. What did they take us for? Bloody fools, but one of these days they'd be wrong. They think they've settled our hashes with their insurance cards and television sets, but I'll be one of them to turn round on 'em and let them see how wrong they are. When I'm

bombs they like for all I care: I'll never call it war and wear a soldier's uniform, because I'm in a different sort of war, that they think is child's play'.[58] Smith's war (which is also Arthur's) can only be fought through 'violent' noncompliance and insubordination – through the *sabotage* of power relations. In this context, Smith's refusal goes beyond the refusal to acquiesce in the productive rhythms of the factory – or, in this case, the social factory. It rests on the determination to subvert the logic of 'honesty' by deliberately refusing to win the race. Sabotage is, in this sense, and as Antonio Negri has observed in one of the classic statements of Autonomism, tantamount to working-class self-valorization.[59]

By refusing to win the race (while deceitfully keeping the 'In-laws' under the false impression that he is fully committed to it), Smith sets out to dismantle the expropriating dynamic of capitalist society beyond the factory, which his role in Borstal literalizes. Sabotage is thus, primarily, the reappropriation of estranged social value through the constitution of an autonomous, oppositional subjectivity. As he declares: 'I only want a bit of my own back on the In-laws and Potbellies by letting them sit up there on their big posh seats and watch me lose this race.'[60]

Smith's inflection of the proletarian 'strategy of refusal' takes the structural conflict between the classes to the institutional heart of capitalist power. By aiming his antagonism at the repressive State of capitalism, his class autonomy emerges as pure anti-institutionalism, and hence as the strict negation of the State-form itself.[61] The crucial difference between Smith's and Arthur's approaches lies in the articulateness of their respective positions with respect to the subsumed functions of the social, and consequently, to the real distribution of power beyond the factory. Arthur's anti-institutionalism is impaired by his partial absorption into the dialectic of the wage, which disables his autonomy and ultimately results in self-defeat. Smith's stance, by contrast, takes up the 'separatist' vocation expressed by Arthur on the assembly line,

---

on my fifteen-days' training and I lay on my guts behind a sandbag shooting at a target board I know whose faces I've got in my sights every time the new rifle cracks off. Yes. The bastards that put the gun into my hands. I make up a quick picture of their stupid four-eyed faces that blink as they read big books and papers on how to get blokes into khaki and fight battles in a war that they'll never be in – and then I let fly at them. Crack-crack-crack-crack-crack-crack', Sillitoe, *Saturday*, 132.

[58] Sillitoe, *Loneliness*, 16.
[59] Negri, *Books*, 258.
[60] Sillitoe, *Loneliness*, 45.
[61] Negri, *Books*, 234, 279.

pursuing it beyond the constrictive parameters of the wage and developing it into a fully-fledged revolt against capital's subsumed forms. His autonomist checkmate thus articulates the necessity of affirming working-class independence as an anti-power to the organized (institutional) power of 'managed' or 'socialized' capital; as a mode of pure exteriority which both 'destructures' the system of capitalist appropriation and valorization and indexes the constitution of a free, creative and independent margin – in other words, of living labour reconfigured as an open and ongoing construction of the individual *in* the collective.

2.3 Capitalist subjectivation in David Storey's *This Sporting Life*

Sillitoe's 'The Loneliness of the Long-Distance Runner' offers a rather exceptional formalization of the antagonistic relationship between capital and living labour, one that breaks with the mediatory function of the factory and the wage (which, as we have seen, had become hegemonic in post-war capitalist society). If in this piece Sillitoe managed to articulate a figure of working-class independence by presenting it as an indomitable subjectivity locked in an immediately political struggle with the State, the prevalent dynamic in writing from the period remains one of displacement and obfuscation of this antagonistic immediacy.[62] In this section, we will see how a novel such as David Storey's *This Sporting Life*, published in 1960, engages the theme of exploitation outside or beyond the factory (in this case, in professional sport) as a dynamic of subsumption that closely follows the pattern analysed by Sillitoe and theorized by Tronti and Negri. However, in contrast with Sillitoe's breakthrough in his later text, Storey does not allow a direct route of access to the class antagonism underpinning his narrative, situating his focus instead on the work of 'abstraction' through which the money-form enveloping the exchange between labour and capital confuses the political relationship of exploitation. This confirms the Operaist hypothesis regarding the socialization of capital in its post-war incarnation, or what Negri, following Marx, refers to as the 'real

---

[62] The novels of Stan Barstow, Keith Waterhouse and Barry Hines, among others, can serve as examples of this far less confident representation of proletarian emancipation.

subsumption' of society within the capitalist cycle of valorization. But it also offers a penetrating insight into what this might signify once the centrality of the technical, industrial, factory system diminishes, and the watertight separation between production and reproduction begins to crumble. As we will see in succeeding chapters, this effect of socialization or real subsumption will induce a radical transformation of the exploitative relations embodied within the factory as described by Sillitoe in *Saturday Night and Sunday Morning* and, consequently, a rediscovery of antagonistic politics in the (increasingly) undifferentiated spaces and times of social life.

This Sporting Life reinscribes the naked exploitation of athletic ability (revealingly reconstructed here as the sheer physical power of a professional rugby league player)[63] in a less exceptional context than that represented by the Borstal school to which Smith had been confined by the repressive apparatus of the capitalist State. By focusing on a *professional* relationship rather than a penal/disciplinary one, Storey re-situates money at the centre of the social dynamic of exploitation (insofar as money was the element that had been excluded in the passage from *Saturday Night* to 'The Loneliness'). And by insisting on professional *sport* as his object of representation and means to engage with the working-class realities of post-war Britain, he puts emphasis on the unfolding shifts and displacements at the heart of the capitalist process of valorization: the appropriation of living labour, its transformation into dead labour, into capital (or, in this case, into professional sportsmanship), and its monetary expression in earnings and spending, posit those aspects and segments of the cycle of valorization that Marx had deemed 'unproductive' in *Capital*, as directly expressive instances of the post-war dynamic of exploitation.

Storey's novel narrates the progress of Arthur Machin from young factory worker with an aptitude for rugby to professional player, detailing the process of conversion of his raw physical power into the objective property of the team that 'buys' him. Critics like William Hutchings have insisted on this aspect of the dynamic of capitalist appropriation, which is customarily described in

---

[63] As Jeffrey Hill has pointed out, until the 1990s, 'most of rugby league's players were semiprofessionals who earned modest wages from the game and were required by the league regulations to be employed in a respectable job ... Thus, work and sport were linked, and because of this the rugby league players remained close to their community', 'Sport Stripped Bare: Deconstructing Working-Class Masculinity in *This Sporting Life*', *Men and Masculinities*, 7: 4 (2005), 411.

terms of commodification,[64] but the precise articulation of the character's position within the social cycle of capitalist valorization has been somewhat neglected (or insufficiently accounted for). It is important to note that, in this novel, the opposition between 'productive' (factory) work and 'unproductive' work (sport) is displaced onto a level of social generality signified and contained within the figure of money. *This Sporting Life* draws a movement of abstraction from the concreteness of work and the wage that was absent from *Saturday Night and Sunday Morning*, and that re-stages the phenomenon of post-war affluence (the expansiveness of the cycle of commodity circulation and consumption) as directly expressive of a more general, more *socially diffuse*, relation of production.

The novel begins with a description of Machin's labour power as sheer physicality, in what is a rather typical construction of working-class masculinity in twentieth-century writing: 'I was big, strong, and could make people realize it. I could tackle hard and, with the kind of deliberation I took a pride in later, really hurt someone. I was big. Big! It was no mean elation.'[65] The appeal to size and strength, compounded with the emphasis on youth that becomes pervasive through the early stages covered by the novel, offers an immediate qualification of Arthur Machin as quintessential living labour, as a high stake in the relation of exchange that the worker naturally engages in with capital. Strength and ability equal here (greater) bargaining power, and thus point to the concreteness of the primary form of exchange contained within the labour relationship. The fact that Machin both works (like Arthur Seaton, as a lathe operator) at the local factory and plays professionally for the team owned by the same factory managers underscores the basic symmetry between his two callings and their fundamental continuity in terms of the exchange of his labour power. In this context (as much as in Sillitoe's Borstal universe), there is no possible confusion between 'sport' and 'play', between the professionalized relationship between a seller of athletic 'labour power' and his capitalist buyers and the root notion of play as the antithesis of waged work.[66] As Machin soon admits to Mrs Hammond (the widow with whom he lodges and with whom he maintains a

---

[64] Hutchings, 'Work', 38.
[65] David Storey, *This Sporting Life* (London: Vintage, 2000), 22.
[66] Apropos of this notion of play as the antithesis of work, see, for example, Harry Cleaver, 'Foreword', in Ben Carrington and Ian MacDonald (eds), *Marxism, Cultural Studies and Sport* (London: Routledge, 2008), xvii–xviii.

troubled sentimental relationship throughout the novel): 'It's only a job. If I play well I might collect three or four hundred quid.'[67] In this sense, nothing substantially separates or distinguishes this from his other job at the factory: both are equated on the basis of a unitary identification of Machin's physical qualities as formative of his labour power, and both result in the latter's exchange for a wage.

Wage labour is thus the standard, the measure against which the world of the novel is set in its opening pages. The characterization of Johnson, Machin's older acquaintance and unofficial manager in the early days (as well as surrogate father figure), is particularly interesting for the sharp contrast it offers, for the moment of rather devastating exclusion from the abovesaid measure or standard it represents. If Johnson is cast in a negative light by characters like Mrs Hammond, and is even spurned by Machin himself, that is, fundamentally, because he has been excluded (or has voluntarily opted out – a far more 'dangerous' possibility no doubt) from the logic of wage labour:

> Perhaps I'd never come across a man who was quite as broken down as Johnson. I might have been a bit startled by his limitless simplicity. How small does a man get? I wondered every time I saw him stumping along... He was fairly conspicuous to all the women and kids on Highfield estate because when all the men were at work Johnson would still be seen walking about the streets, the only man in sight. I suppose solitariness encouraged him to the idea of premature age – he pretended to be ten years older than he actually was. This of course was added to the oddity of his persistent idleness.[68]

The system of oppositions rehearsed by this passage reinforces a fundamental endorsement of work as a category of concrete, material production, and, secondarily, of the factory as the indisputable guarantee of the symbolic order underpinning working-class life. By contrasting Machin's strength to Johnson's fragility, the conversion of living labour into dead labour, into the primary subjective form of capital in this industrial universe, is naturalized (and thus distanced from the antagonistic openness that became evident in Sillitoe's writing). This is not, however, a state of affairs that will remain unchanged in *This Sporting Life*. Rather, with the deepening of Storey's analysis of Machin's

[67] Storey, *This*, 21.
[68] Ibid., 18.

life as a professional rugby player, and also of his life outside work, in the domestic realm, a new dimension of abstraction and immateriality will emerge at the centre of working-class existence that will complicate the initial binaries and oppositions. As we will see below, Storey's novel offers a fundamental departure from the partial and incomplete engagement with the realm of domestic life and, in particular, reproductive (female) labour developed by Sillitoe in *Saturday Night and Sunday Morning*. By focusing on the troubled and confused relationship between Machin and Mrs Hammond, and by insisting so fundamentally on the complex power relations implied by the penetration of money into the realm of the household (at first, in the relatively trivial form of the 'rent' paid by Machin to Mrs Hammond as his lodger, and, subsequently, in the more complex form of his earnings as a professional rugby player), Storey displaces and alters the terms of definition of value (that is, of the production and accumulation of value in society) that had initially enabled the contrast between Johnson's 'oddity' and the normality implied by industrial work.

However, one central disjunction seems to preside over all the other displacements operated by the novel: that which concerns the transformation of Machin's wage as a professional sportsman (which is the image that governs his initial understanding of his engagement with the team as 'only a job') into a monetary form that seems to have lost all correspondence or equivalence to the temporal measure of the working day. It is at the point where the concrete scenario of exchange between labour and capital transmutes into an abstract figure of bargaining, which is soon reinterpreted (by the capitalists, but also by Machin himself) as 'gambling', that the measurable profile of the wage is lost to the immeasurable logic of money understood as social generality, as diffuse valorization:

> 'Now Arthur', Wade said, 'you're putting us in the position of a gambler. If we accepted your way we'd have no guarantee that we'd see adequate returns for our investment. I'm not saying it isn't a good gamble, and that, but on principle alone we try to avoid circumstances like that. You see, you're not dealing with us as individuals. Personally we might think you're worth every penny of what you're asking. But it's not our money we'd be paying you. You see – that's the point', he added after discovering it. 'This is a company. We've responsibilities stretching beyond this football ground.'[69]

---

[69] Ibid., 54.

The movement of abstraction implied by the transformation of wage bargaining into 'gambling' induces an initially defensive response from the bosses, who rush to reinstate the links between their ownership of the rugby club and that of their other, ostensibly 'productive', ventures. But this soon proves to be a futile effort that the new kind of relationship established between the professional player and themselves – that the new *unmediated* monetary link between the two – reveals in its full starkness. As Machin puts it in response to Wade's reasoning: 'It's still a gamble, whichever way you look at it.'[70] In this sense, what the reality of 'professional', capitalist sport uncovers is nothing but a new autonomy of the exchange relation between labour and capital: a relation that is not constructed dialectically around the measure of necessary and surplus labour time and the mediation expressed by the wage, but one that is *immediately* posited in the form of abstract, general sociality – of money. As Negri points out in his discussion of Marx's *Grundrisse*: 'Money has the advantage of presenting me immediately the lurid face of the social relation of value; it shows me value right away as exchange, commanded and organized for exploitation.'[71] According to Negri, what the emphasis on money announces (both analytically, in the *Grundrisse* and, from his own perspective, in the historical transition of the 1960s and 1970s) is the crisis of the law of value as the focus on industrial production and the commodity form had framed it, with its insistence on the temporal articulation of the labour process determined by the factory. Money – that is to say, the autonomization of money as the exclusive form of exchange value – points on the contrary to a demystification of the relation between the classes (between labour and capital) that leads to an immediacy of conflict, to a laying-bare of their structural antagonism. It also confirms the process of socialization of capital as an indisputable fact of capitalist development, insofar as money is regarded as a function of the increasing generality and diffuseness of the productive process (which in turn makes the latter, in its strict definition as factory work, increasingly alien to the reality of value, of exchange, of money). As Marx himself puts it:

> The need for exchange and for the transformation of the product into a pure exchange value progresses in step with the division of labour, i.e. with the

---

[70] Ibid., 54.
[71] Negri, *Marx*, 23.

increasingly social character of production. But as the latter grows, so grows the power of *money*, i.e. the exchange relation establishes itself as a power external to and independent of the producers. What originally appeared as a means to promote production becomes a relation alien to the producers.[72]

It is so that the fiction attempted by Machin's bosses to connect – through an invocation of their general duties as a part of the collective capitalist – the realm of money (of monetized sport) to the realm of production (of the factory) collapses. The *political* consequence of this, as Negri suggests, is that the mystifications operated in the name of production and the alleged proportionality of the wage can no longer be maintained in this context. In *This Sporting Life*, money represents a full disclosure of the antagonistic difference between bosses and workers, and especially of the oppressive immediacy of command, of exploitation, exerted by capital. It is not so much that Machin realizes and experiences this immediacy, but that in becoming fully subsumed within this autonomous figure of exchange, of money, he will eventually incarnate the directness of the exploitative relationship, bearing the marks and traces of the generated suffering, and imprinting them upon others.

This becomes apparent as Machin stops referring to money as an external object, as the objectification of his sale of labour power to the club owners (or in other words, as he stops referring to it as a 'wage', however incommensurate with or disconnected from his experience of productive labour),[73] and accepts it as an autonomous subjective figure that he himself will soon embody. Machin's return to the domestic realm of Mrs Hammond's house after his 'transformation' into a professional player marks the actualization of the antagonistic immediacy represented by money: at this stage, once the semblance of proportionality linked to wage labour has been shed, once Machin has *become* money, the encounter between capital and living labour – in this case, as embodied in the figure of Mrs Hammond – can only be expressed as an unmediated confrontation, as crude and naked exploitation. This violent immediacy comes across very clearly when he says to her: 'So

---

[72] Marx, *Grundrisse*, 146.
[73] This initial 'objectivity' is expressed in passages like the following: 'For a minute I hated the stinking money. It burnt a hole in my pocket. Then I remembered it was mine, and I was smiling', Storey, *This*, 58.

just guess how much you think I'm *worth*. How much solid cash do you think *I* am?'[74]

By *being* 'solid cash' and not merely *owning* it, Machin assumes the subjectivity of capital expressed in the autonomous figure of money, of value torn from the mediated relations of production. And this is a subjectivity that, having dismantled mediation and equilibrium, can only interact with living labour (with working-class life in its pure, bare incarnation) through the logic of command, negating its autonomy and self-worth, exploiting and ultimately destroying it:

> I looked at her afresh. I'd never seen her much as a person. She didn't want to be seen. Her life, while I'd known her, had been taken up with making herself as small, as negligible as possible. So small that she didn't exist. That was her aim. And it was exactly opposite to mine.[75]

The theme of smallness returns here – note that it had already been invoked in relation to Johnson's exclusion from the logic of wage labour – as a cipher of working-class life's absolute exposure (and at the same time, obscurity, invisibility) to the predatory subjectivity of capital. The exploitative immediacy that money brings to the relationship (between Machin and Mrs Hammond, but also between capital and living labour) results in a dynamic of destruction from which there can be no stabilizing escape, no confused neutralization à la *Saturday Night and Sunday Morning*. Thus the cycle of wealth and consumption that Machin's 'transformation' entails, and in which he involves Mrs Hammond with eventually fatal consequences, does not point to a mere process of incorporation or de-activation of the resistant profile of the worker as it had done in the case of Arthur Seaton. Under the figure of the wage and its social extension in consumption, we witnessed an ambivalent oscillation between belligerence and neutralization, between resistance on the factory floor and domestication in the pub (or the supermarket).

But now, in *This Sporting Life*, the dominant figure is that of money, and the social terrain the latter defines is revealed as increasingly diffuse and undifferentiated. Machin's declared intent to raise Mrs Hammond's standard of living, from that of an impoverished widow with two small children to his

---

[74] Ibid., 68.
[75] Ibid., 68–9.

own 'level', comes across as a brutal, if perhaps unwitting, form of expropriation. The subjective figure of money – of Machin-as-money – thus replaces the mediated exploitation of unwaged, reproductive workers under the hegemonic relation of the wage, with immediate violence. We will see in the following chapter that this dynamic becomes predominant (and consequently, that the relevance of reproductive work within the antagonism between capital and labour grows exponentially) as the centrality of the factory diminishes. In contrast with the subordination of women by the male worker in *Saturday Night and Sunday Morning* (which was presented as an obscuring or screening of their self-worth through an almost exclusive focus on Arthur Seaton's subjectivity), in *This Sporting Life*, structural subordination is transformed into inter-subjective violence.

It would not be exact – or, at any rate, sufficient – to claim that Mrs Hammond is objectified by Machin. The immediacy and violence of the social relation expressed in money results in a crude dynamic of antagonism and conflict that goes beyond the passivity of reification. Having assumed the abstract subjective form of capital, Machin goes on to prey upon Mrs Hammond as a fresh, hitherto untapped, source of living labour that her relegated position within the realm of social reproduction had kept concealed from the mediated dynamics of exchange between workers and capitalists. By breaking into this reproductive – bio-social – rearguard in the violent form of money, Machin exposes his (and capital's) own inability to transform this woman into a mere object. There is a fundamental will, a basic autonomy, that his deployment of power cannot conquer, a primary elusiveness that iterates her subjectivity as essentially impenetrable. This becomes apparent in those passages where his sexual advances repeatedly run into a dispassionate resignation on her part; a radical unwillingness that cannot be disciplined or appropriated – that is, turned into an object – but only destroyed qua antagonistic subject:

> I waited until she'd made the bed and was tucking in the sheet, hoping she'd sense the atmosphere and do something to break it. But she carried on with what she was doing, until disbelievingly I had to put my hands out and touch her hips ... We didn't do it very often ... She suffered it. She thought, I imagine, there was no alternative. She didn't care.[76]

---

[76] Ibid., 96–7.

Machin can only 'imagine' her subjectivity as an alien entity that will not submit to his own, that will not accept the terms of appropriation laid down by the capitalist form of his 'success'.[77] Sex expresses here an incommensurability whose relational logic lies in the violent mystery of money, and which transposes the dynamic of struggle that presided over the exchange between capital and labour in the factory to the submerged terrain of reproduction. The subjectivity of capital that Machin embodies or enacts is fundamentally premised, as we have seen, on an abstraction of value, on a disconnection of exchange from the forms of temporal mediation expressed by the wage. Money can only think of itself as autonomized capital, as a 'tautology for power' that 'attacks things and transforms them in its own image and resemblance'.[78]

The increasing violence of the interactions between Machin and Mrs Hammond reflects this destructive tendency from which no reinstatement of equivalence, no restoration of measure or stability, can follow. Against her desperate protestations that his very presence in the house has become unbearably oppressive to her, Machin insists that he can only 'see the food you eat. The clothes you wear, the pleasure you get'[79] – in other words, a universe of commodities, of objectified values, that leaves no room for the self-valorizing, unobjectifiable, realm of subjectivity. His attempt to reduce her will and desires (which throughout the novel remain indecipherable mysteries to him) to a commodified and essentially unfree version of 'pleasure' leads her to angrily respond: 'Pleasure, pleasure, pleasure! You say pleasure! You standing over us! Like a bloody lord and master ... You *made* us enjoy anything we ever did. You *made* us.'[80] This characterization of affluence as command, as negation of subjectivity, is sharply distinct from the tantalizing and ideologically disabling universe of consumerism portrayed in *Saturday Night and Sunday Morning*. Affluence is converted here into a violent immediacy encroaching upon the subordinated (domestic, unwaged) worker's possibility of self-valorization. In this context, death literalizes the tragic defeat of the latter, inscribing the power

---

[77] In an earlier episode, the terms of opposition between her reproductive labour and his 'success' had already been clearly established: 'I ... sat down, annoyed, like a visiting inspector, to find her still stuck in her den of unventilated air, cluttered spaces, unused rows of crockery, completely unaware of the success I brought into the room', ibid., 44.
[78] Negri, *Marx*, 35.
[79] Storey, *This*, 176.
[80] Ibid., 176.

of money as a boundless expression of the subjectivity of capital, one which cannot contemplate the survival of any other, opposing or antagonistic, subjectivity.

After the death of Mrs Hammond, it could be said that Machin's foundational identification with capital, with the money-form, begins to recede. The novel presents this as a gradual process of exhaustion of his youthful energy, of that labour power which, having undergone an exceptional form of exchange within the ambit of professional sport (rather than ordinary factory work), led to a reconstruction or embodiment of capital itself in/as his own subjectivity. But as strength begins to fade, so does this fundamental subjective impetus around which his character had been constructed. In the final pages of the novel, a very different, almost defeated, Machin begins to emerge:

> I began to resent the activity around me. An old way of escape. I looked to the life that wasn't absorbed in the futility of the game – to the tall chimney and the two flowering cylinders of the power station, half hidden by cloud, the tops of the buses passing the end of the ground, the lights turned on inside the upper decks, the people sitting uncommitted behind the windows. The houses were lit too, in their slow descent to the valley. I moved back to the centre, imitating the figures whose activity suddenly tired me. I was ashamed of being no longer young.[81]

There is here an attempted reorientation of Machin's subjectivity from the immediacy of his earlier success (and its monetary expression) to the search for an estranged sociality, of a concrete context from which his stardom had only represented a destructive uprooting in the exclusive interest of capital. The factory, the town, and the suggestion of a domestic space that he himself had savagely exploited in his 'youth', now represent for him a lost sense of value as social quality and not merely abstract quantity, a lost opportunity for self-valorization and recognition of the self-valorization of others.

The process of capitalist socialization – or 'real subsumption' of society within capital – is thus contained in this figure of the generalization of value (of pure, abstracted or autonomized exchange value) that Storey rehearses in *This Sporting Life*; in this figure of subjectified money that simultaneously

---

[81] Ibid., 251.

invades time and space – reconstructing it in its image – and negates the possibility of alien, independent subjectivities. Although this is the concluding point articulated by this novel, it is worth noting that the expansiveness of capital in its socialized phase cannot simply presuppose the teleological inevitability of its triumph (something that Sillitoe's 'The Loneliness' had made apparent). Rather, the full inclusion of the social within the circuit of capitalist valorization and its articulation as an unmediated relation of power lead to a fresh redeployment of antagonistic politics, to a discovery, even in the hitherto muffled spaces of social life, of a new resistant energy and oppositional immediacy – of refusal as subjectivity and struggle.

3

Reproductive Work and Proletarian Resistance in Transition

Nell Dunn and Pat Barker

3.1 Desire and the labour of subjectivity: On Nell Dunn's proletarian women

As we anticipated in the previous chapter, the 'real subsumption' of society within capital that characterized post-war developments implied a valorization of areas of experience and subjectivity that were traditionally subordinated to the objectifying function of the factory (that is, to the transformation of living into dead labour operated by the latter). A whole range of activities, of relations, affects and desires, which writers and thinkers had typically excluded from the matrix of production (and hence, from the central axis of representation), were now accorded a strategic role. In the 1960s and 1970s, working-class fiction would increasingly turn towards hitherto marginalized proletarian subjects, especially women, their sexuality and domestic labour, in an attempt to capture the unmediated dynamics of exploitation, the direct encroachment of capital upon social life that was beginning to define this historical phase.

As a number of feminist theorists influenced by Operaismo were able to observe in these years,[1] the increasingly social quality of post-war capitalism implied that women's hitherto ambiguous position at the intersection of waged and unwaged work, of production and reproduction, now came to represent a

---

[1] See Mariarosa Dalla Costa and Selma James, *The Power of Women and the Subversion of the Community* (Bristol: Falling Wall Press, 1975), Leopoldina Fortunati, *The Arcane of Reproduction: Housework, Prostitution, Labor and Capital*, trans. Hilary Creek (New York: Autonomedia, 1995), Silvia Federici, *Revolution at Point Zero: Housework, Reproduction, and Feminist Struggle* (Oakland, CA: PM Press, 2012). For an important, recent addition to this debate, see Kathi Weeks, *The Problem with Work: Feminism, Marxism, Antiwork Politics, and Postwork Imaginaries* (Durham: Duke University Press, 2011).

general standpoint from which labour's subsumption within capital could be countenanced. The socialization of capitalism thus involved a fundamental levelling of pre-existing qualitative distinctions in the realm of work, and the unveiling of a dynamic continuity in the processes of extraction and accumulation of value.

I will begin with an analysis of Nell Dunn's portrayal of working-class women in 1960s London in *Up the Junction* (1963) and *Poor Cow* (1967). The first book consists of a series of semi-documentary vignettes depicting the lives of women factory workers both inside and outside the factory, while the second one follows the misadventures of a marginal woman without any direct ties to the realm of productive labour. In these two works (and especially, in the passage from one to the other), Dunn charts the effects of capitalist socialization upon working-class women who are presented as both exploited and assertive in their vindication of subjective areas of autonomy. The picture painted by this author is neither one of obliteration – as in the case of Sillitoe's and Storey's women – nor one of fully realized emancipation. It is, rather, a complex and socially dense canvas of affirmative brushes and systemic traps, of subjective movements against a background of generalized exploitation on which no stabilization, no pacification, can be achieved.

Nell Dunn's quasi-documentary investigation of the living conditions of women factory workers in 1960s London is characterized by a strong emphasis on subjectivity, on the complex and unquantifiable universe of desires and affects, which effectively presents labour as a dynamic articulation – as *living* labour in the strictest sense – extending beyond the narrowly objective determinations of the industrial process. As we have seen, Storey's novel anticipated a process of autonomization of exchange (of capital as money) that becomes generalized in postmodernity and that marks the completion of the process of capitalist socialization (the real subsumption of society within capital). Sillitoe's texts, for their part, insisted on the separation that constitutes working-class subjectivity and its antagonistic interactions with capital in the age of massified industrial work. With Dunn, we are again in the midst of this struggle, of this irrepressible affirmation of class difference that characterizes the labour process in the post-war years, while witnessing the development of the crisis of value presented by Storey. The latter is articulated, however, as a crisis of discipline that inheres in the affirmation of the working-class subject, in its extension and projection beyond the factory as a fluid entity capable of anticipating the molecular spread of capital's own command over the entire society.

As in the case of Sillitoe and Storey, the point of departure for Dunn is also the centrality of the factory, of a factory that reflects the transformation of work into a mass process technically defined by advanced automation and the deskilling of its workforce. But this is a factory universe in which the protagonists are women, and in which working-class subjectivity is not constructed as mere resistance to the concrete manifestations of capital (whether in the form of the machine, the State's repressive apparatus, or an autonomized version of money), but as so many unrestrained expressions of desire, alternately tentative and insecure, whimsical and riotous. In effect, Dunn's novels have been praised (and in her own time, condemned) on the basis of this commitment to the representation of 'women's sexual desire and autonomy' in a thematically candid and formally raw manner.[2]

In *Up the Junction* we are immediately presented with a desiring logic that departs from the segmentations and compartmentalizations (between pleasure/consumption and work/production) enacted by *Saturday Night and Sunday Morning*. In the latter text, sexual desire had not only been the subjective preserve of the male worker, but also, ominously, the royal road to the dismantling of his autonomy, a blurring effect working against the antagonistic clarity of vision attained on the factory floor. Here, by contrast, desire in not subordinated to pleasure or objectified in consumption (although pleasure and consumption are functional elements of these women's daily lives). Its articulation is primary and non-derivative, a constitutive moment of their socialization as working-class subjects. The book opens with one such scene of socialization through desire, with three girls standing in a pub, intently gazing at men. One of them, the more passive character, is the middle-class narrator (a thinly fictionalized version of Dunn), while the other two, the local factory workers Sylvie and Rube, are presented as active, desiring subjects: 'Rube, neck stiff so as not to shake her beehive, stares sultrily round the packed pub. Sylvie eyes the boy hunched over the mike and shifts her gaze down to her

---

[2] Stephen Brooke, '"Slumming" in Swinging London: Class, Gender and the Post-War City in Nell Dunn's *Up the Junction* (1963)', *Cultural and Social History*, 9: 3 (2012), 430.

breasts snug in her new pink jumper.'[3] As Stephen Brooke has pointed out, the word 'gaze' is indeed key in this passage,[4] insofar as it suggests a scopic articulation of female agency that subverts the traditional position of women as objects within a male-dominated field of vision. Rube's 'sultry' and sweeping stare across the gallery of masculine bodies on display, together with Sylvie's sensuous awareness of her own physicality, are the true actors, the irreducible agents in this passage, in which men are remarkably transformed into targets and vehicles of their autonomous desire.

This is not a dynamic that presides exclusively over the social world outside the factory. The logic of desire as socialization also colonizes the factory itself, almost transforming it into an internal moment of the women's subjective constitution, into a function of their autonomy. Dunn's stylistic choices, the largely passive role played by the narrator as a participant, and the seemingly unmediated quality of the women's voices, further reinforce the presentation of this working-class universe as an independent variable that, within the structural conditions of the massification of industrial work, has managed to impose itself as autonomous subjectivity. The psychological withdrawal that, for Arthur Seaton, had been a tactical necessity in his resistance against the onslaught of fixed capital, of the machine and the bosses, is here replaced by a playful overtness that is neither individualized (as in Arthur's case) nor directly subordinated to the productive rhythms of the assembly line. As we can see in the following passage, the factory routines described in the book are still harsh and physically demanding. The sickening fumes of the bicycle factory where Arthur Seaton worked are replaced by the damp and cold of the chocolate factory portrayed by Dunn. However, in the latter case, these conditions are effectively subordinated to, or mediated by, the subjective and desiring density of the collective exchanges, of the impudence of the women's speech, and of their laughter:

> 'Anyone lend me their husband for the weekend?'
> 'Yeah, you can 'ave mine, he's a dirty sod on the quiet.'
> 'I'd lend you mine, only he wouldn't be much good to yer!'
> 'Send them all up. You know where I live – just by the church.'

---

[3] Nell Dunn, *Up the Junction* (London: Virago, 1988), 13.
[4] Brooke, '"Slumming"', 438.

'Do you like 'em fair or dark?'

'It's not the 'air I'm interested in!'

We laugh, twenty-five women hunched over three long tables, packing cheap sweets for Christmas. Thick red fingers, swollen with the cold, flash from tray to box. In a matter of seconds it's neatly packed, a little circle of sweets with three pink mice in the middle.[5]

The technical organization of the extraction of value (the industrial process of the modern factory) is thus framed within an affirmative extension of the subjectivity of living labour. Once again, this is not to say that in this text the working-class subject has broken free from the logic of capital, but rather that in the context of the latter's massification and socialization, the subjective density of living labour is increasingly asserted and posited as an irreducible element in the process of valorization. The expansiveness of the mass relation initiated in the factory finds, in the essential insubordination and 'separateness' of working-class subjectivity, its fundamental driving force. This relational paradox is constitutive as much as it is irreducible. In *This Sporting Life*, the capitalist relation of exploitation had been autonomized, rendered abstract and independent from the logic of waged labour, and transformed into a subjective figure of command – into money. This dynamic (personified in the character of Arthur Machin) had in turn provoked an antagonistic confrontation with living labour, with 'naked', unmediated labour (embodied in the figure of Mrs Hammond), that could no longer be mystified or confused by the logic of consumption and affluence. The diffuse ubiquity of money, its subjective assertion as the socialized form of capitalist command, dictated a symmetrical construction of the worker as equally diffuse and abstract, at the same time that it exerted its violence upon the latter.[6]

And yet, simultaneously chased and socialized, exploited and abstracted by the onslaught of capital, labour ceases to be a localized, individualized and easily mystifiable entity (as it had been in the case of Arthur Seaton). Instead, it becomes a 'real abstraction', a socialized subject operating in and beyond the factory, and delineating with every moment of its existence an autonomy of needs and desires that capital will be increasingly unable to discipline.[7] By the

---

[5] Dunn, *Junction*, 25.
[6] Mrs Hammond's work was, in this sense, eminently social – socially reproductive labour.
[7] This is Antonio Negri's summary of the development described above: 'Remember how, from the first pages of the analysis, when money began to represent the rarified but powerful space of social

time we get to Dunn's desiring women, the structural subordination of individual needs to the dictates of capital has been broken, and the phenomenological confusion suffered by Arthur Seaton has been replaced by an affirmative and undisciplined *social* behaviour. At this point, as Negri puts it, the 'relation with capital breaks the subjection to economic necessity, comes to life in the only way that matter can come to life: as behaviour, as *power (potenza)*. This power is subjectivity. It is irreducible.'[8]

It is in this precise sense that Dunn's emphasis on female sexual desire should be understood. This essentially represents or announces the coming-to-life of labour in its post-war, socialized, configuration. It marks the transformation of an actually existing functional generality (of labour power as a 'mass' formation, as 'abstract labour') into a subject. With this crucial mutation, the capitalist deployment of the wage as an attempt to capture and discipline the vitality of labour becomes obsolete and useless,[9] and must be replaced with an equally abstract, diffuse and *powerful* operation. Dunn's eminently insubordinate women are thus recurrently confronted with a faceless or indefinite logic of social oppression, which often takes the form of a dramatic reversal of their sexual freedom. In *Up the Junction*, this is tellingly exemplified by the crude description of Rube's abortion. After realizing that she is pregnant ('About three months', by her reckoning),[10] and after seeking help from an illegal abortionist, she finally gives birth to a living, five-month foetus that dies soon afterwards, in what constitutes perhaps the most shocking scene in the book. The spare quality of the narration savagely underscores the drama of social exposure and vulnerability that now characterizes this working-class universe:

> When I came back from ringing, Rube was shrieking, a long, high, animal shriek. The baby was born alive, five months old. It moved, it breathed, its heart beat.

---

command, living labor began to rise up untiringly before it? Remember how, in its development, living labor takes the form of *"real" abstraction*, of workers' society, of mediator of production? *The red thread of abstract labor traces a constituting process.* The more work becomes abstract and socialized ... the more the sphere of needs grows. Work creates its own needs and forces capital to satisfy them', *Marx Beyond Marx: Lessons on the* Grundrisse, trans. Harry Cleaver, Michael Ryan and Maurizio Viano (New York and London: Autonomedia/Pluto Press, 1991), 133.

[8] Ibid., 133.
[9] 'The *wage* is formed ... on the basis of these needs – to *mystify* the individuality, henceforth clear, of the masses of necessary labor that this process has consolidated', ibid., 133.
[10] Dunn, *Junction*, 63.

> Rube lay back, white and relieved, across the bed. Sylvie and her mum lifted the eiderdown and peered at the tiny baby still joined by the cord. 'You can see it breathing, look!'
> Rube smiled. 'It's nothing – I've had a look meself!'
> ...
> Finally the ambulance arrived. They took Rube away, but they left behind the baby, which had now grown cold. Later Sylvie took him, wrapped in the *Daily Mirror*, and threw him down the toilet.[11]

The affirmative quality of desire that punctuates the social world of the novel is now turned on its head and presented as socialized violence and affective indifference. The crudeness of the image of the dead baby, compounded with the emotional unresponsiveness of the characters, contribute to the devalorization of the affirmed and autonomized life of the working-class subject, to its reconstruction as a figure of social deprivation rather than constitutive richness. Thus, the antagonistic dialectic between exploitation/ oppression and affirmation/resistance is displaced to the diffuse spaces and dynamics of social life and recast as general and immediate violence (of the kind that we had begun to see in *This Sporting Life*).

In a slightly different idiom, we could say that the antagonism becomes *biopolitical*. In other words, life itself (including, and especially, life's more 'intimate' spaces and dimensions) becomes not only the passive object of a general extractive arrangement at whose strategic centre lies the factory, but also a productive subject in its own right, an autonomous target of systemic exploitation.[12] By encroaching upon the free potentialities released by these unruly female subjects in the form of diffuse social oppression, of an 'immaterial' poverty that expresses their exclusion from capitalist freedom in this universe of supposedly reigning affluence, the system sets out to disarticulate the subjective power of their socialization, to turn their autonomous 'behaviour' against them. Thus capital is forced to adopt the form of what Michel Foucault calls 'biopower' and to render the entire process of the social exploitation of labour into an operation of management, of 'conduction' or 'conduct',[13] that

---

[11] Ibid., 65–6.
[12] See Michael Hardt and Antonio Negri, *Commonwealth* (Cambridge, MA: Harvard University Press, 2009), 131–49.
[13] Foucault plays on the double meaning of the French word *conduite*, 'conduct' (understood as 'behaviour' and the act of 'conducting'). See Michel Foucault, 'The Subject and Power', *Critical Inquiry*, 8: 4 (1982), 777–95.

presupposes a fundamental freedom on the part of the exploited subject. According to Foucault, power is only possible if the subjects upon which it is exerted are free, if they embody a 'field of possibilities', a range of behaviours and responses, with which it can engage. In this sense, power 'is a total structure of actions brought to bear upon possible actions; it incites, it induces, it seduces, it makes easier or more difficult'.[14] The fact that it can only occur 'by virtue of [a subject's] acting or being capable of an action' permanently refers to 'the recalcitrance of the will and the intransigence of freedom' on which that subject is predicated.[15] Yet this is not an essential or transcendent freedom; it is the freedom of life's unfolding as a tapestry of possible behaviours in a social continuum of countervailing pressures. In such a saturated and power-driven social universe, the outcome of subjective freedom may well be, for example, the iteration of racist stereotypes, and consequently the promotion of divisive attitudes with respect to the very social composition of labour power. Thus, the occasional derogatory references to 'coloureds' in *Up the Junction* attest to the profound ambivalence of the increasing autonomization of proletarian subjectivity in this context.[16]

Capital, in its socially diffuse, post-war development, is increasingly found operating as such a structure of actions upon possible actions, inducing and inciting a dynamic of freedom, of subjective self-valorization that it will seek to manage and 'conduct', to exploit and use for its own benefit. Yet (as Foucault and Negri have stressed in their different ways) the irreducibility of autonomy, of free actions both possible and actual, on which power rests, means that the prospect of a final stabilization (of a final operation of ideological incorporation or material annihilation such as those portrayed, *in extremis*, by Sillitoe and Storey) becomes increasingly distant and improbable. Under the sign of the abstraction of labour, of the socialization of the relationship of capital, the ambivalence of power (the irreducibility of resistance and the inescapability of the exploitative operation) is absolute. As Dunn's novel *Poor Cow* will demonstrate, the expansive dynamic of subjectivation undergone by these 'socialized' female workers will lead them steadily away from the traditional

---

[14] Ibid., 789.
[15] Ibid., 789, 790.
[16] See, for example, the racial othering of 'black Moira' undertaken by some of the girls in Dunn, *Junction*, 43–6; or, later, the narrator's own rehearsal of ambient racial stereotypes: 'Down a basement coals are burning, hot jazz is playing, and the room is thick with Coloureds', ibid., 71.

disciplinary enclosure of the factory, presenting them as ever more complex and fluid, as simultaneously more empowered and more vulnerable, more autonomous and more exposed to new mechanisms and relations of biopower or biopolitical exploitation.

In *Poor Cow*, Dunn takes the examination of female working-class life initiated in *Up the Junction* to its social (one might say, 'lumpenproletarian') limits. Joy, the novel's protagonist, is a young, jobless mother married to a thief, Tom, who is arrested and imprisoned early on in the novel. She then becomes emotionally involved with Dave, her husband's former partner-in-crime, until he too is sent to prison. The novel is then for the most part a reconstruction of Joy's thoughts, feelings and experiences as a single (and independent?) woman, as she waits for both men's release (expressing a passionate impatience in relation to Dave's, and a tired, and perhaps somewhat fearful, indifference in regard of her husband's). The ambivalence and complexity surrounding the position of autonomy/subordination of working-class women within the socialized dynamics of post-war capitalism in *Up the Junction* is greatly amplified in the case of *Poor Cow* and its protagonist. It has been noted by critics, for example, that the choice of name, Joy, while ironic given the title of the novel (she is, after all, the eponymous 'poor cow'), is not entirely so, since 'she is by no means a helpless victim: she is a survivor who admits to herself that she can't take too much security'.[17] In effect, the lack of psychological depth that was a fact of Dunn's construction of her characters in the previous book (characters who, for the most part, remained pure sketches, pure *subjective tendencies* within a compressed exercise of semi-documentary analysis), is now replaced by a sustained attempt at narrative complexity whose principal ingredient, it might be argued, is a central ambivalence in Joy's attitude towards 'security'.

Security comes across in her internal monologue as a labile aspiration, as a sign of material status ('something out of life that everybody's got')[18] that seems appealing if it remains transitory, yet becomes unsatisfactory – and even unsettling – once it is shaped into a permanent state of affairs: 'When I'm walking down the road I see people happy, I want that, but when I come to think of it I can have it one day and I may not want it. I'm not going to have

---

[17] Margaret Drabble, 'Introduction', in Nell Dunn, *Poor Cow* (London: Virago, 1988), xi.
[18] Dunn, *Poor*, 28.

much excitement once I settle down.'[19] The notion of security is recurrently subordinated, for Joy, to the 'excitement' its loss might entail, to the experience of flight and break it typically brings in its wake. It is so that her unhappy marriage to Tom is vindicated as the necessary prerequisite to her subsequent unravelling of desire: 'Let's face it, if I wasn't married I'd never have had all the excitement I've had.'[20] But 'excitement' is from the outset an ambivalent and contradictory category, one that is often reduced to the status of a possession, of an object or a commodity ('something that was mine'),[21] yet which systematically proves far more elusive and immaterial. Joy's fundamental confusion (which Dunn reflects in the logical breaks and twists of her internal monologue) arises from her inability to detach the nature and intensity of her ontological insubordination as a desiring subject – as a subject in flight from 'too much security' – from the still prevalent narrative of affluence. The result is a reified phenomenology in which security stands as an ideal (or ideological) deviation from the actual process of subjectivation through which her character is constituted.

Thus, while security remains an abstract standard of fixation or stabilization, the real movement of Joy's subjectivity is characterized by an increasing expansiveness and dynamism, by an outward movement of desire that cannot be fixated or stabilized. As I have already suggested, this is the specific profile of a dynamic of socialization of the capitalist power relation through which the poles of resistance and subjection, of insubordination and exploitation, are simultaneously reinforced and integrated. Joy's rejection of security expresses the duplicity of a process through which her freedom becomes increasingly functional to the diffuse system of discipline to which the traditional form of the factory was giving way in the 1960s, at the same time that the unruliness of her conduct (of the field of possible actions constitutive of her subjectivity) is consolidated.

It is in this sense that Joy's relationship with her lover Dave is so defining of her subjective development in the novel. Unlike Tom, who is a mere reminder of a foregone material stability that, when carefully examined, is neither genuine nor effectively desirable, Dave represents, for the most part, an invisible

[19] Ibid., 28.
[20] Ibid., 28.
[21] Ibid., 28–9.

presence around which her subjective development unfolds – almost a blank screen upon which her desire and affects are projected in cumulative fragments and tentative sketches. Indeed, Dave only briefly appears in the chapter entitled 'Love' before he is arrested and sent to prison, and there, his contribution is almost exclusively that of encouraging, or even serving as the material support for, Joy's sexual discoveries.[22] After that, Dave becomes the largely absent addressee of a series of letters without reply,[23] virtually a formal excuse for Dunn to carry on the process of Joy's autonomous self-making.

These letters in effect articulate Joy's process of subjectivation as that ambivalent, simultaneously liberating and enslaving, figure through which the general movement of the socialization of living labour within the capitalist relation can be summarized. The idiosyncratic misspellings that pepper her writing sometimes offer a particular insight into this ambivalent biopolitical logic: 'We got a LOVE no one else got and it terrific its sending me mad. I'm so raped up in Your love I never wont to be un raped and I want to stay like it for ever I Love You – Dave I do.'[24] Rather than merely signal a condescending exposure of Joy's naivety on the part of the author,[25] this is surely a revealing instance of the irreducibility and interpenetration of freedom and exploitation in this subjective construction and its wider social context. What this fragment so playfully suggests is nothing but the constitutive indivisibility of autonomy and power, of the founding act of freedom (possible or actual, as Foucault remarks) upon which the latter in turn operates. It is only through the expansive and productive freedom expressed by Joy's sexuality that the socialized, diffuse and decentralized relation of power can function and proliferate: throughout the novel, Joy remains 'raped up' in and through the freely constituted acts of love and desire that she in the first place calls forth.

---

[22] There is a clear sense in which the sexual enjoyment that Dave's presence enables is foreshadowed (and thus effectively provoked or *produced*) by Joy. Thus her confession that 'I shall get very perverted in time to come, very perverted', ibid., 29, seems to directly link to her first sexual encounter with Dave: 'Over the top of the bed was this plastic chandelier – and all the beams started falling like crystals, falling down on top of us, he was going so slow and I was coming so much', ibid., 31.
[23] He is only reported by the narrator as annotating the letters he receives from Joy with the presumable aim of filing them: 'And at the bottom Dave wrote, "FIRST LETTER FROM JOYSY AFTER SENTENCE 12 YEARS OH GOD"', ibid., 45.
[24] Ibid., 50.
[25] Which is the suggestion made by, for example, Dominic Head in his *Cambridge Introduction to Modern British Fiction, 1950–2000* (Cambridge: Cambridge University Press, 2002), 91.

The more immediately obvious and pervasive of these acts is the one that her relationship with Dave inaugurates, an intense sexual desire that will soon be emancipated from any monogamous structure. While a declared amorous faithfulness to her imprisoned lover remains the central feature of her letters, Joy's sexuality is gradually transformed into a free-floating 'lust' without exclusivity, attachment, or transcendence: 'Proper lusty I was getting – it used to be love but it's all lust now – it's so terrific with different blokes. Sometimes you fancy it all soft and other times you want them to fuck the life out of you. Well you can't get that from the same bloke can you.'[26] The crude directness of the interior monologue contrasts with the stylized ambiguity of her letter-writing, suggesting the uncompromising and absolute radicality of the founding act of freedom. This 'lust' is the generative matrix upon which dependency and subordination (her being 'raped up') will be constructed without possible abolition or definitive surrender. Once desire is discovered as the motor of her subjectivity, it becomes the irreducible foundation of her subsumption within the total structure of socialized relations of power.

A second fundamental aspect of Joy's paradoxical subjection through autonomy concerns her status as a single mother. Apart from her sexual forays and experimentations, the other central aspect of her affectivity that is constantly engaged throughout the novel is her love for her little son Jonny. This is a love that runs in parallel to and in many ways surpasses the physicality of her sexual encounters; a love that, in a sense, takes bodily intimacy to a new level of sensuality. There is a subtlety and intensity (a 'lyrical' quality, as Margaret Drabble puts it)[27] in the description of Joy's attentions to her baby child that may induce us to regard this relationship as a further, actualized, dimension of her constitutive freedom. Although the book does open with an expression of Joy's misgivings about her motherhood ('What did I go and get landed with him for, I used to be a smart girl?'),[28] the affective quality that unfolds in those passages where she dresses, caresses, or plays with little Jonny points to an equally if not more powerful affirmation of her subjectivity than that represented by sexual desire.[29]

[26] Dunn, *Poor*, 64.
[27] Drabble, 'Introduction', xiv.
[28] Dunn, *Poor*, 9–10.
[29] 'She loved doing this, holding his small warm body on her lap, pulling the T-shirt over his head "pee boo Mama", he'd shout and fall back in laughter. She couldn't get over his lovely legs and little square

I would like to suggest that this figuration of maternal freedom, articulated as corporeal intimacy between Joy and Jonny, indicates a further – and absolutely central – development of the foundational autonomy on which her subjective construction rests, and thus a crucial instance of her subsumption within the diffuse power relations of capitalist exploitation. Her previous stints as a model, as a waitress, and even, for a brief period, as a prostitute all come to represent, in retrospect, a temporary detour from the central subjective constituency defined by her maternity (or the alternative pathway to follow in the catastrophic event of losing her child).[30] As the novel draws to a close, Joy comes to the conclusion 'that all that really mattered was that the child should be all right and that they should be together'.[31] This brings her to one final consideration regarding her sustained ambivalence towards security/stability throughout the novel that has the final effect of re-presenting her – primarily to herself – as a 'poor cow': '"Oh gawd, what a state I'm in", she said, as, hand in hand, they walked back down the deserted road. "To think when I was a kid I planned to conquer the world and if anyone saw me now they'd say. 'She's had a rough night, poor cow'".'[32] Following what I have suggested above, it would not be exact to claim that this final realignment with the 'security' provided by the presence and well-being of her child (which is certainly very different from the kind of security provided by her husband Tom, or even her lover Dave) is merely a reflection of her relinquishment of freedom. The affective closeness and protective physicality of the mother–child relationship does not represent a momentary retreat from the subjective affirmation traced in the central chapters of the novel. Rather, it expresses the radical interpenetration of freedom and subjection, of autonomy and exploitation, in an immanent continuum through which the socialized and biopolitical logic of power comes into being.

---

feet. She let his dark hair grow long and thick so it curled in great feathers around his ears. She would sit for a long time looking at him as he played around the room or crawled out onto the balcony', ibid., 40; '[S]he felt an overpowering love for him – a love which didn't seem to have a beginning or an end. They would spit Spangles into each other's mouths as they lay in bed in the mornings, listening to the small throbbing transistor', ibid., 57.

[30] 'I spose I could be a brass – if anything happened to Jonny that's what I would do – go professional. It would be terrible. You have nothing. You become numb to everything. You never really think of settling down and having a family, that doesn't ever come into it. You never think of that sort of thing. All you think of is good times and the money. And you find that somebody is going to cut your throat for each penny', ibid., 126.
[31] Ibid., 140.
[32] Ibid., 140–1.

We could say that this dynamic of interpenetration, that this indivisible logic of mutual dependency between capital's social power and the proletarian subject's affirmative capacities, summarizes the historical level of development attained by capitalism at the point where the traditional factory begins to decrease in importance. As Dunn's fiction demonstrates, the focus is increasingly shifted from the *external* spaces and temporalities of the older industrial process to the *internal* potentialities of subjectivity. This implies a fundamental recognition of the productive qualities of areas of social and individual life that had traditionally played a secondary role. After all, the logic of the factory had effectively relied on the objectification of living labour, on the transformation of human capacities into a commodified matrix of production. But as the factory begins to lose its centrality within the social cycle of the production of value, the untapped resources of human life, the unobjectified, raw, and multifarious potentialities of *living labour* become a fundamental constituent of the capitalist apparatus. The paradoxical aspect of this extension of the productive franchise – so to speak – is that there is a direct and insurmountable correlation between the subjectivation of these potentialities, between the 'becoming-subject' of raw social life and its multiple dimensions, and their incorporation or subsumption within the mechanisms of extraction and appropriation of value; in other words, that, as the material differentiation of the proletariat qua polymorphous and increasingly self-affirmative subject grows, so does its 'capture', its integration within the social textures of the capitalist machine. This, as we have seen, closely approximates the dialectic of power without sublation (without resolution or cancellation in the Hegelian mode) described by the later Foucault.[33]

In this context, the fictional representation of proletarian resistance, of the working-class attempt to break the deadlock of mutual presupposition and dependency, will increasingly turn towards figures in which resistance is no longer necessarily understood as subjective growth and consolidation, as expansive 'behaviour' in the sense suggested by Negri above,[34] but as intensive

---

[33] See, for example, Michel Foucault, *Discipline and Punish: The Birth of the Prison*, trans. Alan Sheridan (London: Penguin, 1991); *The Will to Know: The History of Sexuality*, vol. 1, trans. Robert Hurley (London: Penguin, 1998); and *Society Must Be Defended: Lectures at the Collège de France, 1975–6*, trans. David Macey (London: Penguin, 2004). For a good overview of the development of Foucault's thought, especially in this period of the mid- to late 1970s, see Judith Revel, *Foucault, une pensée du discontinu* (Paris: Milles et Une Nuits, 2010).

[34] See Negri, *Marx*, 133.

diminution, as contraction or reduction of the subject's capacities (of those capacities that capital seeks to appropriate), or as deviation, *détournement*, or even dissolution. As society becomes the central stage on which the capitalist machine of value extraction is deployed, the proletarian subject, as we will see, undergoes a process of self-estrangement and unworking. While the 'intimate' dimension of the (especially female) proletarian subject – its sexuality, its reproductive 'labour power' – will increase in importance, it will often appear in excess of subjectivity itself, more as a line of flight that escapes the interiority of the power scenario described by Foucault than as a point of support for the latter.

As we will see in the following sections, Pat Barker's early novels signal a fundamental development in this direction. The exploitative and resistant dynamics depicted in novels such as *Union Street* (1982) and *Blow Your House Down* (1984) represent a radical intensification of the areas and forms of vulnerability and exposure through which the proletarian subject is exploited. Yet this intensification also prompts, ultimately, an evacuation of the increasingly accepted and recognized forms of subjectivation, of self-affirmation, on which, as we have seen, the process of capitalist socialization rests. Thus, beyond Joy's discovery of sexual desire as an ambivalent strategy of defence against capital's onslaught, beyond the anarchic quality of these women's laughter and spontaneity, we will find in Barker's women an experiential extremity that brings subjectivity to the limit, even recreating refusal – proletarian refusal – as a suicidal strategy of rupture with the system.

3.2 Reproduction in revolt: Pat Barker's *Union Street*

The British 1970s have been customarily depicted as a decade of unstoppable decline. According to historian Nick Tiratsoo, when

> [l]ooked at in detail, the conventional charge sheet against the 1970s is long and damning. Britain was beset by economic failure. The trade unions acted like robber barons, holding the rest of the country to ransom. Inflation stalked the land, destroying the social fabric. Ordinary people constantly

found themselves bullied by powers outside their control. This was a period of strikes, power-cuts and discontent.[35]

This bleak picture, painted many times over by right-wing ideologues throughout the 1980s in an attempt to justify the thrust of Thatcherite policy, tends to obscure the complexity of a historical period which saw the widespread rejection of the so-called 'post-war consensus' and the generalized intensification of class antagonisms and expressions of proletarian autonomy. The centrality of working-class resistance has often been downplayed in accounts of the rise of neoliberalism in Britain, often presenting the latter as an endogenous development of capitalist ideology. However, as we have seen, the cumulative effect of working-class resistance and self-valorization in the preceding decades cannot be overestimated as a determining factor in the explosion of ideological, economic, social and political crises in the 1970s. Indeed, the increased radicalism of organized industrial labour (suggested by Tiratsoo's reference to the trade unions above), after their relatively passive and incorporated position within the political establishment of previous years, pointed to a new set of attitudes within the working class itself rather than to a sudden conversion of its institutions. This process reached a climax in the miners' strikes of 1971–2 and 1973–4, which would eventually topple the Conservative government of Edward Heath and represented, in the words of Raymond Williams, 'a return to real class politics' and a 're-emergence of genuine socialist militancy'.[36] The 1970s effectively culminated in an episode (the so-called Winter of Discontent, during which a flurry of strikes spread over the country) that would lead straight to Margaret Thatcher's electoral victory in 1979; but first and foremost, the 1970s epitomized the British working class's revitalization of proletarian struggles. The depth and intensity of the 1970s crises – which, despite specific national characteristics, had a truly global reach – was abetted by the spread of antagonisms across the entire social body. As we have already seen in the context of 1950s and 1960s writing about the breakdown of Fordist industrial and social discipline, proletarian resistance could no longer be confined to the factory, and the struggle over the wage was increasingly regarded as concerning not only paid labour, but also a

---

[35] Nick Tiratsoo (ed.), *From Blitz to Blair: A New History of Britain since 1939* (London: Phoenix, 1998), 163.
[36] Raymond Williams, *Politics and Letters* (London: New Left Books, 1979), 376.

whole range of social provisions, both formal and informal, direct and indirect.[37]

Barker's fictional engagement with working-class women's lives in the crisis-ridden North of England of the 1970s situates domesticity and reproductive labour at the centre of social conflicts and transformations. While the period's miners' strikes and structural readjustments lurk in the background, supplying an ill-defined temporal frame to the narrative, the dramatic foregrounding of women's exposed existence, of their resilient corporeality and indomitable psychology, offers a radical redefinition of working-class experience and subjectivity in post-war Britain. Although some critics, such as Sarah Brophy, have rightly identified Barker's interest in 'women's reproductive and domestic labors as a mode of economic production',[38] the extent to which these novels engage with capitalism's *biopolitical* turn (that is, with capital's shift of focus from the factory and its specific staging of labour power to *life* itself, understood as a far more diffuse and productive social resource) has not been sufficiently explored. I argue here that Barker's early fiction situates reproduction at the centre of both capital's penetration of the fabric of social life and of the articulation of working-class resistance and self-valorization.

As feminist theorist Leopoldina Fortunati has written, 'the female worker, in order to reproduce herself, can exchange her labor power *as capacity to reproduce* either for the male wage or, if she works in the production of commodities, for her own wage. But in reality this dual aspect is never posited as an *alternative* at a general level; instead it takes place contemporaneously.'[39] Most of the adult women portrayed by Barker show that this dual exchange often translates into a near-complete subsumption of life under labour; whether it is the mind-numbing labour of the assembly line, the sordid selling of one's own ageing body, or the mass and invariably bloody business of childbirth. Women's reproductive labour is constructed, across the different characters in the book, as a relentless exertion, as an all-pervasive form of

---

[37] As Michael Hardt and Antonio Negri have observed: 'The enormous rise in the social wage (in terms of both working wages and welfare) during the period of crisis in the 1960s and 1970s resulted directly from the accumulation of social struggles on the terrain of reproduction, the terrain of non-work, the terrain of life', *Empire* (Cambridge, MA: Harvard University Press, 2000), 273.

[38] Sarah Brophy, 'Working-Class Women, Labor, and the Problem of Community in *Union Street* and *Liza's England*', in Sharon Monteith et al. (eds), *Critical Perspectives on Pat Barker* (Columbia: South Carolina University Press, 2005), 26.

[39] Fortunati, *Arcane*, 13.

exploitative socialization which leaves no room for respite or withdrawal. The work of reproduction – literally, the hard labour of pregnancy and childbirth, of unwaged housework and conjugal violence – alternates in a seamless continuum with the drudgery of sub-employment as an unskilled factory hand, a home helper, or even a prostitute. This is a gendered universe in which life is effectively co-opted or subsumed by labour, and in which the chances of survival are defined by the nature of the exchanges into which the female subjects enter (with boyfriends, husbands, foremen, clients and other 'proprietors').

In the crowded rooms and parlours of this proletarian women's world, the possibility of turning off, of withdrawing from, the exploitative machinery of socially imposed labour is simply non-existent. Joanne Wilson's situation, as described in the second chapter of the novel, is revealing in this regard: the isolation produced by the assembly line is still the same as in earlier accounts of male 'productive' labour, but the psychological recourse to a defensive, and even properly resistant, escapism (à la Arthur Seaton, for example) is no longer available to Joanne. While still physically chained to her productive, waged, routine at the cake factory, her mind concentrates on the implications of her impending, unwaged, reproductive burden – an unexpected pregnancy – and on how she will break the news to her boyfriend Ken:

> The first sponge cake reached Jo. She began the sequence of actions that she would perform hundreds of times that day. It took little effort once you were used to it and, provided the cakes continued to arrive in a steady stream, it could be done almost automatically.
> Almost. But not quite. Now that she was alone – for in this roaring cavern of sound each woman *was* alone – she wanted to think about Ken, she wanted to plan the evening, to work out exactly how she was going to tell him about the baby. She couldn't do it. Each half-formed thought was aborted by the arrival of another cake. She was left with a picture of his face floating against a backcloth of sponges: dark-haired and sallow-skinned, the rather prominent Adam's apple jerking when he laughed.[40]

This interference between the demands of production and reproduction, between the psychological alertness imposed by the factory, on the one hand,

---

[40] Pat Barker, *Union Street* (London: Virago, 1982), 85.

and by sexuality, on the other, makes Joanne doubly exposed, doubly vulnerable to the mechanical thrusts of capitalist exploitation. By using explicitly reproductive language in her characterization of the mind-numbing productive rhythm of the factory (note that Joanne's thoughts are repeatedly 'aborted'), Barker insists on the reigning confusion between the two ambits under the unitary control of capital. Intercourse itself becomes an extension of the impersonal rhythms of production,[41] a corporeal mark of the workers' real condition of expropriation and subordination and of their inability to break off from its control, however momentarily. Sex does not represent for her, or for any of the women in *Union Street*, an outlet or getaway from capital and its circuit of valorization. Rather, it signifies an extension of its mechanical rhythms to the intimate realm of life, an internal disciplining of living labour at the most basic level.

The process of subsumption whereby life itself becomes a dependant feature of the capitalist production of value reaches its apotheosis in sexual intimacy. In this universe, the spontaneity and naturalness of sex is subordinated to the exigencies of a social organization predicated on the universality or pervasiveness of labour – to a socialized form of exploitation in which it is increasingly difficult to distinguish between work and non-work, between capital and life. Sex is thus, in a very concrete sense, the paradigmatic site of expropriation. Two extremes – rape and prostitution – frame this circumscription of life itself within the axis of capitalist accumulation. While rape embodies the most direct and extreme form of primitive accumulation, prostitution, as we will see later on, represents the proletarianization of women's reproductive labour power.

The story of Kelly Brown, which gives the novel a dramatic start, provides an allegorical treatment of the emergent biopolitical nature of capitalist exploitation in postmodernity. Kelly, a neglected eleven-year-old who lives with her single mother and sister, is raped one night by an older man as she roams the rundown streets of this northern town. Significantly, the rape is committed in a dark back alley just outside a closed-down factory, as if underlining a crucial – and savage – conversion and displacement of exploitation, which is no longer necessarily mediated by the wage or contained

---

[41] Ibid., 100.

within socially recognized structures. By opening her narrative exposé with such a radical form of abuse as the rape of a child, Barker allegorizes the range and intensity of exploitation in advanced capitalism, the capacity of power (understood as a general expropriating agency, in whichever guise) to prey upon life itself from start to finish. Yet sexuality comes across in this context as not only a primary site of expropriation but also of resistance. Even in the extreme form of Kelly Brown's rape, the flat linearity of exploitation is subverted, giving rise to a two-way dialectic in which the victim acquires radical traits of empowerment, and the sexual predator is ultimately rendered helpless. As David Waterman has noted, 'Barker never allows such simple binary categorizations as assailant and victim',[42] for there is always a dimension of frailty in the former and a source of resistant strength in the latter. The brutal back-street event thus surprisingly morphs into an opportunity for the exploited subject to contest her subaltern position and literally make the exploiter pay. Immediately after the rape, Kelly refuses to follow the man's indications on how to get home and insists on going with him to a nearby fish and chip shop. The initial feeling of helplessness rapidly transforms into a sense of being in charge, of effectively being able to subdue her abuser:

> They crossed the street together. She thought, I don't have to be quick. I don't have to be anything I don't want. Though in spite of his words he lagged behind until she turned and hauled him on to the pavement. The more he hesitated, the more obviously afraid he became, the greater was her rage, until in the end she seemed to be borne along on a huge wave of anger that curved and foamed and never broke. She pushed him into the shop in front of her.[43]

This passage captures the profound ambivalence of even the most extreme form of oppression. The partial empowerment which ensues from this scene does not dissolve the pain and trauma of the exploitative event, but rather turns them (in a way which the different stories in the book develop to one extent or another) into enabling features, into resources of resistance.

In *Union Street*, as Waterman has pointed out, 'sex and violence seem almost inseparable ... whether in the form of a rape in a public place or conjugal

---

[42] David Waterman, *Pat Barker and the Mediation of Social Reality* (Amherst: Cambria, 2009), 18.
[43] Barker, *Union*, 31.

violence'.[44] It should be added that these do not constitute an exceptional aspect of the broader social regimes of exploitation to which the novel makes constant reference, but rather a particular modality of the systemic violence underpinning the sexual division of labour. Thus, the submerged quality of reproductive work (which perhaps reaches its culmination in sex itself)[45] conveys a sense of the naturalization of violence in this proletarian universe from which Kelly Brown's rape only represents a partial departure or deviation. The violence implied and often made explicit by unwanted pregnancy and vulnerable maternity, for example, showcases a complementary dimension of Barker's portrayal of women's expropriation.

The story of Lisa Goddard is a good example of the 'ordinary' form which reproductive exploitation adopts in this book. In her early twenties, burdened with two babies and already well into her third pregnancy, Lisa represents reproductive exploitation at its purest. A practical inability to manage her situation often leads her, as in an early scene at the supermarket, to lose control and vent her anger and frustration on the children.[46] With her husband Brian out of work, and typically away at the pub, Lisa is left to confront the crude and lonely experience of subsumed life, or, in other words, of a life fully absorbed, shaped and devastated by the privatized rhythms of housework and nurture. Violence – both exerted and endured – is not a pathological deviation from a normal state of affairs in capitalist reproductive relations, but a likely manifestation of the extraction of surplus labour in the reproductive domain.[47]

The wageless condition of domestic labour implies a structural dependence on the male wage, leading to a profound but revealing imbalance whenever the latter dwindles or is cut short by unemployment. The novel's 1970s background of capitalist crisis and restructuration thereby supplies a further dimension to the subsumption of women's reproductive work in the form of exceptional saving and provision in the absence of a steady income:

> For the last four or five months she had been saving up for the baby. Most of the things she'd got for Kevin were worn out now, and the maternity grant

---

[44] Waterman, *Mediation*, 20.
[45] On this point, see, for example, Federici's article 'Why Sexuality is Work', in Federici, *Revolution*.
[46] Barker, *Union*, 108–9.
[47] As Federici notes: 'When capital or the State does not pay a wage, it is those who are loved, cared for, also wageless and even more powerless, who must pay with their lives', *Revolution*, 35.

wouldn't cover replacements. At first she saved whatever was left in her purse at the end of the week. But that was usually just a few coppers. Then she made herself save all the 50p pieces. Sometimes when she saw a shopkeeper about to give her a 50p in her change she would pray for him to change his mind. She needed the money now.

But she made herself stick to her self-imposed rule. And was rewarded. The sum quickly mounted up. By now the jar was almost full.[48]

When Lisa finds out that Brian has stolen from the jar to pay for his drinking habit, further violence ensues, further despair which follows upon the woman's taking over the man's role as financial purveyor (although outside the formal labour market), and along with the latter, his direct relationship with capital.[49] This confusion of production with reproduction in the absence of a wage makes the subsumption of the social under capital ever more fraught and visible. In the face of serious economic difficulty, domestic work becomes a matter of survival for living labour, for working-class life in its entirety, and hence even more important for capitalist valorization.

Union Street is replete with male figures who have somehow deviated or been displaced from traditionally 'productive' roles (as waged labourers and family breadwinners), resulting in a general landscape of crisis which is not only punctuated by relative material poverty, but also by a radical disturbance of the sexual division of labour. John Scaife, for example (who, unlike Lisa's husband, is neither a drunk nor has been laid off), embodies a form of disempowerment which is still intimately connected to the fact that he cannot work. Seriously ill, he is simultaneously confronted with his subalternity as a bed-ridden invalid who can neither perform his heavy industrial job nor act his part as a husband and a father. This growing sense of impotence (which, one could argue, contributes to his eventual death almost as much as the actual disease) is underlined by his illiteracy, which he desperately tries to conceal from his wife Muriel and, most of all, from his academically gifted adolescent son. Family life as Muriel Scaife views it is a fight of a different kind from that of other women like Joanne or Lisa, yet one equally predicated on her ability to confront and survive the unrelenting onslaught of material hardship and subjective deprivation:

---

[48] Barker, *Union*, 114.
[49] Ibid., 117.

> She had never been able to take happiness for granted, perhaps because she had lost her father while she was still a child. She must always be aware of time passing, of the worm that hides in darkness and feeds upon innocence, beauty and grace. John's hands on her breasts, the children asleep upstairs: nothing was to be taken for granted. Love, security, order: these were achievements painfully wrested from a chaos that was always threatening to take them back. She remembered the children playing in the lamp-light. Life was like that. *Her* life was like that. A moment in the light. Then the lamp goes out, the circle is broken, the chanting voices are silenced forever.[50]

The precariousness of existence is matched here with the need and the determination to resist, to draw fresh strength and power from pain and hardship in order to make life continue, in order to pursue her entrusted duties of care and nurture. For Muriel, the loss of her loving husband cannot represent the surrender of her reproductive work, which must continue against all odds as a real work for life (both in terms of duration and quality).

This quiet grappling with pain contrasts with Iris King's extraordinarily vital and empowering approach. For Iris, the daily struggle against suffering and exploitation, which is the substance of these women's collective universe, can only lead to a powerful recreation of her subjectivity, to an ever greater freedom from the threatening chaos which, according to Muriel Scaife, defines their lives. This is a recreation that always points towards the collective, towards the shared or common dimension of their existence as exploited working women. Iris King seems to confirm Antonio Negri's claim that '*Pain is a key that opens the door to the community*', an ontological buttress on which shared suffering comes into being, coalescing in a collective subjectivation and transforming the experiential form of the 'expropriation of the time of life by Power' into its liberated opposite.[51]

Iris's life is an ongoing struggle against subalternity – an unceasing effort to transform oppression and suffering into something more than a structurally determined expression of impotence. Thus, the way in which she handles her subordinate position as a housewife dependent on her husband's wage is far more confrontational and empowering than that of other women in the novel.

---

[50] Ibid., 152.
[51] Antonio Negri, *The Labor of Job*, trans. Matteo Mandarini (Durham: Duke University Press, 2009), 90.

On the occasion of her first fight with her husband Ted, for example, she does not emerge as a passive victim, but as a resistant subject ready to strike back against normalized violence:

> When he came back she was waiting for him behind the door with the meat chopper in her hand. The blow glanced off him, though there was enough blood around to scare the pair of them stiff. It didn't stop him hitting her again, but it did free her from fear. She never lost her self-respect.[52]

Her attitude towards the wage itself is similarly characterized by a determination to break the spell of victimhood and subordination, and to reclaim the centrality of her position within the family, the community and the productive structure itself. As her daughter Brenda bitterly reminds her, 'You used to go round the pub and fight me Dad for his wages. I used to get that thrown up at me at school', to which Iris responds sternly and unrepentantly: 'I did. I did fight your Dad for his wages. I'm not ashamed to say it. And think on, Brenda, there was many a week you'd've gone hungry to shit if I hadn't.'[53]

Here, the work of reproduction develops a radically independent quality, a will to carry forward its struggle for survival regardless of capital's assessment of it in terms of value. Reproduction thus becomes something more than a subordinate appendix of production, opening the gates to self-valorization and autonomy. Through her sustained rejection of the subaltern position accorded to working-class women, and of the attendant devaluing of their reproductive labour power, Iris King embodies an attitude of refusal, which in large measure corroborates the paramount importance accorded by revolutionary feminists like Federici to reproduction as the strategic axis of the class struggle: '[T]hese struggles are fought by women who, against all odds, are reproducing their families regardless of the value the market places on their lives, valorizing their existence, reproducing them for their own sake, even when the capitalists declare their uselessness as labor power.'[54]

This interweaving of suffering and emancipation under the sign of a freshly empowering labour of reproduction leads to a communitarian enactment of hope, to a construction of the community as an autonomous and redemptive space of subjective constitution. The working-class community does not retain

---

[52] Barker, *Union*, 190.
[53] Ibid., 183.
[54] Federici, *Revolution*, 92–3.

here any of its organic and romantic overtones of continuity with a pristine past, for the latter is acutely recognized as truly standing for pain and brutality rather than cosiness and harmony. Instead, the community enacted by the resistant labour of reproduction, as Iris demonstrates, points to a self-affirmative refusal of the chaos and darkness feared by Muriel Scaife, which routinely floods the existence of working-class women. By 'mother[ing] half the street' ('Kelly Brown and the Scaife children, Lisa Goddard's little lads – they all knew and loved their Iris'),[55] Iris King offers a glimpse of the kind of 'production of community'[56] embodied in reproductive work as the latter becomes less of a subordinate feature of the broad social organization of capital, and proceeds to its self-reconstruction as resistant and autonomous.

The kind of subjective resistance and autonomy which *Union Street* situates within the realm of domestic, reproductive exploitation does not necessarily entail a victorious outcome for the women involved. From start to finish, devastation and despair colour the particular strategies of survival and the subjective universes of the individual women. In Kelly Brown's case, for example, the sense of empowerment which follows her traumatic experience leads to dead-ends of destructive rage, whether breaking into a plush, comfortable house in a wealthier neighbourhood or defacing the Headmaster's office at her school during the night.[57] It seems as if her denial of victimhood can only replicate the destructive form of the original trauma, adopting and adapting the endured violence to the purposes of painful resistance. In a context of ritualized violence, of socialized expropriation and, consequently, of human devastation, resistance can often only take this quasi-suicidal form.

The latter may turn overtly suicidal when the physical energy of resistance fades towards the end of life, while the determination, the *potentia* (to say it with Spinoza), remains. The story of the septuagenarian Alice Bell, with which the novel concludes, is a compelling instance of this. Against the injunctions of doctors and social assistants, as well as her own son, Alice refuses to accept the consequences of her physical frailty as a mark of subordination and dependency. Rather than accept these as facts leading to a necessary surrender of her subjectivity, she insists on recognizing them as painful signs of an

---

[55] Barker, *Union*, 196.
[56] Negri, *Labor*, 91.
[57] Barker, *Union*, 49–56.

independence that she is determined to defend to the very end: 'Her home. They were taking it away from her. The dirt and disorder, the signs of malnutrition and neglect which to them were reasons for putting her away were, to her, independence. She had fought to keep for herself the conditions of a human life.'[58]

When the prospect of being transferred to a home for the old becomes inevitable, Alice decides to exert the ultimate form of refusal and take her own life. Her final excursion from the house becomes, as she describes it, 'an act of faith which, if it was ever known at all, would appear to others as folly or madness or mere senile confusion.'[59] Alice's final exertion, not unlike Kelly Brown's acts of destruction, points to a common horizon of autonomous despair, to a tragic production of subjectivity as refusal, as discontinuation of power's injunctions. The two characters meet briefly as the end approaches, sitting side by side on the park bench where Alice will eventually die from hypothermia. Through this final and symbolically charged encounter, Barker makes a direct and emphatic link between the commonality of suffering and the irreversibility of resistance. For Alice and Kelly – despite their obvious differences – as for the other women in *Union Street*, vulnerability and suffering cannot be accommodated as acceptable subjective modes under the rule of this or that exploitative power. The realities of exploitation must be confronted, rather, with the full force of an act of refusal, even if it involves (self-)destruction or sacrifice of some kind.

Tasked with the 'invisible' labour of reproduction, the women inhabiting these pages are compelled to forms of resistance that are often ambiguous, contradictory and even self-defeating. If the muted forms of domestic exploitation and sexual violence are presented here as an extreme version of life's subsumption within labour (that is, within capital's complex machinery of value-production); if labour in all its complexity (but especially in the socially unrecognized forms of unwaged labour) is configured as the zero-degree of the subordination of life to capital – of the *becoming-capital* of life itself – then suicide may constitute the ultimate form of rebellion and denial of this state of affairs. As Jean Baudrillard writes in *Symbolic Exchange and Death*: 'Labour is opposed as deferred death to the immediate death of sacrifice ... Does capital exploit the workers to death? Paradoxically, the worst it inflicts on

[58] Ibid., 260.
[59] Ibid., 262.

them is refusing them death. It is by deferring their death that they are made into slaves and condemned to the indefinite abjection of a life of labour.'[60] Capitalist labour is premised, according to Baudrillard, on the continuation of life as (re)productive servitude, on the indefinite deferral of death for the sake of subservience and protracted exploitation. The story of Alice Bell offers a good illustration of this point. There is a clear suggestion in her narrative that the prospect of institutional care in a 'home' away from her real home, away from the site of her independence, marks an encroachment of regulated, socially controlled life upon the subject and, hence, a denial of the self-determination implied by the possibility of dying – willingly – on her own. In this context, the sacrificial prospect of suicide (or indeed, of any abrupt break with the subaltern life dictated by capital) constitutes a radical and incontestable negation of the latter's dominion. *Union Street*'s ending is therefore to be read in this light, not as concession of defeat or confirmation of women's victimhood in this rapidly changing (post-)industrial universe, but as a rehearsal of the logic of separation – of the imagination of working-class independence vis-à-vis capital's power over life.[61]

The biopolitical agenda unlocked by sexual violence and unwaged domestic labour is one that concerns itself both with disruption of the normalized state of exception imposed by capital outside the factory, in the reproductive sphere, and with the possible production of innovation in the form of tentatively free subjectivities. Biopolitics in this sense is, as Michael Hardt and Antonio Negri have written, an 'event': 'The biopolitical event comes from the outside insofar as it ruptures the continuity of history and the existing order, but it should be understood not only negatively, as rupture, but also as innovation, which emerges, so to speak, from the inside.'[62] This dual aspect of biopolitics thoroughly informs *Union Street*, offering a sustained alternation between the constructive and destructive dimensions of resistance and placing them at the centre of reproductive life. All the way from Kelly Brown's traumatic experience at the beginning of life to the insidious and 'humanitarian' attempts to rein in

---

[60] Jean Baudrillard, *Symbolic Exchange and Death*, trans. Hamilton Grant (London: Sage, 1993), 39.
[61] This notion of working-class separation, autonomization or – in a far more consolidated expression – 'self-valorization' has been most forcefully developed by Antonio Negri in his militant writings of the 1970s, where he describes class consciousness 'as a moment of intensive rooting within my own separateness. I am *other* – as is the movement of that collective practice within which I am included', *Books for Burning: Between Civil War and Democracy* (London: Verso, 2005), 237.
[62] Hardt and Negri, *Commonwealth*, 59.

Alice Bell's autonomy towards the end, through the whole range of intermediate situations of violence, exploitation and resistance, the gendered universe explored in this novel points to a profound desire for subjective transformation which nevertheless avoids any flat or linear teleology of liberation. The perspective of pain and suffering is forever present in Barker and does not allow for easy resolutions. Nor does the possibility exist, however, to settle for a discourse of subalternity from which subversion and the (self-) production of alternative subjectivities would be excluded. As we will see in the next section, Barker's second novel, *Blow Your House Down*, confronts these problems by delving deeper into the crisis of reproduction and, in particular, by making suggestive links between prostitution, death and subversion/resistance.

3.3 Prostitution, death and the subversion of life in *Blow Your House Down*

Prostitution is a very special case of reproductive labour in which the sex worker effectively sells her labour power, yet does not directly engage in an exchange with capital. In fact, the prostitute is, as it were, waged 'at second hand', receiving payment for her work typically from another (male) waged worker. Here, the buyer of labour power does not appropriate or extract value in the way that the capitalist employer does, but rather seeks to satisfy his needs (strictly, to 'reproduce' his own labour power). It is then really capital, as Leopoldina Fortunati observes, 'that appropriates the value of the labor-power of the female sexual reproduction worker when she sexually reproduces male labor-power'.[63] This ambivalent connection to value-extraction sets prostitution apart from the invisible exploitation of domestic work (sexual and otherwise), making the possibility of withdrawal and rupture that we have seen in *Union Street* somewhat limited and curtailed by the formal dependency on a wage (even if it is – or precisely because it is – an unofficial or non-legal wage). This limitation or curtailment can manifest itself as a loss of the presumptive autonomy indexed by the domestic sphere itself; by the home which, as in the

---

[63] Fortunati, *Arcane*, 43.

case of Iris King or Alice Bell, is not only the assigned workplace for the woman but also a potentially emancipated territory for self-determination. In *Union Street* this becomes clear in the chapter dedicated to Blonde Dinah, which, in addition to being considerably shorter than the others, does not fully, or even directly, engage with its titular character's life story (nor is it narrated from her point of view). Dinah is an ageing prostitute about whom we learn very little in the novel, and most of it through the eyes of a local man who buys her services. It is as if the particularity of prostitution made this story an unwieldy fit within the general universe of domestic violence and resistance traced in the novel. It is therefore very telling that Barker's next book would confront this – in principle very different – universe so directly.

By turning her attention now to the one aspect of reproductive labour that her first novel had virtually sidestepped, and by framing it within a semi-Gothic narrative of serial killings of prostitutes (a thinly fictionalized version of the Yorkshire Ripper murders of the late 1970s and early 1980s), Barker seems to emphasize the increasing alterity and 'unreliability'[64] of women in this transitional period of crisis and postmodernization, as well as the increasing separation of reproductive or biopolitical work from traditionally 'productive' industrial work. *Blow Your House Down* is made up of four parts. The first two follow Brenda, a single mother of three, in her descent from precarious employment at the local chicken factory to prostitution in the streets of a northern town. The factory is presented here as a physically repugnant and not merely alienating form of labour, emerging not only as a site of exploitative subjection but also of abjection, of repulsion at the object and conditions of the productive routine, in a way that recalls the naturalist depiction of the meat-packing industry in Upton Sinclair's 1906 classic *The Jungle*:[65]

> She was frightened, she needed the job so badly. In her anxiety to get the interview over, she blundered in at the wrong entrance and saw a line of live

---

[64] In the sense suggested by Mariarosa Dalla Costa and Selma James: 'The day to day struggles that women have developed since the Second World War run directly against the organization of the factory and of the home. The "unreliability" of women in the home and out of it has grown rapidly since then, and runs directly against the factory as regimentation organized in time and space, and against the social factory as organization of the reproduction of labor power. This trend to more absenteeism, to less respect for timetables, to higher job mobility, is shared by young men and women workers', *Power of Women*, 3.

[65] Upton Sinclair, *The Jungle* (New York: Oxford University Press, 2010).

chickens fastened to a conveyor belt by their legs. They jerked past. At the end of the line a man hit them with something to stun them and another man chopped off their heads.

The tiles were spattered with blood. They must've been able to smell it, but there was no struggling, no panic after the first frantic clapping of wings.

They didn't even squawk.[66]

The abattoir section of the factory embodies, beyond the merely alienating routines of Fordism, what is 'abject', what is radically and unassimilably other, about labour in industrial capitalism. The fact that the woman worker's first encounter with industrial work is one characterized by a radical disjunction, by a radical difference between the female subject and the specific 'object' of this type of work places the latter in a relation of abjection with the former, in a relation of mutual exclusion. According to Julia Kristeva's definition, 'What is abject is not my correlative, which, providing me with someone or something else as support, would allow me to be more or less detached and autonomous.'[67] Factory work, represented now by the gory image of a headless chicken, appears, in the eyes of the woman worker, as a 'jettisoned object', as a site where 'meaning [the meaning of industrial work itself] collapses'.[68] In this context, the retreat to reproductive labour in whichever guise, including prostitution (which significantly combines the wage-form of production and the 'intimate' quality of reproduction), signifies a deliberate break with the world of industry and production, as well as an emphatic thematization of the biopolitical nature of exploitation in late capitalism. Brenda's refusal of factory work, after she realizes its incompatibility with the tasks of housework and looking after her children, brings to the fore a renovated concern with the centrality of reproduction for capital, making it both a ripe field for fresh expropriation and a potential site of resistance for the subject.

Barker boldly combines in this novel an emphasis on the crude and brutal possibilities inscribed in reproductive work with the paradoxical suggestion of the 'freedom' it offers when compared with industrial labour. The link between the two seems to be, ironically, an overarching presence of bloodshed and death. Thus, the taylorist butchering of the birds in the abattoir is seemingly

[66] Pat Barker, *Blow Your House Down* (London: Virago, 1984), 33.
[67] Julia Kristeva, *Powers of Horror: An Essay on Abjection*, trans. Leon S. Roudiez (New York: Columbia University Press, 1984), 1.
[68] Ibid., 2.

replicated on the streets where the prostitutes work. However, a fundamental difference sets them apart, marking the life of the latter with a sacrificial quality which, not unlike Alice Bell's 'decision' at the end of *Union Street*, conceals the promise of subjective autonomy, of biopolitics understood not only as reproductive exploitation but also, crucially, as an 'event of resistance'.[69] The choice of prostitution is, or at least can be, for these women, a relative choice of life under capital entailing the possibility of tragic, sacrificial death, that is, of a radical subversion of the indefinite deferral of death to which Baudrillard alluded and which the chicken factory literalizes. By choosing prostitution, Brenda restores a measure of the subjective autonomy that her abject response to the factory had initially placed under erasure. Her choice is thus, in an important sense, a deliberate, biopolitical option *against* productive regimentation and *for* reproductive freedom (although, to be sure, under conditions of generalized or socialized exploitation). Thus, in response to the police branding her, and her fellow women, as a 'common prostitute', she retorts:

> Right, if that's what I am, OK, I'll bloody well be it. It wasn't all bad, not by any means. There was a lot of things you could enjoy. Oh, not the sex, not that side of it, but there was the company, the excitement, the chance of a drink whenever you fancied it, going out and looking in the shops and not having to think all the time, Eee, can I afford it? And she had the best-dressed kids in the street. That made up for a lot.[70]

Prostitution is cast here not only as the material possibility of surpassing ordinary wage labour, but also as the possibility of wresting life – however partially – from the 'normal' discipline of exploitation. This possibility is even more overtly appealed to by Jean, another woman whose interior monologue occupies the third section of the book, and who represents what we could describe as the peak of separation and otherness attained by prostitutes in the novel. Jean's story designates prostitution as a conceivable reversal of the naturalized exploitation embodied in housework, on the one hand, and in factory work, on the other. Speaking in her own voice, Jean confirms a measure of adequation between her desires and the particular form of exchange between labour power and capital represented by this kind of work:

[69] Hardt and Negri, *Commonwealth*, 61.
[70] Barker, *Blow*, 50.

I like this life. I'm not in it because I'm a poor, deprived, inadequate, half-witted woman, whatever some people might like to think, I'm in it because it suits *me*. I like the company. I like the excitement. I like the feeling of stepping out onto the street, not knowing what's going to happen or who I'm going to meet. I like the freedom. I like being able to decide when I'm going to work. I like being able to take the day off without being answerable to anybody.[71]

Even if, she adds, the money is not bad either, it is this aspect of the subjective freedom afforded by prostitution that makes it incomparably better than work at the factory, where, as Brenda had noted: 'It wasn't enough to say you needed a job and you'd work hard and all that. You had to go on as if you'd wanted to gut chickens all your life, as if you couldn't imagine a better way of spending your time.'[72]

Jean's embrace of prostitution as a free alternative to unwaged reproductive and factory work marks a significant departure from the embedded (or second-degree) regime of subordination which links the prostitute to capital and typically leaves her in a doubly subaltern position (as illustrated by the story of Blonde Dinah in *Union Street*). In *Blow Your House Down*, and in particular in the case of Jean, this regime is subverted and replaced with a largely autonomous affirmation of individual choice and freedom of decision. The Gothic backdrop to the narrative announces, in a certain sense, the collapse of the role that prostitution work had been traditionally assigned under the law of value. If prostitution first appears as 'corollary', as 'support and complement' to housework, 'mak[ing] up [for] any deficit in domestic sexuality',[73] it also represents a transgressive opportunity for denaturalizing reproductive activity itself. As Andrew McCann has argued, apropos of Walter Benjamin's treatment of the figure of the prostitute in *The Arcades Project*, the latter conceals a 'politically disruptive potential ... to displace a sphere of life deterministically defined by biology'.[74] Thus, beyond the contrived naturalization of prostitution as the required appendix of domestic exploitation, the uncanny figure of the autonomous and free sex worker emerges on the

---

[71] Ibid., 112.
[72] Ibid., 34.
[73] Fortunati, *Arcane*, 18.
[74] Andrew McCann, 'Walter Benjamin's Sex Work: Prostitution and the State of Exception', *Textual Practice*, 28: 1 (2014), 101.

horizon, threatening to subvert the edifice of subaltern reproduction, and with it, the entire edifice of the capitalist law of value.

The Gothicism – the *monstrosity* – of Barker's second novel reaches its peak in this figure of the free prostitute, rather than in that of the serial killer. Its otherness resides in its capacity to break down the measure of value (its subordinate and indirect reliance on the wage) through which capital characteristically harnesses it, and to imagine an existence beyond its law – an excessive and 'immeasurable' existence which may only be arrested tragically, through an event of violence commensurate with its event of resistance. As Negri has argued: 'In postmodernity, the eminent form of rebellion is the exodus from obedience, that is to say, from participation in measure, i.e. as the opening to the immeasurable.'[75] The only form of containment that may live up to the 'excess' and 'otherness' of the prostitute's challenge is one that, beyond the ordinary state of affairs of reproductive exploitation, would restore the regime of (extraction of) value which the prostitute has threatened with her free subjective movement. In other words, it is necessary *to make the prostitute pay*. In one of the key passages of Jean's interior monologue, we learn about an attack she suffered in London several years earlier, which left her with a terrible scar across the neck. On that occasion, it was not the slashing of her throat that captured the essence of the attacker's act, but rather the pre-climactic violent fantasy of – literally – making her pay:

> He got me bag open and took what bit of money I had, which was only the notes he'd given me, plus a few odd coppers, and he screwed it all up into a ball and he started pushing the coins against me teeth, and all the time he was saying, 'You're gunna pay *me*.' He wasn't having much trouble at the other end now, the thought of me paying *him* was a real turn-on.[76]

The sexual immediacy of rape is superseded here by the possibility of violently subverting the sense and direction of capital's extortion of value from the prostitute. This original attack, which both predates and foreshadows the subsequent attacks in the novel, typifies the desperate nature of capital's violent reaction to a potentially free and self-determining sexuality or reproductive labour, operating both within and against its valorization process. There is a

---

[75] Antonio Negri, *Time for Revolution*, trans. Matteo Mandarini (London: Continuum, 2003), 258.
[76] Barker, *Blow*, 108.

family likeness here to what Baudrillard described as 'ecstatic' or 'fatal' in the event: 'An event – or a being, or a word – resolves all efforts at explanation; it imposes itself with a force which is no longer of the final or causal order. It is more final than final: it is fatal.'[77] The ecstasy is of course not that of discharge or orgasm, but that of abolition and cancellation of the ordinary directionality of sex work, and of the authorized position occupied by the prostitute vis-à-vis capital. The fatal unfolding of the event confirms the radical subversiveness of her choosing to be a prostitute and 'enjoying it' in the first place.

Death in *Blow Your House Down* is not a consequence or a function of subalternity (of being, as Jean puts it, 'a poor, deprived, inadequate, half-witted woman'), but a 'fatal strategy' through which the entire system of value collapses, killing and being killed on account of its confrontation with an 'immeasurable' experience of resistance. This radical convulsion cannot lead to justice or even to (successful) retribution, as this would restore measure and value to a dynamic of rupture and catastrophe. It is in this sense that Jean's actions, after her lover Carol dies at the hands of the serial murderer, offer no solace or comfort, but only a pervading sense, or rather non-sense, not of injustice either, but of the fatal or the ecstatic in Baudrillard's definition: 'Ecstasy is the quality proper to any body that spins until all sense is lost, and then shines forth in its pure and empty form.'[78] The equilibrium, the symmetry and the meaning of revenge are displaced and abolished by a self-serving yet profoundly antagonistic logic of the monstrous which cannot fall back on the pre-existing state of affairs. When Jean stabs an innocent man, whom she mistakes for the murderer, in the neck, the entire (moral) order of value on which ordinary exploitation rested (all the way from everyday sex work to the reverse, 'punitive' act of making the prostitute pay) collapses, and only the immoral, monstrous and sense-less form of ecstasy can take its place:

> He didn't twist and turn or anything like that. He just stared at me. Then his mouth opened, it opened very wide, and he was gasping and gurgling and trying to speak and I held onto the knife and I watched his lips and I held onto the knife and finally it came, one single word, with a rush of blood like a baby splitting open a cunt, one single word: '*Why?*'[79]

---

[77] Jean Baudrillard, *Forget Foucault* (Los Angeles: Semiotext(e), 2007), 85.
[78] Jean Baudrillard, *Fatal Strategies* (Los Angeles: Semiotext(e), 2008), 28.
[79] Barker, *Blow*, 132.

The bottomless abyss of the man's opening mouth (which is significantly presented in crude reproductive language), just like the unbearable stare of the dead prostitute elsewhere in the novel, bring proportion, balance and meaning to an end, materializing the Nietzschean reference of the book's epigraph, which reads: 'Whoever fights monsters should see to it that in the process he does not become a monster. And when you look long into an abyss the abyss also looks into you.'[80] The strategy of refusal which *Union Street* had often deployed in subjective figures of resistance, of wilful withdrawal, self-assertion or even sacrifice, gives way here, in this climactic moment of *Blow Your House Down*, to a 'fatal strategy' of abolition or monstrous metamorphosis from which there can be no recovery (for either the resisting subject *or* the system).

After this point of no return in the novel, the course to follow is one deprived of finality, of meaning, of transcendence; one whereby the subject *dissolves* and gives way to the pure singularity of what Gilles Deleuze called 'a life'.[81] What succeeds the ecstasy of murder (of unsuccessful revenge, of doomed retribution) is the release of life from the signifying regimes which presided over its universe – its 'liberation', in other words, from the system of (re)productive work (of life *as* work) under which all these women are placed in one way or another. Maggie, a worker at the chicken factory, whose ordinary life differs greatly from that of the prostitutes, is attacked by the killer one night as she walks home from the local pub. Unlike previous victims, she is neither sexually assaulted nor murdered: she sustains a serious wound to the head leading to a slow and painful recovery through which the entire universe of work and value will become gradually, but irrevocably, estranged and defamiliarized. The organized world of working-class life, of factory and community, from which prostitution had marked a fundamental (but often limited) departure, fades with Maggie in a gradual process of desubjectification, of virtual vanishing from the here-and-now of exploitation. As if pushing the effect of dissolution of Jean's catastrophic revenge forward, to a dimension outside the marked territory of back alleys in a derelict northern town, Maggie's plight opens up a fresh space for subjective transformation. Like Kelly Brown before, Maggie follows a spatial course of deterritorialization, which leads her

---

[80] Barker, ibid., n.p.
[81] Gilles Deleuze, *Pure Immanence: Essays on a Life*, trans. Anne Boyman (New York: Zone Books, 2001).

away from the hollow sympathy of neighbours and family. It is in the open countryside, in the presence of wildlife, against a background of immeasurable and unsignifiable otherness, that healing can take place. But this healing cannot entail a return to her pre-existing subjectivity or to a validation of her previous, (re)productive life. Rather, her life-in-recovery will be disclosed as 'a life', a pure singularity or a becoming-imperceptible of subjectivity, where the subject appears at its most distant and irreducible to the universe of meaning, value and exploitation. This is life placed in the vicinity of death, singular life poised on the brink between subjective existence and pure nothingness. This is, as Deleuze says, the moment at which '[t]he life of the individual gives way to an impersonal and yet singular life that releases a pure event freed from the accidents of internal and external life, that is, from the subjectivity and objectivity of what happens'.[82] The following is the moment of bliss which Maggie reaches on one of her excursions, towards the end of the novel:

> She would have liked this rain to last forever, to close her eyes and not open them again, sealed off in the privacy and intimacy of the wood. It would have been easy to die here. She thought of the bodies of small animals she'd seen on her walks, shrews and voles, how they seemed not to rot but rather to fade into the leaves and grass, growing a little fainter day by day, like the after images you see when a light is switched off. That kind of death held no terror.[83]

This kind of death holds no terror because it implies a foreclosure or dissolution of the subject – a post-catastrophic release of singularity from the embattled life of the exploited and resisting subject. The metamorphosis achieved by Maggie returns us to the immanent figure of resistance evoked by Alice Bell's own fading at the end of *Union Street*. In both cases, the release of the event – of the singular event of refusal – complements and contrasts with a catastrophe that serves as background and that throws the system into irreversible crisis. After Kelly's rape, the system of production and reproduction cannot go on undisturbed. After the killer's murders, and especially after Jean's failed retaliation, it cannot be reimagined as an outlet or channel for individual autonomy. The 'fatal strategy' of dissolution appears here as the disavowal of

---

[82] Ibid., 28.
[83] Barker, *Blow*, 168.

the system's hold on the subject, as the aftermath of the event – of the crisis – into which the latter had strenuously lured the former.

As we will see in the following chapters, this 'ecstatic' logic will increasingly impose itself as a last-ditch form of resistance against a system that has already foregone spatial and temporal distinctions between life and work, between the 'inside' of value-production and the 'outside' of social and even biological life. The historical crisis to which this post-subjective logic responds will receive many names and accrue a plurality of experiential and semantic valences. However, the changes it brings in its wake will deliver an integrated image of ubiquitous and multifarious control, of phenomenological destruction of the subject's life-world, and yet also of renewed antagonism. The growing exposure of the 'postmodern' worker (to mention just one of the possible historical denominations), her increasing vulnerability to the expropriating mechanisms of capital, paradoxically results in an ontological opening, in a radical mutation, that will threaten the system's coherence. The proletarian struggle can no longer be understood as primarily a matter of inter-subjective conflict, as a symmetrical engagement between *formed* subjects, but rather as a process of unworking, of gradual inundation and decomposition of the assailed proletarian subject (of her symbolic and material world), and of re-emergence of the latter as an inassimilable, irreducible and ungovernable singularity.

In the next chapter, I will trace this transformation in the work of two remarkable Scottish writers, James Kelman and Irvine Welsh. I will present their work as offering a sequential unfolding of the fate of the postmodern proletarian, from the reconstruction of late capitalism's abolition of temporal and experiential boundaries, and the transcription of exploitation as State violence offered by Kelman, to Welsh's imagination of a resistant, uncapturable and ecstatic form of life (not unlike that proposed by Barker) amid the social debris of neoliberal Britain.

4

Beyond Civil Society

Proletarian Exodus in James Kelman and Irvine Welsh

Antonio Negri has insisted that postmodernity – or rather, postmodernization, that is, the transition to and unfolding of postmodernity – should be identified with what he calls 'real subsumption'. As we have seen in the preceding chapters, the integration of society as a whole within the matrix of capitalist valorization is a protracted historical process that really commenced with the transformation of the factory (of the mass relation inaugurated by the Fordist factory) into the centrepiece of a wider social network. With the displacement of the factory, with its relegation by capital from the frontline of value-production (the process commonly known as 'de-industrialization'), the subordination of society to the logic of capital becomes complete. The rise of new forms of production of value, of new strategic sites of expropriation, brings about an abolition of temporal and spatial differences, and, consequently, a dismantling of the working subject's perceived autonomy. The resulting experiential universe is immediately oppressive, immediately violent (even in a strict physical sense). As we will see, under these circumstances, proletarian subjectivity can either fade out, collapse into the brutal ontology of work/exploitation without bounds, or come out the other end, as it were, transformed into a thin – but undefeated – line of flight. James Kelman has explored this alternative in many of his novels. The three I have selected for analysis here, *The Busconductor Hines* (1984), *A Disaffection* (1989) and *How Late It Was, How Late* (1994) (three novels that essentially engage with and respond to the ideological and political conjuncture of Thatcherism) rehearse a hopeful and politically unyielding development from the first to the second option.

4.1 The collapse of measure: Postmodern abstraction and proletarian flight in James Kelman

James Kelman's first published novel, *The Busconductor Hines* (1984), offers a penetrating analysis of the destructive temporal effects of post-industrial labour upon the working subject. By charting the subjective universe of its eponymous protagonist Robert Hines – especially his mental ramblings and unfolding psychic crisis – the novel presents the working experience of the post-industrial proletarian as a closed circuit, as a self-referential temporal structure over which he has no control. As Simon Kővesi has noted: 'Time is a burden for Hines because it is exterior, it measures and orders the universe but he cannot get the measure of it.'[1] For the bus conductor, working time is not indexed to an identifiable productive routine or even to an active role in the provision of a service, as in the case of the bus driver. The work performed by Hines is almost indistinguishable from the shifts he works and the timetabling of his daily existence that these impose. The object of labour has been replaced here by a temporal continuum which frames the worker's existence and dissolves his direct agency or control over it. There is a sense in which, as Cairns Craig observes, Hines' life is dominated by the 'need for *over*time' and the 'expectation of his own coming redundancy, when conductors are replaced by the drivers of one-man buses'.[2] Both anxieties point towards a temporal structure which exceeds the possibilities of any qualitative reference, of any concrete productive task or use-value, and which therefore lead to a re-imagination of work as an abstract social generality.

For Hines, time is an indomitable quantity, a phenomenological black hole defying understanding and subjective control: '[H]ow in the name of Christ is a body to keep track of time when the world's crumbling about his fucking ears.'[3] This experiential confusion reaches beyond the conventional distinction between work and non-work which a traditional industrial routine would have naturally upheld. For the bus conductor, the incapacity to 'keep track of time' directly arises from (and greatly amplifies) this blurring of ambits.

---

[1] Simon Kővesi, *James Kelman* (Manchester: Manchester University Press, 2007), 49.
[2] Cairns Craig, *The Modern Scottish Novel: Narrative and the National Imagination* (Edinburgh: Edinburgh University Press, 1999), 103.
[3] James Kelman, *The Busconductor Hines* (Edinburgh: Polygon, 2007), 66.

Kelman provides no formal separation or material distinction between Hines' subjective experience at work and at home: both realms are narratively fused – and confused – into one single, undifferentiated stream of consciousness in which the demotic features of vernacular expression combine and alternate with the crudeness of the protagonist's psychological exposure. The novel's technical experimentation, rather than marking an individualistic departure for working-class literary representation in postmodernity, uncovers a fundamental problematic in the construction of subjective experience when the measuring function of time (and hence, the phenomenological dividing line between work and non-work) collapses. There is virtually no substantive or qualitative difference between the kind of mental rambling that defines Hines' private subjective world and his public persona. Thus, a soliloquizing tendency marks the tone of his interactions with the driver Reilly, rendering his psychological experience of the working routine as a conductor practically indistinguishable from his moments of domestic loneliness and estrangement from his wife Sandra:

> Hines didnt reply. He walked to the rear of the bus, shaking his head and occasionally snorting. He sat down. He sniffed. Naw, christ naw, no now, definitely, definitely not, bastards, the decision's made and that's it final; hh; fuck it; the bastards, them and their fucking promotion, all I wanted to be was a fucking the Busdriver Hines.[4]

Refusing interaction with Reilly (and hence, refusing to recognize a dialogic and interpersonal dimension to his job), Hines remains absorbed in the empty and tautological structure of his mental relation to work: unable to identify the object or content (that is to say, the use-value) of his activity as a conductor, his mind strays to a lingering and indefinitely frustrated dream of becoming a driver. Work on the buses is thus not something that any temporal measure of which the subject may be aware can capture, but rather a displaced past or future – a career path devoid of quality or meaning and thus endlessly void and self-repeating. The erasure of time's qualitative content, its reduction to sameness and repetition, entails a radical redefinition of domestic life itself. There is nothing of the romanticized warmth and closeness of the working-class home evoked by the likes of George Orwell or Richard Hoggart – only a

[4] Ibid., 69.

painful sense of vital stasis and entrapment, of the incommunicability of subjective experience and of the impossibility of progress within the terms of the system:

> It seemed as though there was nothing to say. That that which could be said must have been said already. She was in bed and facing the wall, her breathing inaudible but eyes maybe open, attentive ... They had looked at each other. What could be sadder than that. Nothing could be sadder than that. It is terrible. Nothing has ever been more terrible.[5]

Here, the disorientation induced by the empty circularity of work without content, of deferred, deflected and defeated career aspirations, joins the dereliction of a space of reproduction – of life – which can no longer represent a recognizable outside to the general inertia dictated by work. As work – and in its wake, life – becomes detached from the 'rationality of measure', pain in turn grows immense and immeasurable.[6] The only possible response in this context – and this will become Hines' recurrent gesture throughout the novel – is to escape, to flee from the temporal cage of sameness and quantitative repetition into an undefinable spatial beyond: 'Hines is to get away, away; he is to get away.'[7] Yet the temptation of flight is in this, unlike in later novels (as we will see later on), shot through with contradictions that underscore the profound confusion in which Hines is submerged and that ultimately render his resistant instincts impotent. On the one hand, 'hazy visions of distant travel' – to 'the sunbaked shores of Australasia' – 'did recur',[8] indicating a hopeful point of exit from the implosive reality of abstract work and temporal subsumption, while, on the other, leaving concretizes Hines' obsessive fear of being abandoned by Sandra: 'If she does not return the outlook is entirely bleak. If she does return the outlook is of a bleakness he can handle.'[9]

In both cases, what is at stake is the temporal rootedness of a subject who, torn from the measuring function provided by concrete material work, has been displaced by an experience of indefiniteness which he cannot handle because it mirrors the abstract and unmanageable magnitude of capitalism's

---

[5] Ibid., 91.
[6] Antonio Negri, *The Labor of Job*, trans. Matteo Mandarini (Durham, NC: Duke University Press, 2009), 11.
[7] Kelman, *Busconductor*, 91.
[8] Ibid., 106.
[9] Ibid., 110.

postmodern productivity. Hines' anxiety about Sandra's delay in coming home – which prompts the mental collapse that the novel maps over a number of pages – is thus directly linked to his inability to comprehend the abstract nature of work around him, in particular the office work that Sandra performs. This appears to him an impenetrable mystery that can only add to the confusing circularity and emptiness of his own job as a conductor: '[W]hat he still has difficulty in comprehending is the way an office can be in existence when nothing else seems to.'[10] The ultimate paradox and conundrum of the postmodern experience seems to be, for Hines, the perdurability of a form of work that is by definition immaterial, and thus – he reasons – devoid of the solidity and gravitas that would make it indispensable in an increasingly fluid[11] and fast-moving system: 'There is an office and there is a staff for that office, and they do office work for which they get paid office salaries with the usual office perks. But the money. The actual fucking money. Where does it come from.'[12]

The essence of the mystery revolves around the disjunction between the tangible materiality of office work – embodied in the physical premises, the staff and even the salaries paid within that office – and the irrational phenomenality, the uncaused appearance, of the monetary product that the office generates.[13] As Negri has pointed out, the primary effect of the breakdown of the law of value in postmodernity is the redefinition of money as an immediate correlate to 'the quantity of abstract labour that is expressed by the social processes of production.'[14] It is in this sense, according to Negri, 'that *the central intuition of monetarism* (namely, that money is a reflection of society and of the entirety of exchanges) *is correct*. Money has become ... a numerical expression – not individual but collective, not concrete but abstract, not definite but indeterminate.'[15] Through its lack of individuality, concreteness and definiteness, money presents itself to the disoriented worker as a disturbing

---

[10] Ibid., 104.
[11] 'He had assumed the world as a State of Flux. All things aboard the world are constantly on the move', ibid., 96.
[12] Ibid., 105.
[13] This enigmatic status of money merely extends the process that we had already seen unfolding in Storey's novel.
[14] Antonio Negri, *The Politics of Subversion: A Manifesto for the Twenty-First Century*, trans. James Newell (London: Polity Press, 1989), 120.
[15] Ibid., 120.

enigma, as a symptom of systemic oppression and irresistible command.[16] If Hines cannot comprehend why office workers like his own wife accept the unpaid prolongation of the working day (in sharp contrast to his and his fellow bus workers' obsession with remunerated overtime),[17] that is because money in this context has been coherently and explicitly detached from concrete, individual productivity and perfected as a social form of control to which the still traditional figure of the bus conductor instinctively reacts.

The social abstraction and semantic impenetrability contained in the figure of money prompts the subjective crisis which unfolds at this point and which in large measure accounts for the level of formal and stylistic experimentation that Kelman develops in the novel. The characteristic brokenness of the syntax, as well as the repetitive tone of the internal monologue, are thus directly mapped onto the incommensurability and irrationality of a productive logic based on social abstraction and immateriality. John Kirk is thus partially right in attributing Kelman's repetitive style to the 'endless repetition of commodity production'.[18] However, what is really at stake here is the shift from a social productivity founded on the (temporal) measure of value to an immeasurable social productivity that only the 'uncaused' and irrationally expansive flow of money can properly express.

Just as Hines cannot grasp the nature of work, nor can he understand the act of leaving, around which his mind obsessively circles. Both stem from a matrix of systemic confusion, of ontological subsumption, from which the subject can only emerge as an embattled, antagonistic and suffering entity.[19] Kelman's narrative contortions act in this sense as a precise gloss on the status of subjectivity in this universe, as formal markers of the irreconcilability of antagonism in the subsumed world of postmodern capitalism. Thus the 'voice' of real subsumption, of the phenomenological confusion of the Glaswegian

---

[16] 'From the moment it becomes the numerical expression of a complex of abstract and collective productive quantities ... money is used as a repressive instrument. *The result of this short circuit is an extreme brutality*. The sensation of death against that of life, surrounds it', ibid., 122.

[17] 'Sometimes she did come home late, because of the office, having to stay on to work an extra wee bit – which for some reason seems acceptable to office workers though Sandra receives no extra cash as far as Hines is aware. Office workers may believe unpaid hours are an entry fee into the Big Time', Kelman, *Busconductor*, 104.

[18] John Kirk, 'Class, Community and "Structures of Feeling" in Working-Class Writing from the 1980s', *Literature and History*, 8: 2 (1999), 55.

[19] 'There is no resolution of this conflict. There is only a deep and violent antagonism. Life and death confront one another. The violence manifested by the relationship is inexpressible: only ethical or poetic practice succeeds in capturing it', Negri, *Politics*, 122.

bus conductor, is captured and processed through what Aaron Kelly terms 'unfree direct discourse' – a narrative treatment of subjectivity which, expressing the profound immeasurability of exploitation, rejects the consensual ideology promoted by modernism's free indirect style and stream of consciousness: '[Unfree direct discourse] replaces the concord by which subjects stream into one another with direct antagonism, with the unreconciled and non-identical politics of class that flout the regime of identification by which subjects agree their expression.'[20] A significant example of this stylistic endorsement of the experiential logic of antagonism in the face of immeasurable production and exploitation – one that Kelly cites – is the passage where Hines imagines a conversation with a man in a pub immediately after Sandra leaves:

> Here auld yin my wife's fucked off and left me I mean what's the fucking game at all, your fucking daft patter, eh, leave us alone ya cunt for fuck sake. This isnt Hines who's talking. It's a voice. This is a voice doing talking which he listens to. He doesnt think like it at all. What does he think like. Fuck off. He thinks like anybody else, anybody else in the circumstances, the circumstances which are oddly normal. Here you have a busconductor by the name of Hines Robert whose number is 4729 and whose marital status. What's the point of fucking about. You leave half of the second pint and get off your mark.[21]

As Kelly notes, the shift to a third person narrative does not have an effect of closure or resolution of the antagonism; it cannot 'reconcile his thoughts and agency with an agreed and consensual subjectivity by which all "circumstances" are made homogeneous and universal'.[22] Rather, Hines' subjectivity emerges here as an inexhaustible conflict of viewpoints and subject positions, oscillating between the incorporated generality of an adaptive 'anybody' and the immediacy of a refusal articulated by the first person singular. Unfree direct discourse thus echoes the immeasurability of the social as the production of value can no longer be given a temporal basis and as work is voided of concrete substance.

Hines' desire to leave, to flee the here-and-now of empty, circular work and implosive life, expresses the urge of the postmodern refusal, the radicality of

---

[20] Aaron Kelly, *James Kelman: Politics and Aesthetics* (Oxford and Bern: Peter Lang, 2013), 93.
[21] Kelman, *Busconductor*, 197.
[22] Kelly, *Kelman*, 93.

the challenge presented – often beyond comprehension and rational measure, in the blindness of an instinctual and fundamental rage – against power. Leaving, for Hines, means refusing: refusing to work, refusing to co-operate (with his fellow workers and the institutional forms of continuity with the system of exploitation that these represent),[23] and thus refusing to submit to the integrated or subsumed logic of capitalist valorization. However, if Hines' refusal is ultimately failed and ineffectual, that is because it is still largely aimed at what he considers management's deliberate and unjust tampering with the necessary division between working and non-working time – a division that the general process of real subsumption makes unsustainable. When, towards the end of the novel, Hines is required to turn up for work on his day off, he refuses, claiming a distinction between working time and 'his own time'[24] which his entire experiential trajectory in the novel seems to contradict. His refusal thus becomes an empty gesture of rebellion that fails to identify the abstract and diffuse – the immeasurable – dynamic of social exploitation pervading the entire social body. This failure, which is similarly expressed both in his inability to leave and in his fear of being left, defines an initial position of subjective vulnerability and defeat in the face of postmodern capital's excess, which Kelman will gradually abandon in his later novels. As we will see below, the act of leaving retains its symbolic centrality in *A Disaffection* and *How Late It Was, How Late*, at the same time that it acquires a new strategic effectuality that will eventually lead to a rehearsal of resistant potentialities left unexplored in *The Busconductor Hines*.

*

In postmodernity, as Negri writes, we 'are forced into the peripheral or simply cruel spaces of the exploitation of labour. The most productive labor, the most refined and powerful, the most intellectual and abstract, seems to repeat the course of development of slave labor, of unpaid female labor, of forced labor'.[25] The experience of abstraction and immeasurability is exacerbated in

---

[23] This includes refusing to participate in any collective initiative, such as a strike action, 'on his behalf': 'Anyway, to be perfectly fucking honest with yous all, I dont want anybody going on strike on my behalf. I want to do it on my tod. It's my strike, yous can get your own. I mean they're fucking easy to find', ibid., 244.
[24] Ibid., 238.
[25] Negri, *Labor*, 10–11.

those forms of work that are most directly social and immaterial. To Hines, office work represented a phantasmagoria of insubstantiality that only a magical, uncaused flow of money could match. His own job as a bus conductor embodied the cruelty of work devoid of content; an empty pattern of shifts and frustrated aspirations pointing at the circularity and violence of unqualified social time. In *A Disaffection*, published in 1989, Kelman delves even deeper into the destructive effects of the abolition of the temporal law of value.

This novel follows Patrick Doyle, a 29-year-old school teacher, as he descends into a personal crisis over the sense and purpose of his role and general position in life. For him, the experience of work marks a radical departure from the material concreteness that informs his family background in industrial labour. Working as a teacher represents an immediate, and immediately disorienting, engagement with the social generality and abstraction which, in postmodernity, increasingly defines the labour process. This is the realization that stands at the root of his disaffection: the notion that his work is defined by an abstract content, by an abstract and unquantifiable object, which can only be encountered, after the fact, as it were, in coercive social effects. As an intellectual or cognitive worker in an institutional setting, Patrick deals with intangible products that cannot be charted or accounted for directly, but which nevertheless have transversal and lasting effects across the social body. This indirectness and immateriality is experienced as a crisis of value, as a questioning (which is also, for him, a self-questioning) of the immeasurable magnitude which cognitive work generates within the cycle of social productivity. Thus, for Patrick, the intellectual labour of the teacher amounts to the creation, circulation and perpetuation of '[t]heoretical webs, dirty webs, fusty webs; old and shrivelling away into nothingness, a fine dust. Who needs that kind of stuff. Far far better getting out into the open air and doing it, actually doing it, something solid and concrete and unconceptualisable.'[26]

For the disgruntled teacher, intellectual speculation – the sort of activity that his job keeps bringing him back to – signals a dead-end, a void exercise against a recurring pattern of subjective disempowerment. In this case, it is not

---

[26] James Kelman, *A Disaffection* (London: Secker and Warburg, 1989), 10.

the alienating succession of shifts – the timetabled existence of the bus conductor – that makes the working experience abstract and undifferentiated, but rather the compulsion to theorize in a void, without any sense of real intervention in or connection to the social context around him. The experience of the social as a set of concrete affective, symbolic and communicative continuities (or interventions) is precisely what is lost and replaced by an apparatus of control – the school – that recreates intellectual work as either an instrumental fetish or a futile and empty exercise. In this novel, subsumption takes the form of an institutional incorporation and neutralization of the creative possibilities that the intellect – once it is rediscovered as general, social intellect – harbours.[27] The school no longer merely represents a known locus of ideological reproduction on behalf of the ruling class (an 'ideological state apparatus', in Althusser's classic formulation),[28] but an instance of the disarticulation of relatively autonomous social forms by the neoliberal State. What Patrick primarily resents about his job is the nature of its institutionality, which no longer represents a form of mediation at the level of civil society.[29]

As Michael Hardt and Antonio Negri have argued, the postmodern 'State no longer has a need for mediatory mechanisms of legitimation and discipline'.[30] Rather, the State of late capitalism exerts its rule directly, immediately, through decentralized and fluid 'networks of control'.[31] Gilles Deleuze claims that, in the postmodern period, the disciplinary enclosures of such characteristically modern institutions as the prison, the asylum, or the factory have been replaced by 'smooth' – as opposed to 'striated' – institutional forms that exert

---

[27] The notion of 'general intellect' was introduced by Marx in the *Grundrisse* in relation to the shared cognitive and creative capacities of the species expressed as a productive force of capital in machinery. This has since become a standard reference for Autonomist Marxists. See, for example, Paolo Virno and Michael Hardt (eds), *Radical Thought in Italy: A Potential Politics*, trans. Maurizia Boscagli et al. (Minneapolis: University of Minnesota Press, 1996) and Christian Marazzi, *Capital and Affects: The Politics of the Language Economy*, trans. Giuseppina Mecchia (New York: Semiotext(e), 2011).

[28] Louis Althusser, *Lenin and Philosophy and Other Essays*, trans. Ben Brewster (London: New Left Books, 1977).

[29] According to Gramsci, civil society is the ideological space, the connective tissue, linking the productive forces to the State, and thus the realm of constitution of 'hegemony'. This means that power, in a modern capitalist society, is primarily located in the intermediate institutions of civil society, and that consequently, these need to be seen as the proper targets of the revolutionary struggle. See, for example, Norberto Bobbio, 'Gramsci and the conception of civil society', in Chantal Mouffe (ed.), *Gramsci and Marxist Theory* (London: Routledge, 2014).

[30] Michael Hardt and Antonio Negri, *Labor of Dionysus: A Critique of the State-Form* (Minneapolis: University of Minnesota Press, 1994), 259.

[31] Ibid., 259.

their power, transversally or rhizomatically, simultaneously on each and every level of society.[32] The replacement of discipline with control, as theorized by Deleuze, Negri and Hardt, does not point to an abolition of the disciplinary effects found in the institutional enclosures of modern society (of which the school was a traditional example), but rather to 'the generalization of the logics that used to function within these limited domains across the entire society, spreading like a virus'.[33] In terms of the general process of real subsumption, this proliferation of open, decentralized and viral modalities of control expresses another aspect of the crisis of measure within the social process of extortion and accumulation of value. The disciplinary operations traditionally assumed and exerted by power through a range of institutional mediations and hegemonic/ideological apparatuses are now displaced onto an abstract plane of immediate and smooth control, of direct and pervasive yet possibly intangible interventions on behalf of power. As in the case of the bus conductor's empty and circular experience of work, the experience of the educational state apparatus is rendered immeasurable and hardly resistible by its repositioning as a diffuse and unmediated institution of control.

As the school ceases to function as a disciplinary structure of civil society, the intellectual activity on which it nominally rests is also excluded from the ideological/hegemonic game, re-emerging as an empty and powerless tool for social transformation. The roots of Patrick's disaffection thus lie not only in the immeasurable nature of intellectual work within the social cycle of production of value, but also in its ideological 'abstraction' and exclusion from the dynamics of hegemonic struggle. In this context of the real subsumption of society within the State (which formalizes, in institutional-political terms, the real subsumption of society within capital), the work of the teacher can only contribute to the diffusion of social control: both school and teacher now appear as instruments of the State expressing the balance of power of capitalist social relations through direct, fluid and unmediated mechanisms of regulation and exploitation. Thus, Patrick ironically informs his pupils of the oppressive nature of his role and of their subaltern position in the school:

---

[32] Gilles Deleuze, 'Postscript on the Societies of Control', *October*, 59 (1992), 3–7. The opposition between 'the smooth' and 'the striated' is fully explored by Deleuze and Guattari in *A Thousand Plateaus*, trans. Brian Massumi (London: Continuum, 2011), 523–51.
[33] Hardt and Negri, *Dionysus*, 260. See also Michael Hardt, 'The Global Society of Control', *Discourse*, 20: 3 (1998), 139–52.

> Now, all of yous, all you wee first-yearers, cause that's what you are, wee first-yearers. You are here being fenced in by us the teachers at the behest of the government in explicit simulation of your parents viz. the oppressed poor. Repeat after me: We are being fenced in by the teachers.[34]

Far from signalling a cynical renunciation of his oppositional stance, the playful irony of the exercise – in which the students amusedly participate – reveals a desire to reclaim the intellect from the pressures of control. This desire is nevertheless disabled by a recognition of impotence, of his incapacity to engage the system and attempt any form of contestation within its terms and structures. Guilt seems to be for Patrick the predominant expression of this acknowledgement, the primary subjective effect of his exclusion from the ideological/hegemonic game and of his reduction to a passively instrumental position within the mechanisms of the postmodern State. This guilt constantly oscillates in the novel between a sense of disconnection or alienation from residual working-class solidarities and a pressing feeling of entrapment in a role of functional complicity with the State. Thus Patrick thinks of his parents as 'always secretly trying to figure out how come they wound up with me! How come they wound up with a boy who went in for his Highers and then went to uni and became a member of the polis.'[35]

His role as a teacher is presented as deeply structural, as a central element of the current 'polity'. In this sense, the ideological distance that his playful intellectual interventions in the classroom seem to be calling for are ultimately dissipated by a repressive enactment of the power structure: 'It's us that keep the things from falling apart. It's us. Who else! We're responsible for it, the present polity.'[36] The dynamics of control thus reveal the ontological confusion – already uncovered by the vernacular Glaswegian rendition of the police as 'polis' – between the social and the political, and, consequently, the institutional conflation of the polity with a proliferation of mechanisms of discipline without possible ideological mediation or separation. As Cairns Craig puts it, 'the police dominate the *polis* as envisaged in ancient Greece and replace the ethic of free citizens in a shared community with repression and the continual threat of violence'.[37]

---

[34] Kelman, *Disaffection*, 25.
[35] Ibid., 139.
[36] Ibid., 149.
[37] Cairns Craig, 'Resisting Arrest', in Gavin Wallace and Randall Stevenson (eds), *The Scottish Novel Since the Seventies: New Visions, Old Dreams* (Edinburgh: Edinburgh University Press, 1993), 112.

As the institutional expression of real subsumption becomes apparent (or, in other words, as the apparatuses of discipline and ideological reproduction are reinvented as 'smooth' forms of social control), resistance and oppositionality are in turn redeployed as subjective strategies of flight or exodus. Exodus, according to Paolo Virno, is a form of 'engaged withdrawal' that transcribes the dialectic of enmity embedded in class struggle into the context of late capitalism and real subsumption.[38] In Virno's analysis, post-Fordist work displays the immaterial qualities which had been traditionally assigned to political praxis in modernity. Work is increasingly rediscovered as an activity without a product, closer to the actions of the performing artist than to any form of material creation. But if postmodern work is essentially a mode of 'virtuosity', of public performance, much like the pianist's (in Virno's privileged example), or the teacher's, what, then, is its 'score'? For Virno, 'the *sui generis* "score" of present-day labor is Intellect *qua* public Intellect, general intellect, global social knowledge, shared linguistic ability'.[39] Thus, the immaterial, diffuse, and hence immeasurable character of postmodern labour has its paradigmatic expression in 'conceptual constellations and schemes of thinking that cannot ever be recuperated within fixed capital'.[40] The intellectual work of the teacher is in this sense 'a direct attribute of living labor', which, unlike the material labour of the industrial worker, with its dependency on the factory and the machine, is immediately produced as abstract generality.

With the collapse of the regime of the factory and with the reconfiguration of living labour as an immeasurable social productivity, the general intellect that had hitherto been objectivized in fixed capital – in the machine – is now released into the public sphere, reinvented or rediscovered as a performative potentiality, as virtuosity. However, as Virno points out, and Kelman confirms, this newly acquired publicness of postmodern work is not without its distortions and inhibitions.[41] Precisely because it is reconfigured as performative activity, and thus made similar to political praxis, immaterial labour is permanently at risk of being subordinated and rendered servile to the

---

[38] Paolo Virno, 'Virtuosity and Revolution: The Political Theory of Exodus', in Virno and Hardt, *Radical*, 197.
[39] Ibid., 194.
[40] Ibid., 194.
[41] Ibid., 195.

State: 'What we have here is no longer the familiar process of rationalization of the State, but rather a Statization of Intellect.'[42]

In this context, labour can only organize itself antagonistically by exiting from the institutional orbit of the State, by fleeing its horizon of transversal control of the social. Exodus thus becomes the paradigm of struggle in the epoch of real subsumption. Far from expressing passivity, defeat or acquiescence in the face of the police/*polis*, the figure of exodus offers a reactualization of antagonistic class politics by sketching the possibility of a 'nonservile virtuosity' – of Intellect in revolt against the State of late capitalism.[43] Yet as Patrick's predicament amply demonstrates, no real exit can be envisaged while the general intellect – while living labour – remains encapsulated in the forms of work sanctioned by the State apparatus. Insofar as this subordination prevails, the will-to-exodus (which is the subversive form the will-to-power adopts under conditions of real subsumption) can only manifest itself as impotent 'disaffection'.[44] In effect, 'general intellect can only affirm itself as an autonomous public sphere, thus avoiding the "transfer" of its own potential into the absolute power of Administration, if it cuts the linkage that binds it to the production of commodities and wage labor'.[45] In other words, the active form of resistance can only be articulated in this context through the refusal of work. And since work has itself been rendered diffuse, abstract, immaterial and immeasurable – a feature or a part of the postmodern State's exertion of control upon the subsumed social body – refusal can only appear in the shape of an absolutely radical gesture of desertion. Herein lies the paradox of the politics of exodus: the publicness of the resisting subject – whether we choose to name it general intellect, living labour, or postmodern working class – can

---

[42] Ibid., 196.
[43] Ibid., 200.
[44] This conceptual translation of the Nietzschean will-to-power into the Autonomist will-to-exodus is best understood through the Spinozian opposition (which in turn plays a crucial role in the development of Negri's thought) between 'power' and 'Power', or, in the original Latin, *potentia* and *potestas*. Thus, while the latter is typically associated with the State, with the command exerted by the institutional form adopted by capital, the former refers to the 'constituent' possibility of subjective transformation, of creative flight from the gripping structures of 'constituted' power. Negri's own work on 'constituent power' and Spinoza represents the most exhaustive analysis of this fundamental opposition. See Antonio Negri, *Insurgencies: Constituent Power and the Modern State*, trans. Maurizia Boscagli (Minneapolis: University of Minnesota Press, 2009). See also, Antonio Negri, *The Savage Anomaly: The Power of Spinoza's Metaphysics and Politics*, trans. Michael Hardt (Minneapolis: University of Minnesota Press, 1999) and *Spinoza for Our Time: Politics and Postmodernity*, trans. William McCuaig (New York: Columbia University Press, 2013).
[45] Virno, 'Virtuosity', 196.

only be asserted by exiting a public sphere already colonized by capital and its bureaucratic apparatus: a public sphere that has been 'privatized' by the postmodern State.

This seems to be Kelman's central insight in *A Disaffection*. Patrick's initial withdrawal involves a displacement, a refusal of his role as a teacher in an institutional setting, in favour of a performative approach which would restore the publicness of intellect: thus, throughout the novel, he expresses a determination to leave his job in order to concentrate on playing the electrician's pipes which he has found in the street and subsequently refashioned as musical instruments. However paradoxically, this retreat from the official domain of 'public performance', this desertion of his job, is envisaged as the only possibility of rehabilitating the publicness and performativity of intellect in this subsumed universe:

> To stop being a teacher. To concentrate solely upon things of genuine value, things of genuine authenticity, of a genuine physicality. Teaching by performance instead of pointing the finger.
> But could all that be achieved on the pipes? What was it about them?[46]

The act of leaving is presented here, unlike in *The Busconductor Hines*, where it still functioned as an abstract signifier of defeat, as a concrete form of empowerment and active *resistance* against the suffocating constraints of the institutional system. Under these conditions, the search for a non-subsumed public sphere, for a true performativity of the intellect beyond the control of the State, cannot be regarded as an unproblematic or neutral movement of withdrawal. On the contrary, the dynamic of exodus is experienced as an overt form of class struggle which cannot be entirely separated from the materiality of conflict, from the immediacy of an often physical clash with the apparatuses of control.[47] In other words, if in the case of Hines the act of leaving had essentially represented a conditioned reflex of systemic circularity and abstraction (and thus, in a sense, an 'unconscious' reflection of the 'consciousness' of capital), for Patrick, it constitutes a fully conscious and

---

[46] Kelman, *Disaffection*, 10.
[47] As Hardt and Negri put it: 'Our readers with a taste for combat may be reluctant to accept a notion of class struggle as exodus because it does not have enough fight in it. Not to worry. Moses learned long ago that those in power do not just let you go without a fight', *Commonwealth* (Cambridge, MA: Harvard University Press, 2009), 164.

deliberately oppositional notion of refusal which soon transmutes into a concrete insurrectionary scenario. Thus, in the last few pages of the novel, Patrick's *general* disaffection suddenly morphs into a *specific* vision of rebellion against the institutions of capital:

> Along at the corner of the street he approached was this national bank from whose topmost windows beamed a nightlight and this was the window Patrick's brick would smash. If he was about to become seriously engaged in the world then this was the time and this was the place. And as he progressed towards Cowcaddens he could be smashing in the windows of each and every bank he chanced upon. And also those of building societies and insurance offices – anything at all connected with the financial institutions of the Greatbritish Rulers.[48]

The crux of this passage is not its unrealized threat – or, in other words, its unfulfilled revolutionary promise – but the manifestation of the State and the institutions of capital as combined and coordinated forms of the sequence polity/*polis*/police. Unlike in the case of the bus conductor Hines, Patrick's insurrectionary drive is not defeated by his confused relation to the logic of exodus (or, in other words, by his lack of understanding of the necessity of a total break with the institutional system), but by the pre-emptive power of an apparatus of capture, of an inescapable system of control, capable of – literally – emerging from the shadows 'at the very thought of insurrection':

> So, the banks of the city and big bricks. At least it would be a bloody start. There was a pair of polis across the street who needless to report were observing him openly and frankly and not giving a fuck about who was noticing. But now they watched him watching them ... They had appeared at the very thought of insurrection, the very thought, and there they were.[49]

With this novel, Kelman's attention shifts from the phenomenological drama of subsumption to its socio-political effects, and from the abstract violence of postmodern work to the concrete violence of the postmodern State. The coercive nature of the system, which Hines' confused reflections still identified at a general level, transmute, in *A Disaffection*, into a specifically institutional operation of control. Thus, Kelman draws a clear trajectory in his analysis of

---

[48] Kelman, *Disaffection*, 335.
[49] Ibid., 336.

postmodern exploitative and oppressive dynamics that will climax in the nightmarish and yet, paradoxically, more hopeful universe of his 1994 Booker Prize-winning novel *How Late It Was, How Late*.

*

How Late It Was, How Late articulates the logic of exodus from the subsumed and statified public sphere of late capitalism as an interminable (and interminably antagonistic) process. If Patrick Doyle realizes, at the end of *A Disaffection*, that the State apparatus casts a ubiquitous – and pre-emptive – net of control over every potentially subversive move, Sammy Samuels, the lumpen protagonist of the later novel, proposes an unrelenting strategy of resistant flight from the State, which in turn emerges as an even more brutally bureaucratic and repressive form than before. In this novel, the public sphere has not only been colonized by the State, but has also been effectively shorn of every ideological remnant, of every trace of civil society. The school recedes as the institutional representation of the *polis*/polity and is now replaced by the actual police and by a bureaucratic apparatus which stands in a relation of radical exteriority to the subject: an abstract, faceless machine of administration/repression, which, rather than threaten to thwart his subversive instincts, directly, and sometimes physically, interferes with Sammy's every move.

The novel's opening provides an apt and compact summary of its narrative trajectory: Sammy Samuels, an unemployed ex-convict, wakes up in the streets of Glasgow after a night of binge drinking. Disoriented and penniless, robbed of both shoes and jeans, he is first quietly watched, and then abused and beaten up by a group of nameless and mysterious policemen, whom Sammy militarizes by referring to them as 'sodjers'.[50] The boundless abstraction and immeasurability of the postmodern experience – initially delineated by Kelman in *The Busconductor Hines* – reach in these pages a paroxysm of coercion and overt violence. The subsumption of the social (of Virno's public sphere) within the cycle of capitalist expropriation and valorization is articulated here as a purely physical exertion of command. No more alienation and no more self-contained circularity as in the case of Hines: the institutional form of capital can only be met, can only be experienced, as State violence – as

---

[50] Kővesi, *Kelman*, 128.

faceless and nameless, as abstract and 'unquantifiable', State violence. It is thus no surprise that the main event in the novel is Sammy's becoming blind as a result of this initial aggression by the police. The linguistic condensation of this early passage, the violence conveyed by the expletives and repetitions, evokes an asphyxiating social universe of crushing pressures and blind(ing) forces:

> Sammy couldnay get away; gulping for a breath, he couldnay get one; he tried to crawl, but he was tottering and he spotted the sodjer stepping back the way and wiping his mouth on his wrist ... He could feel them shaking, shaking, so fucking angry man they were just so fucking angry; there was only two of them, that was a thing, fucking hell man, Sammy was thinking, but he was fuckt, fuckt, he couldnay break loose, he fucking couldnay, they had him, they fucking had him man the two of them ... After they straightened him out he was in a patrol car, the cuffs were nipping. It was black, things seemed black.[51]

This blackness and general sense of oppression expressively capture postmodern capital's transformation of measure into command, of social mediation into immediate exploitation. If, as we noted at the outset, real subsumption essentially refers to the process whereby the cycle of capitalist valorization dissolves every dimension of exteriority, every possibility of a use-value, of a labor power, external to the circuit of capital's circulation, then we must recognize in this figure of complete and violent interiority – of blinding immanence, so to speak – a paradigmatic expression of its social effects. The ontological transformation of capital's temporality in real subsumption, from measure to substance and from equivalence to command, is at the root of this exemplary narrative of exploitation. The time of life, which is to say, under the described parameters, the ontological substance of the individual and of society, is placed under the direct and brutal rule of a plurality of coercive apparatuses, ranging from the anonymous policemen who exert the *foundational* violence which leaves Sammy blind, to a legion of bureaucrats who enact the reduction of the social to a state of general captivity. In this case, no phonetic or semantic slippage is required to justify the identification of the State as a whole with the police. The former is now globally and directly

---

[51] James Kelman, *How Late It Was, How Late* (London: Vintage, 1998), 6.

expressive of a police function, of an unmediated and undisguised dynamic of command.[52]

As it has been argued, the transformation of civil society and its ideological mediations into mechanisms of direct control by capital and the State lay at the root of Patrick Doyle's break with the system. What had begun, following Hines' steps, as confused disorientation and existential crisis soon morphed into a deliberate search for disconnection and exodus from the State (and consequently, from the cycle of capital). In Sammy's case, there is no room for negotiation; there is no slow brewing of disaffection: the 'withering away of "social space"',[53] its conversion or reduction to a form of command, expresses itself immediately in the shape of immeasurable – that is, unexplained and irrational – violence. As Sammy soon finds out, the arbitrary and unmotivated brutality of the police is reproduced, at a more abstract level, in the bureaucratic distortions of the Department of Social Security. The physical blows dealt out by the 'sodjers' transmute into immaterial blows, into discursive and procedural operations aiming to subdue the individual and to turn the entire fabric of social interactions into a savage dynamic of control. Thus, as it is 'explained' to Sammy:

> the police department is empowered to restrain the customer Mister Samuels and certainly if the customer is then in receipt of a dysfunction, and this dysfunction is shown to be an effect of the restraints applied then the customer is entitled to submit an application to this department in respect of Dysfunctional Benefit and if it is approved then the benefit is awarded.[54]

The blind(ing) and irrational violence exerted by the police at the beginning of the novel is thus accommodated here within an opaque discursive procedure which transcribes the general thrust of the subsumption of the social under the direct command of the State. The oppressive physicality of the early passages, of Sammy's interrogation and detention at the police station, is replaced by the linguistic and semantic bludgeoning of bureaucrats, who turn an apparently neutral compensation claim into a nonsensical and nightmarish

---

[52] This representation of the State's administrative mechanism confirms Hardt and Negri's claim that 'the postmodern State appears increasingly as a true and proper police State while the police appear as the supreme administrative system', *Dionysus*, 300.
[53] Ibid., 271.
[54] Kelman, *How*, 104–5.

operation of control. The initial assault is refashioned as a commercial transaction between 'the police department' and a 'customer' who may, as a result, 'be in receipt of a dysfunction'. The act of power is no longer defined by a relation of exceptionality, by a suspension of rights as in the classic modern definition of sovereignty,[55] but is, rather, presented as an 'ordinary' and procedural extension of the administrative apparatus of the State (which is moreover given an overtly economic modulation) to the point where it engulfs every interaction, every movement and occurrence in/of the social. Power no longer expresses a contingent – and in that sense, exceptional – possibility of intervention or articulation of a given antagonism. It is rediscovered, rather, as an absolute horizon (as an immeasurable ontological space) from which every intermediate option has been evacuated.

In other words, this novel constructs a world in which power is reduced to an administrative procedure – to an absolute, immediate, inescapably close and *unexceptional* procedure. While Patrick Doyle still experienced – however precariously and confusedly – a certain degree of distance (constructed as 'disaffection') from the institutional apparatus of the State, Sammy, by contrast, is thrust into a black hole, into a universe that cannot be *seen* from however minimal a distance, and that can only be experienced corporeally, through so many *physical* clashes with the boots of 'sodjers' or the words of bureaucrats. Power is thus expressed in this novel as linguistic abstraction, as lexical bluntness, syntactic redundancy, and semantic impenetrability violently impinging on the subject: 'Ye must understand also Mister Samuels that if as you suggest the alleged dysfunction is an effect of physical restraints and is established as such then the secondary factor arises in respect of those restraints, and this secondary factor may become primary, why were those restraints being exercised.'[56]

In this context – and in a way that is much clearer than in previous novels – Kelman's characterization of the protagonist through vernacular expression, through combative and expletive-ridden speech, offers a resistant break with the absoluteness of power. Sammy's language is both insistent and

---

[55] As Carl Schmitt famously put it, in a formula that has been taken up and adapted by a multiplicity of modern and postmodern thinkers both left and right: 'Sovereign is he who decides on the exception', *Political Theology: Four Chapters on the Concept of Sovereignty*, trans. George Schwab (Chicago: Chicago University Press, 1985), 5.

[56] Kelman, *How*, 105–6.

resistant in a way that profoundly subverts the oppressive repetitiveness of official discourse. It reveals a constituent power – a radical ontological *potentia*, in the Spinozian sense – which can only be understood as a frontal blow against the constituted power of the late capitalist State.

From the beginning, Sammy brings his antagonism, his indomitable subjectivity, to the heart of the system through an unrelenting flow of subversive language (which, in the eyes of the literary and critical establishment, has recurrently appeared as an assault on the institution of literature itself).[57] The anarchic quality of a speech filled with variations of the word 'fuck', plagued with syntactic interruptions and dislocations, operates a radical 'deterritorialization' of official discourse and the power relations it entails.[58] In Deleuze's terms, this is a minor form of language making the major language 'stutter' – that is, a mode of expression breaking up the organized and hierarchical system of language and giving way to a radical opening beyond its control:[59]

> He was gony be fine. Across the big junction and onto the bridge and that was him, so okay, so that's that, ye just fucking
> that's all ye do, step by step, ye walk
> step by step, by step, ye keep going, ye just dont cave in man that feeling, hanging there, but ye don't let it cover ye ye keep going christ the times he had had, the time he had been through man he had been through the fucking worst, this wasnay the fucking worst man e had been through it man and this wasnay it, it fucking wasnay, it wasnay, it just fucking wasnay, he had seen it, the worst man he had fucking seen it, cunts fucking dying, getting fucking kicked to death, the fucking lot man he had seen it.[60]

---

[57] As Kövesi observes: 'For many English reviewers – especially those whose interest in Kelman was generated by the glitzy cultural gossiping of the Booker prize rather than by intrinsic literary pursuits – the language of Kelman is brutalising, amoral, desensitised, difficult and unsophisticated: [Simon] Jenkins compared reading his work with being accosted by a Glaswegian drunk on a train', *Kelman*, 156–7.

[58] This 'deterritorialization' suggests a radical ontological transformation – prompted, in this case, by language – rather than a literal displacement or loss of territory. It is clear that, despite the level of temporal abstraction condensed in the text, there are sufficient pointers to frame this and Kelman's other novels within the concrete 'territoriality' of Glasgow. Deterritorialization should be understood here in the strict Deleuzian sense, as that transformative process that invokes creation of 'a future form ... that does not yet exist'. See Gilles Deleuze and Félix Guattari, *What is Philosophy?* trans. Hugh Tomlinson and Graham Burchell (New York: Columbia University Press, 1994), 108.

[59] Gilles Deleuze, *Essays Critical and Clinical*, trans. Daniel W. Smith and Michael A. Greco (London: Verso, 1998), 107. For a full account of the opposition between 'minor' and 'major' forms of language and literature, see Gilles Deleuze and Félix Guattari, *Kafka: Toward a Minor Literature*, trans. Dana Polan (Minneapolis: University of Minnesota Press, 1986).

[60] Kelman, *How*, 57.

Sammy's hammering repetitions express an inexhaustible determination to resist – a powerful *conatus* mobilized against the brutal formalisms of bureaucratic discourse and procedure.[61]

As Kelman further puts it, in one of the narrative's characteristic changes to third-person: 'He kept going. A battler man that was what he was. One thing about the Sammy fellow, a fucking battler. If ye asked him he would have telt ye: nay brains but he would aye battle like fuck.'[62] This concise characterization would suggest an inversion of the position represented by Patrick Doyle, who could be seen as embodying the impotent situation of intellect under conditions of real subsumption. Sammy, on the contrary, marks a direct passage to action, an effectuation of Patrick's imagined withdrawal, which is somehow facilitated or enabled by his relative distance from intellect. Even if, strictly, it is not true that Sammy has 'nay brains' in the conventional sense,[63] it is undeniable that he occupies a more peripheral position within the system than the school teacher in *A Disaffection*. After all, Sammy is a petty criminal, and to him the violence of the State is – as he immediately avows during his initial captivity at the police station – 'the usual ... more of the same'.[64] This exteriority from the State, this subjective heterogeneity with the institutional mechanisms of postmodern capital, which presents him as fundamentally indomitable, makes his progress throughout the novel an incontestable trajectory of flight, of effective exodus from the regime of late capitalist power. Sammy's dynamic of resistance can be linked, in this sense, to Deleuze and Guattari's model of the nomadic 'war machine' as delineated in *A Thousand Plateaus*. In this account, the figure of the nomad is defined, both historically and theoretically, by a relation of mutual exclusion with the State that cannot be overcome:

> It is not enough to affirm that the war machine [of the nomad peoples] is external to the [State] apparatus. It is necessary to reach the point of

---

[61] In Spinoza's philosophy, as Laurent Bove has shown, the notion of *conatus* is the 'strategic', warlike, form that resistance takes: 'Puissance singulière d'affirmation et de résistance, le *conatus* spinoziste est une pratique stratégique de décision des problèmes et de leur resolution' (A singular power of affirmation and resistance, the Spinozist *conatus* is a strategic practice of decision and resolution of problems), *La stratégie du conatus: affirmation et résistance chez Spinoza* (Paris: Vrin, 2012), 14.

[62] Kelman, *How*, 47.

[63] As Kövesi has pointed out: 'Sammy has frequent recollections of fiction, which range from explicit references such as *John Barleycorn* by Jack London ... to the more frequent unnamed references ... Nevertheless it is clear that literature is unproblematically a part of *his* culture, something which reactions to the novel almost always ignore, whether positive or negative', *Kelman*, 137.

[64] Kelman, *How*, 6.

conceiving the war machine as itself a pure form of exteriority, whereas the State apparatus constitutes the form of interiority we habitually take as a model, or according to which we are in the habit of thinking.[65]

The interlocking notions of nomadism and war express an ontological disjunction (which nevertheless maintains a formal symmetry) between the operations of internalization – of incorporation or subsumption – carried out by the State and established as the model of constituted power, and the contrary dynamics of refusal, of subversion and resistance which find in exodus from the latter's sovereign interiority their principle and essence. Just as the State of real subsumption – the State of late capitalism – emerges as an abstract and immeasurable configuration through the effects of its molecular and rhizomatic power, the war that Sammy – the petty criminal, the perpetual outsider, the nomad – wages upon its oppressive apparatus cannot be properly measured (and hence finally controlled or pacified) due to its constitutive otherness and exteriority.

Sammy's existence is defined by *insistence* and by *resistance*, in other words, by an inexhaustible drive to 'battle on' against the odds and in spite of the absoluteness of power. In a subversive mirror reflection of the immeasurability of the exploitative system, Sammy's 'strategy' of struggle emerges as equally immeasurable and powerful:

> Some folk just keep going man they push ahead. And that's what the cunts dont like, they want ye to fucking do yerself in. See if ye dont but, see if ye go and fucking attack, then that's them man they're fuckt. Ye have to start looking on the bright side. Whatever: ye dont take it lying down – that's an invitation to stick in the boot man that's all that is.[66]

Sammy wages his war – his war of withdrawal or exodus, for the most part – as a nomad minority of one surrounded by an abstract multiplicity of apparatuses of control. But insofar as he presents his challenge – his act of refusal – as an unstoppable movement, as an interminable line of flight, the institutional complex of postmodern capital is permanently haunted by the menace of an indomitable outside, of a nomadic incommensurability which threatens to

---

[65] Deleuze and Guattari, *Thousand*, 390.
[66] Kelman, *How*, 118.

make the 'dream' of power (a hallucinatory dream of perfect and total submission) an everlasting impossibility.[67]

4.2 Beyond civil society: On Irvine Welsh's *Skagboys*

As we have seen, postmodernity is characterized by a tendential suppression of the institutions of mediation that characterized modernity. If Antonio Gramsci theorized the notion of civil society as the connective tissue linking the productive forces of capital to the institutional apparatus of the State, and situated here the axis of the ideological struggle for hegemony, more recent authors, such as Antonio Negri and Michael Hardt, have identified, in the suppression of this connective tissue, the true profile of postmodern society. Kelman's novels offer a penetrating – and often devastating – insight into the collapse of the mediatory function of civil society and its replacement by a new institutionality characterized by the saturation of the public sphere and the transversal colonization of the entirety of social relations. Kelman's focus is thus placed on what Deleuze called 'the society of control' – the decentralized and flexible form that power takes in the context of capital's fluid expansion across society.

As I argued above, resistance is articulated in this context as a movement of exodus or withdrawal from the new dynamics of institutional immediacy. However, if the social field is now characterized by saturation, if the mere existence of a physical 'outside' to the system of power and production is negated by the suppression of all spaces of mediation, the movement of exodus can only be conceived of as a process without completion, as a journey without destination or terminus. It is in this sense that the postmodern exodus is, in Deleuze and Guattari's terms, a form of nomadism. According to these authors, the nomad does not behave in the way that the migrant does. While the latter moves from one point to another, upon an essentially 'sedentary space' that is

---

[67] It should be noted that this trajectory of exodus, that this 'line of flight', does not point to a physical 'outside'. In the system of control, under postmodern capitalism, the notion that there may still be a possibility of *actually going elsewhere* (say, Australia, in Robert Hines' ill-fated conception) has been disproven as a vain illusion. As Sammy Samuels confirms, the horizon of exodus, the nomadic dynamic of resistance is but a perpetual movement without a final resting place. As Deleuze and Guattari rightly point out, it is only 'by leaving the plan(e) of capital, and never ceasing to leave it' that a genuine revolutionary subjectivity can be constructed in this epoch, *Thousand*, 521.

'striated' 'by walls, enclosures, and roads between enclosures', the space of the nomad 'is smooth, marked only by "traits" that are effaced and displaced within the trajectory'.[68] This suggests that the nomad cannot be properly defined by extensive or relative movement from one place to another, but by intensive, 'absolute' movement, by speed: '[A] speed may be very slow, or even immobile … [it] *constitutes the absolute character of a body whose irreducible parts (atoms) occupy or fill a smooth space in the manner of a vortex*, with the possibility of springing up at any point'.[69] The resistant dynamic of exodus rehearsed by Sammy Samuels in *How Late It Was, How Late* offers a clear instance of the 'vortical or swirling movement' of the nomad.[70] Faced with a 'smooth' institutionality without breaks or segments, without gaps or intermediacies, Sammy's struggle consists of a movement without a point of departure or arrival – a movement that is not really a movement, but rather, a 'stationary process', an intensive release of speed.[71] Kelman's protagonist, like the Bedouin, 'is one who does not depart, does not want to depart, who clings to the smooth space left by the receding forest', or, in this case, the receding institutions of civil society, 'and who invents nomadism as a response to this challenge'.[72] Such a response is only commensurate, as I have argued, with the 'smooth' immeasurability of postmodern social space, and thus, rather than offer a *relative* movement away from the oppressive dynamics of the late capitalist State, inaugurates an *absolute* one without a measurable or tangible outside.

In this section, I will further explore this nomadic dynamic of exodus without movement or outside in relation to an author who both radicalizes and departs from Kelman's strategy of resistance: Irvine Welsh. I will argue that Welsh's engagement with extreme forms of marginality in his 1993 literary breakthrough, *Trainspotting*, and, especially, its more recent prequel, *Skagboys*, offers a historically grounded elaboration of the themes explored by Kelman in *How Late It Was, How Late*, and a far more extensive – if arguably less conclusive – rehearsal of the same logic of exodus/nomadism within the smooth space of late capitalist society. In contrast to Kelman's high levels of

---

[68] Ibid., 420.
[69] Ibid., 421.
[70] Ibid., 421.
[71] Ibid., 420.
[72] Ibid., 420.

formal and thematic abstraction, which provide a compelling, if contextually opaque, outline of the violent encounter between the postmodern complex of State and capital and the proletarian subject, Welsh fully inscribes his narratives within a precise historical framework. *Skagboys* thus commences with an extended journal entry, in which Mark Renton retrospectively details his participation in the 'Battle of Orgreave' during the 1984–5 Great Miners' Strike. Although these longhand passages are only written at a later stage in the novel, as part of his treatment at St. Monans (the rehab facility for heroin addicts where Renton and some of his friends temporarily recover), the fact that they are used as a 'prologue' to the novel indicates Welsh's interest in situating his narrative within a specific historical process. The bloody standoff between the police and the striking miners at the South Yorkshire coking plant provides a concrete backcloth to the subjective dynamics of withdrawal and exodus that Mark and his friends will thereafter rehearse through drugs.

In the specific context of subsumption and institutional defeat of the organized working class represented by Orgreave (and more generally, by the strike as a whole), the abstract exodus described by Kelman gives way to a concrete dynamic of flight, of withdrawal from the violent immediacy of postmodern power. By fleshing out this concrete dynamic as a crude story of addiction, Welsh gives us a sense of the profound ambivalence of the resistant process, but also – crucially – of the need to emphasize its radical immanence, its being an internal/interminable dynamic within the social totality subsumed by capitalist power.

Commenting on the concept of flight (of the 'line of flight'), as developed by Deleuze, Giorgio Agamben has insisted on separating it from any notion or meaning of evasion, of pure disengagement from the here-and-now of a concrete situation: 'For me, it's a question of thinking a flight which would not imply evasion: a movement on the spot, in the situation itself.'[73] This is the kind of movement *without movement*, the kind of stationary yet profoundly *active* dynamic, that nomadism points to: an exilic gesture that cannot physically escape the immediacy of conflict (whether it is the ever-receding forest or the ever-advancing 'police' State of postmodernity). Welsh's junkies will impersonate, in the wake of the collapse of the structure of mediation represented

---

[73] Jason Smith, '"I am sure that you are more pessimistic than I am ...": An Interview with Giorgio Agamben', *Rethinking Marxism: A Journal of Economics, Culture and Society*, 16: 2 (2004), 121.

by union power, a nomadic dynamic of resistance 'on the spot', which, instead of revoking the immanent configuration of postmodern power and projecting a transcendent opening beyond its plane, threatens to subvert it from within.

Skagboys' point of departure, as delineated by Renton's journal entry, thus coincides with the collapse of the mediatory function of civil of society, which such authors as Hardt and Negri have identified as one of the defining traits of postmodern society. In the classic modern definition initially proposed by Hegel, civil society is paradigmatically found in the form of the institutional trade union, which represents 'a fundamental point of mediation between labor and capital, and between society and the State'.[74] The neoliberal assault on the trade unions, which in Thatcherite Britain reached its climax during the Miners' Strike of 1984–5, thus marks a crucial instance of the reconfiguration of the relations between the State and the productive fabric of society and, consequently, of the dynamics of antagonism and resistance between the working class and capital.

Orgreave functions here as the unambiguous sign of the convulsive transition to postmodern institutionality, as the symbolic marker of the 'withering of civil society' and its replacement with a new violent immediacy of the State apparatus. Mark Renton describes his journey, together with his father and a group of Scottish pickets from a variety of sympathetic unions, to the coking plant at Orgreave, South Yorkshire, that the National Union of Mineworkers (NUM) was planning to blockade. His account – which is a faithful and detailed transcription of the historical event – makes it clear that this was no ordinary occurrence within the strike, or, rather, that it traumatically established a new logic of 'the ordinary' in the relations between the State and the institutions of the working class. Orgreave (and by extension, the whole strike) epitomizes the dramatic mutation of the public status of the more left-wing trade unions – in particular, the NUM – from a relatively successful instance of actualization of the Hegelian notion of civil society into a bleak incarnation of the militant threat against the survival of the State itself (into an 'enemy within').[75] At Orgreave, the civil/public dimension of the industrial dispute becomes absorbed by the sovereign interiority of the State apparatus, and the police consequently cease to operate as the strikers' opposite number

---

[74] Hardt and Negri, *Dionysus*, 258. See also G. W. F. Hegel's *Elements of the Philosophy of Right*, trans. H.B. Nisbet (Cambridge: Cambridge University Press, 1991).
[75] For a comprehensive overview of the NUM's postwar history, see Andrew Taylor, *The NUM and British Politics*, 2 vols. (Aldershot: Ashgate, 2003 and 2005).

within a regulated system of mediations between labour and the State, turning into enemy troops, into a hostile army. As Mark writes in his journal:

> On oor side there's banners fae every trade union and political group ah've ever heard ay joining the gathering. But ah'm startin tae feel edgy: thaire's still mair polis. For every load ay pickets that swells oor ranks, the polis force seems tae increase tae correspond, and then some mair. Andy gies vent tae the growin sense ay trepidation in the air. 'They've been preparing fir this for years, since the miners done ower Heath'.[76]

Mark's father's friend Andy observes that something fundamental has changed in the attitude of the State towards the striking miners since 1974. If that previous strike had been fought and won by the workers on the still-relevant terms of post-war industrial conflict (of a dynamic of conflict still regarded as *internal* to the intermediate space of civil society), the situation in 1984 indicates that the State was now willing to embrace exceptional measures and to redefine the role and actions of the police. The conflict is no longer constructed as a labour dispute within the institutional space of civil society, but as an *exceptional* confrontation requiring exceptional measures. The generally 'unexceptional' logic of control examined by Kelman in his novels, whereby the disciplinary/administrative apparatus of the State was universally deployed over the social body, is replaced here by a moment of sovereign assertion.

As Giorgio Agamben has explained, following Carl Schmitt's classic formulation, sovereignty is defined by the decision made on the state of exception. State power, articulated as sovereign power, is thus the power that can decide over life and death, suspending the guarantees of positive law and reconstructing the latter as pure exceptionality, as pure sovereign decision. For Agamben, the defining element of the state of exception on which State power is founded is the isolation or extraction from within the autonomous field of social life – that is, from the multiplicity of actual or potential forms-of-life internal to the social body – of a measure of bare or naked life whose existence is exclusively guaranteed by its dependency on the sovereign, who can in turn, at the point of *decision*, choose to annihilate it. Agamben finds in the figure of the *Muselmann*, of the physically and morally devastated prisoner of the Nazi

---

[76] Irvine Welsh, *Skagboys* (London: Vintage, 2012), 11.

extermination camp, the paradigmatic figure of bare life, and in Auschwitz, the archetypal sovereign dynamic of modern political power. The camp is that space where the continuity of positive law and of socially autonomous forms-of-life is suspended and replaced by State power's foundational violence, by what Walter Benjamin referred to as law-making violence.[77] There is a fundamental ambiguity in the relation between (State) power and violence, which the German word around which Benjamin weaves his analysis (*Gewalt*) perfectly captures insofar as it expresses both meanings at once. According to Benjamin, law-making violence (and its correlate, law-preserving violence) is characterized by the adequation of means to ends (the latter being, precisely, the ends of the State itself). The State thus cultivates violence, understood as the sovereign decision over the state of exception, over life and death, as the necessary means, first, to its constitution, and second, to its self-preservation. This suggests that sovereignty is to be encountered, primarily, in those institutional expressions of State power that are furthest removed from the ordinary continuity of the positive legal system. In other words, the military and the police, insofar as these embody exceptional measures or exceptional means, represent the two purest manifestations of the State from the point of view of its sovereign, self-constitutive power.

A political situation such as that played out at Orgreave thus manages to isolate, beyond the ordinariness of a State dynamic which has virtually managed to subsume society within its ubiquitous institutionality (thereby negating the autonomy of social forms-of-life, such as those embodied in traditional working-class culture), the foundational principle of its power: violence. Welsh neatly captures this aspect of the neoliberal State by explicitly presenting the standoff between the police and the pickets in terms that powerfully evoke the decisionist logic of the Schmittian state of exception and of Agambenian bare life. Renton's account begins by reconstructing the ordinary setting of the industrial dispute as an exceptional, camp-like setting:[78]

---

[77] See Walter Benjamin, 'Critique of Violence' in *Reflections: Essays, Aphorisms, Autobiographical Writings*, trans. Edmund Jephcott (New York: Shocken Books, 1978).

[78] It is apposite to recall Agamben's definition of the camp: '*The camp is the space that opens up when the state of exception starts to become the rule*', Giorgio Agamben, *Means Without End: Notes on Politics*, trans. Vincenzo Binetti and Cesare Casarino (Minneapolis, University of Minnesota Press, 2000), 39.

> Ye cannae miss the plant we intend tae blockade; it's dominated by two huge phallic chimneys, risin out ay a series ay industrial Victorian buildings. It looks ominous, but the polis have goat us aw herded intae this big field on its north side. Then thaire's a sudden stillness in the air as the chants fade away; ah look at the plant and it feels a bit like Auschwitz and for a second ah get the queasy notion that we're gonnae be corralled <u>intae</u> it, like thaire's gas ovens thaire, because no only are the polis outnumberin the pickets, they're now positioned oan three sides ay us, and we're cut off oan the fourth perimeter by this railway line.[79]

The Auschwitz reference indicates a situation of radical imbalance in which violence is fully rediscovered on the side of the State (and is thus definitively torn from any legitimate use by the institutions of civil society)[80] and then reinscribed as a constitutive exertion beyond the parameters of the existing legal system. As Benjamin points out: 'The assertion that the ends of police violence are always identical or even connected to those of general law is entirely untrue. Rather, the "law" of the police really marks the point at which the state ... can no longer guarantee through the legal system the empirical ends that it desires at any price to attain'.[81] Thus, police violence marks that place, that blindspot filled by power that juridical-positivist appeals to the rule of law cannot properly account for, insofar as the former's aim is not 'the promulgation of laws but the assertion of legal claims for any decree';[82] insofar, in other words, as its proper end is the assertion of a law-making and law-preserving capacity that is strictly external to the formal logic of the legal system and that depends on the pure decision of a naked power.

The latter's nakedness is captured by Welsh as a direct correlate to the naked or bare life that serves as its foundation and which, in the context of Orgreave, is expressed in the brutalized bodies of the strikers: 'A boy in a red lumberjack shirt, oan his knees, tendin tae his decked mate, gets smashed across the skull fae behind by a riot copper and collapses oan top ay his pal. It's like an execution.' As Renton points out, 'This isnae about policing or containment, this is a war against civilians' in which the legitimate terms of conflict contemplated by the institutions of civil society (including, primarily, the

---

[79] Welsh, *Skagboys*, 12.
[80] Hardt and Negri, *Dionysus*, 293.
[81] Benjamin, 'Critique', 287.
[82] Ibid., 288.

legitimate 'use of violence' by the trade unions) are replaced by a previously unseen 'military' dialectic of 'Winners. Losers. Casualties'.[83]

The phantom of a militarized civilian police force, together with the Auschwitz-like profile of the setting, suggests a dynamic of exceptionality which is first of all constructed as a spatial dialectic. Thus the sovereign manifestation of state power is articulated in these pages as a space beyond the interiority of the legal system, as an outside on which the inside of the State-form is founded. It is in this sense that the camp, for Agamben, represents the degree zero of sovereign power: '[T]he camp is a piece of territory that is placed outside the normal juridical order; for all that, however, it is not simply an external space. According to the etymological meaning of the term *exception* (*ex-capere*), what is being excluded in the camp is *captured outside*, that is, it is included by virtue of its very exclusion.'[84] What the camp – like Orgreave – represents spatially is thus an exteriority that serves as a foundation to the political/juridical interiority of the State. More precisely, it presents the topology of power as 'a zone of indistinction between the outside and the inside, the exception and the rule, the licit and the illicit',[85] thereby providing a model on which not only the State, but also its proletarian antagonists, will be forced to operate. If the institutional space of civil society, of the unions and the sanctioned conflict they represented, was essentially a space of *distinction*, of differentiation, the social space that emerges at the point where civil society recedes and is replaced by a reinvigorated sovereign State (for which the exception *is* the norm) is thus best defined by this figure of indistinction, by this topological confusion expressed by Deleuze and Guattari's notion of smooth space.

Welsh's novel suggests that power's zone of indistinction, that its sovereign dynamic of subsumption of the social, can only be contested by starting from a recognition of the impossibility of restoring to the proletarian strategy of resistance its former institutional 'distinction' as part of an organized labour movement. The disappearance of the autonomous spaces of civil society and their replacement by the 'captured' spaces of postmodern sovereignty impose a nomadic 'flight' *on the spot*, an intensive or absolute movement from which

[83] Welsh, *Skagboys*, 18.
[84] Agamben, *Means*, 40.
[85] Ibid., 40–1.

new degrees of being may be extracted, and, hence, new possibilities of existence, new forms-of-life beyond the exceptionality of naked life, may be constructed. In *Skagboys*, the moment of institutional defeat marks the working class's entry into this indistinct ontological space. Orgreave announces, in this sense, not the dismantling of the working class as such, but a condition of being of the latter which remained intimately connected to the topological distinctions expressed by the institutions of civil society (and in particular, by the latter's mediation between the 'inside' of the State and its social and economic 'outside'). The condition in question can be described as a *representable* form of working-class subjectivity and belonging, as the mode of working-class being on which the protagonist role of the trade unions had been predicated and which, in the novel, is characteristically expressed in Mark's father's committed and militant outlook.

The defeat of this working-class mode of being is best captured in the way that Mark's family, who come to represent in the novel the paradigm of 'decent' working-class life, are essentially defined by vulnerability and exposure. The sense of political impotence associated with Mark's father is symbolically amplified by the mental and physical disability of his younger brother, Wee Davie, who stands as the fragile axis holding the family's affects, hopes and fears, together. His severe condition ('He not only has chronic cystic fibrosis, he's also been diagnosed with muscular dystrophy *and* extreme autism')[86] has turned the Rentons' family life into a protracted episode of collective self-abeyance and inaction, into a suffering inertia from which every possibility of joyful subjective empowerment has been excluded. When Wee Davie finally dies from complications, his condition, his 'bare life', is revealed as the buttress on which their 'decent' working-class family life had been essentially predicated. Without this fragile nexus, without this 'naked' condition to which working-class existence has been reduced after the withering of its social institutionality, life is presented as a sad and empty temporal continuity:

> At the kitchen table, Cathy Renton silently gaped into space, smoking her cigarette, occasionally pretending to read the *Radio Times*. Her husband Davie could hear his own breath, heavy with fatigue and stress, over the bubbling pot of stovies on the hob. Time seemed to hesitate, as frail and

[86] Welsh, *Skagboys*, 73.

weary as either of them; Davie found the burden of his wife's silence even more heartbreaking in its insidious, levelling way than her sobs and tortured soliloquies. Standing in the doorway, letting his fingers pick at the paint on the frame, he considered just how much they had all interacted through Wee Davie. Now he was gone, and Billy, idle and unsettled in civilian life since his discharge, was in bother with the police. As for Mark, well, he didn't even want to think about what he was up to down in London.[87]

Mark's opting out from this inertial situation appears as a deliberate strategy of flight from and refusal of the unavoidable stasis into which 'decent' working-class life seems to have turned around him. If it is true that heroin addiction represents the absolute nadir of social and biological life in the novel, it is no less true that the sanctioned alternatives, that the *settled* forms of life that make up the general backdrop to the narrative of addiction, in particular the forms of family life from which Mark and his friends hail, are tragically branded with such signs of paralysis, exhaustion and death.[88]

In this context, marginality, the embodied rejection of the terms around which the accepted definition of 'life' is constructed, signals a movement away from the colonized territories of the social, from the subsumed spaces previously occupied by a 'healthy' and dynamic civil society. By contrast, the prospect of settling into such an existence as this conventional and rather dated paradigm of respectability warrants appears to him as synonymous with a defeat which would amplify and extrapolate into the private realm the public defeat sustained by the working class at Orgreave. Mark soon acknowledges this in a gesture of refusal which will make him break not only with the prospect of conjugality which he associates with his girlfriend, Fiona, but more generally with the working life presupposed by a university education:

> She'd talked about us findin a flat together next year. Then graduation, nine-to-five jobs and another flat wi a mortgage. Then engagement. Then marriage. A bigger mortgage on a house. Children. Expenditure. Then the four Ds: disenchantment, divorce, disease and death. For aw her protestations tae the contrary, that's who she was. That's what she expected. But ah loved her and thus fought to conceal the ugliness she brought out in me. Ah kent

---

[87] Ibid., 285.
[88] A similar case is that of Alison, whose mother is reduced to a 'sack ay skin, bone and tumour, wrapped in bandages across the chest the surgeon's made flat', ibid., 241.

... that ah could never be like that: Could never have her: *really* have her, in the sense of giving masel tae her. Or perhaps ah wis just being a bam: There was mair than a degree ay acceptance for me in her world. My ma and dad's aspirations were decent. Ah fuckin hated the word. It made my skin crawl.[89]

The discourse of decency and the logic of acceptance that underpins it amount in this context to a redefinition of life as insuperable subalternity, as a form of deferred death from which every trace of agency, of subjective *potentia*, has been eradicated by the system. The alternative embraced by Mark is a gesture of refusal proclaiming the irreducibility and autonomy of life, but of a life inevitably modified by the contextual conditions of a suppressed or subsumed sociality. As we will see below, this is a rather paradoxical form of life, radically removed from the institutional forms of intervention from which postmodernity signalled such a crude and violent departure (from the forms of organized working-class life that Orgreave had pronounced defunct), and fundamentally at odds with the productivist and utilitarian logics to which it remained harnessed. Welsh creates in the figure of the heroin addict a paradigm of non-appropriable life, of non-internalizable, marginal, existence placed at the heart of a system developed on the principle of illimitable appropriation, internalization and instrumental exploitation. This form of life is neither 'decent' nor 'bare'; neither subsumed within the institutionality of power nor reduced to a symptom of vulnerability and exposure. It marks, rather, a moment of inconsistency or interruption in the smooth ontology of the system and, hence, a possible opening, a possible exodus beyond its functional limits.

The trajectory of addiction, the 'fall' from 'decency' pursued by Renton and his friends in the novel, enacts a gradual process of dissolution through which the expansive continuities of power will ultimately be called to a halt and replaced by an inoperative – or *workless* – form of life.[90] In this sense, the junkie will impersonate a cancellation of the functional valences on which capital's colonization of society is predicated, notably the category of work itself. Indeed, the rejection of incorporated life articulated by Welsh's addicts commences with the rejection of work, with the negation of capitalist power's injunction to submit to its productivist imperative. Thus, the point of departure

[89] Ibid., 172.
[90] I propose these terms as equivalents of Agamben's *inoperosità*.

of the non-incorporated form of life impersonated by the junkie is the embrace of worklessness as a condition exceeding the instrumental provisions of the system (in the form of structural unemployment, for example), as a mode of being-in-the-social that indicates a radical insubordination to the logic of functionality on which the very process of social incorporation rests. It is noteworthy that the book opens, immediately after the prologue section on Orgreave, with an immensely cynical *and* revealing declaration of refusal by Mark's friend Simon 'Sick Boy', who responds to the subaltern attitude towards work in the following terms:

> Working chappies fail to understand the minds of men of leisure. I am not employed through *choice*, you fucking cretins; please dinnae mistake *me* for one of those hapless drones who wander around town in a trance, searching for non-existent labour. *Garage attendant. Not in this fucking life, Milksnatcher and Bike Boy. Get the Billionaire Playboy cairds up in your shitey offices, and I just* might *be interested!*[91]

By juxtaposing this internal monologue with Mark's account of his experience at Orgreave, Welsh underlines the radical break operated at the heart of the working class at the point of realization of the defeat of its public institutionality. While Orgreave represented the sacrificial moment of a fading working class desperately clinging to a form of life predicated on a specific form of labour (or rather, clinging to a form of labour that constituted a 'whole way of life', in Raymond Williams' terminology),[92] Sick Boy's irresponsible and cynical pronouncement effectively identifies the new horizon on which proletarian resistance is bound to operate: an ontological horizon rather than a social one (after all, the social *is* what has been defeated/incorporated at Orgreave) – the horizon of a life seeking to escape from the 'smooth' strategies of an increasingly exploitative and increasingly sovereign power. The terms in which Sick Boy articulates his refusal allow for no intermediation and for no containment in a way that mirrors, and is thus much better prepared than the organized miners to confront, the neoliberal State's onslaught.

The rejection and the avoidance of work is thus immediately identified in this context as a crucial strategy of survival and liberation from capital's

---

[91] Welsh, *Skagboys*, 22.
[92] See Raymond Williams, *Culture and Society* (London: Hogarth Press, 1958).

apparatuses of capture, as a way of side-stepping and simultaneously undermining the integral logic of capitalist control and of offering an exit 'on the spot'. Welsh's investigation of this fundamental strategy of refusal is at its most suggestive in those passages where the dogmatic rulings of neoliberal capitalism are confronted with the playful – and yet, in its own way, also quite serious – irresponsibility of the junkie. Thus, when Renton and a number of his friends find a temporary job with one of the ferry companies operating on the English Channel, their stance is not one of fearful acquiescence (in the precarious – or 'flexible' – logic governing waged labour under neoliberalism), but one of riotous and carnivalesque refusal 'from within'. As Renton sarcastically observes:

> So we were in work. Three, four or six million unemployed, nae cunt kent cause the calculation methods changed wi the frequency ay keks, and the most motley crew yev ever seen, a combo ay junkies, poofs and fuck knows what else, are engaged in gainful employment for the start of the spring season at Sealink.[93]

This (self-)presentation of Renton and his friends as 'a combo ay junkies, poofs and fuck knows what else' resonates with the classic Marxian definition of the 'lumpenproletariat'. It has been noted that, in Marx and Engels, the etymology of this term refers not only to poverty (as suggested by the German word *Lumpen*, meaning 'rag') but, more importantly, to social deviancy and marginality (insofar as the main root would be *Lump*, meaning 'knave').[94] This notion of the lumpenproletariat as a knave or criminal class not necessarily identified by their economic position is clearly conveyed by Marx in his description of the December 10 Society formed by Louis-Napoléon Bonaparte in the lead-up to his election as President of the French Republic:

> Decayed *roués* with dubious means of subsistence and of dubious origins, ruined and adventurous offshoots of the bourgeoisie, rubbed shoulders with vagabonds, discharged soldiers, discharged jailbirds, escaped galley slaves, swindlers, mountebanks, *lazzaroni*, pickpockets, tricksters, gamblers, *maquereaux*, brothel-keepers, porters, *literati*, organ-grinders, ragpickers, knife grinders, tinkers, beggars – in short, the whole of the nebulous,

---

[93] Welsh, *Skagboys*, 264.
[94] See Nicholas Thoburn, *Deleuze, Marx, and Politics* (London: Routledge, 2003), 52.

disintegrated mass, scattered hither and thither, which the French call *la bohème*.[95]

Marx's roll-call of social outcasts, while appearing to inscribe itself under the sign of difference and heterogeneity, remains isolated from the complex dynamics of the socio-historical process and is therefore far more susceptible than the proletariat to incorporation or subordination to the systemic demands of the bourgeoisie.[96] After all, as Marx notes, this apparently diverse constituency *was* the social platform on which the restorative political project of Louis Napoléon had been based. On the other hand, the Marxian proletariat can be read as the truly differential figure that emerges with the negation of capitalist relations founded on waged labour. In other words, the proletariat is to be understood, beyond any positive or empirical dimension,[97] as 'the class of the overcoming of work and its identities'.[98] It would be inaccurate, then, to include Renton's 'motley crew' within the traditional Marxian category of the lumpenproletariat, for, despite its declassed and anarchic appearance, the logic of marginality it exhibits is directly predicated on the negation of work as the organizing principle and fundamental hierarchical relationship of capital. Thus, Renton and his friends' overtly *proletarian* outlook – that is to say, their actively antagonistic, and not merely evasive, stance towards work – is expressed, however paradoxically, in their radically frivolous and hedonistic approach, in that militant irresponsibility already announced by Sick Boy at the outset, which now translates into a playful sabotage of capitalist discipline:

> The first week at Sealink wis certainly eventful enough; a riot, a bit ay gear, n some barry sex. You *cannae* fucking well say fairer than that. Oan toap ay it aw, Marriott's planned the first walk-through for the night. There's nae chance ay us lasting the month here.[99]

---

[95] Quoted in ibid., 53.
[96] As Thoburn puts it: 'We would be wrong, however, to interpret this nebulous non-class as a force of difference. Across all its various manifestations there is, in fact, a key defining characteristic: it is a mode of practice oriented towards the bolstering of identity cut-off from the flows and relations of the social', ibid., 54.
[97] 'If Marx's lumpenproletariat as a category of identity emerges through the amassing of attributes and historical examples, the non-identity of the proletariat – what I will call the "proletarian unnamable" – is formulated with a decided lack of empirical description and hardly any sense of its positive content', ibid., 60.
[98] Ibid., 64. As Michael Denning puts it: 'You don't need a job to be a proletarian: wageless life, not wage labour, is the starting point in understanding the free market', 'Wageless Life', *New Left Review*, 66 (2010), 81.
[99] Welsh, *Skagboys*, 348.

Far from representing a possibility of individual advancement in the context of rampant unemployment, work (or more strictly, 'employment') is almost dialectically transformed here into its negation, cast as a sex- and drug-fuelled explosion pointing towards the breakdown of the system of discipline and hierarchy on which the wage relationship rests. The refusal of work (which is, let us not forget, the first level of refusal of an entire way of life captured by capital's apparatuses) thus no longer takes the form of an attempt to stay 'outside' or 'beyond' work (as Sick Boy had initially formulated his refusal), but of a fluid or molecular penetration of its disciplinary praxis alternating active avoidance with playful subversion:

> We're experts at avoiding work; no just the seasonals, but the established staff tae. They've aw been issued new contracts ay employment, which means longer hours fir far less pay, so motivation is non-existent. Therefore any passengers with enquiries cannae find us. Oan occasions when we ur visible, we strut around the ship wi a phoney expression ay purpose oan oor faces, eywis in flight fae real graft.[100]

The outcome of the increasing precarization of labour is thus not a growing sense of vulnerability, but of the workers' psychological distance from the tasks at hand. Renton describes how sex and drugs come to fill in this gap, turning the habitual pattern of wage slavery into an occasion for proletarian mockery and autonomization.

As the passage describing Renton and his friends' engagement with the ferries makes clear, the success of this approach lies in its independence from any attempt to reconstitute or reclaim the social space and institutionality of the working class. Its functional premise, as it were, is the reconstruction of proletarian life as the exit-point from such formations (and their corresponding identities): as an exodus, in other words, that weaves the ontological texture of the overcoming of capitalist labour at the same time that it recognizes the non-existence of an empirical, tangible outside to the smooth patchwork of postmodern capital. Renton thus harbours no doubt that the 'welfare state, full employment, the Butler Education Act were all gone or compromised to the point of being rendered meaningless. It now really was everyone for themselves.'[101] The collapse of the mediatory structures on which the post-war

[100] Ibid., 348.
[101] Ibid., 359.

settlement had been secured now force resistance into new forms and spaces of being, into new strategies beyond those traditionally identified and exploited by the organized working class. The consumption of drugs represents in this context a radical possibility of ontological transformation beyond the fixity of traditional social and political subject positions. It marks an opening towards what Deleuze and Guattari call 'becoming', namely, that molecular and imperceptible mode of being where identification and capture (by the 'plane of organization' on which the institutionality of civil society had been mapped) fail and are replaced by intensity and ecstasy.

In true Deleuzo-Guattarian fashion, Renton further makes a direct link between this ontological form and the minoritarian position of Scotland – or rather, the Scots – within the UK. Thus, in response to his English friend Nicksy's suggestion that heroin is not going to help his having been abandoned by his latest girlfriend (or any of his other failures), he observes:

> It isnae about helping, it's aboot *being*. If being Scottish is about one thing, it's aboot gittin fucked up, Renton explains, working the needle into his flesh. – Tae us intoxication isnae just a huge laugh, or even a basic human right. It's a way ay life, a political philosophy. Rabbie Burns said it: whisky and freedom gang thegither.[102]

The position of a 'minoritarian' nation like Scotland is thus not only defined by its political subordination within the structure of the British nation-state, but, more importantly, by its fundamental irreducibility to the instrumental condition that capitalism imposes on the category of the nation itself.[103] Thus, far from resonating with the identitarian figures promoted by established nationalist discourses and their capitalist-systemic frameworks, Renton's evocation of a minoritarian Scotland founded on intoxication suggests a radical reconfiguration of the nation as an inoperative form of collective belonging. This is the nation conceived of as that which exceeds the positivity of any group identity and which therefore eschews any practical or functional ascription; a nation that cannot be internalized or subsumed by the sphere of

---

[102] Ibid., 359.
[103] In an attempt to extricate the differential logic of the 'minoritarian' national movements from the 'majoritarian' dynamics of established nationalism, Guattari speaks of 'nationalitarian' (*nationalitaire*) projects of resistance to global capitalism, in a way that matches Renton's emphasis in this passage, Félix Guattari, *Les Anées d'Hiver 1980-1985* (Paris: Les Prairies Ordinaires, 2009), 88-95.

capital or the capitalist state since it presents itself as an uncapturable moment of collective being. Construed in this manner, the nation becomes synonymous with the proletariat insofar as the latter signifies the tendential overcoming of the system of waged labour (or, in other words, insofar as it announces the successful exodus from capital's ubiquitous system of exploitation and control). In this sense, intoxication, understood as a general condition of inoperativeness/ worklessness (but also, as a generalized ontological refusal of capitalist work *and* life), marks the point at which the process of capitalist valorization – of the production and accumulation of value – fails and is superseded by an ecstatic and unrepresentable mode of being.

Irvine Welsh's fictional exercise in *Skagboys* and *Trainspotting* presents us with the challenge of imagining, against the social debris field left behind by neoliberalism, the possibility of a life without identity, of a life without transcendence, or simply – as Deleuze puts it – of '*a* life'. What is at stake in Welsh's presentation of intoxication, of the drug addict, as the possible paradigm of the proletarian exodus is thus the search for a singularity that may not be reappropriated by the universal machine of reappropriation that is postmodern capitalism; the search for a mode of individuation that may not fall prey to the instrumental/productivist rationalities of subsumed life or to any of its constituent categories.[104] In other words, the junkie confronts us with the possibility of undoing the contrived discourse of free choices and decisions, the ideological texture of subjective interpellation on which capitalism rests. As Renton expresses it in a well-known passage from *Trainspotting*:

> Choose life. Choose mortgage payments; choose washing machines; choose cars; choose sitting oan a couch watching mind-numbing and spirit crushing game shows, stuffing fuckin junk food intae yir mooth. Choose rotting away, pishing and shiteing yersel in a home, a total fuckin embarrassment tae the selfish, fucked-up brats ye've produced. Choose life.
>
> Well, ah choose no tae choose life. If the cunts cannae handle that, it's their fuckin problem.[105]

---

[104] 'There is a mode of individuation very different from that of a person, subject, thing, or substance. We reserve the name *haecceity* for it. A season, a winter, a summer, an hour, a date have a perfect individuality lacking nothing, even though this individuality is different from that of a thing or a subject', Deleuze and Guattari, *Thousand*, 287–8.
[105] Irvine Welsh, *Trainspotting* (London: Minerva, 1996), 187–8.

Turning this logic on its head, the junkie chooses instead to suspend his subjective functionality and to refuse identifying with socially prescribed roles. He *chooses* to escape the gravitational pull of capitalist choice and individual subjectivity and to move instead towards a zone of indistinction governed by pure, subjectless intensity – by ecstasy. A number of thinkers have insisted on the conceptual linkage between this mode of individuation or singularization without identification and the concept of ecstasy. For Jean-Luc Nancy,[106] for example,

> singularity never has the nature or the structure of individuality. Singularity never takes place at the level of atoms, those identifiable if not identical identities; rather it takes place at the level of the *clinamen*, which is unidentifiable. It is linked to ecstasy: one could not properly say that the singular being is the subject of ecstasy, for ecstasy has no 'subject' – but one must say that ecstasy (community) happens *to* the singular being.[107]

According to Nancy, singularity ('*a* body, *a* face, *a* voice, *a* death, *a* writing') is that which occurs at the point of fading of individuality, at the point of *clinamen* or 'inclination', where the latter becomes inoperative and uncapturable by identity. This inclination, this ecstasy, expresses the collective nature of singularity, the impossibility of thinking beyond the abstract fiction of the individual without acknowledging the opening where co-belonging, where being-in-common, becomes unavoidable. It is in this sense that the figures of addiction explored by Welsh oscillate between the 'deconstruction' or undermining of functional individuality and the drive towards community. To be sure, the latter is never hypostatized or produced as a stable and substantial form (as a group identity) but, rather, as an inclination formed in the milieu of need. Such is the account provided in *Trainspotting* of this community of singularities:

> The group entering the pub are also driven by need. The need for more alcohol to maintain the high, or to regain it, and fight off the onset of grim, depressive hangovers. They are also drawn by a greater need, the need to belong to each other, to hold on to whatever force has fused them together during the last few days of partying.[108]

---

[106] See also Agamben, *The Coming Community*, trans. Michael Hardt (Minneapolis: University of Minnesota Press, 1993), 69.
[107] Jean-Luc Nancy, *The Inoperative Community*, trans. Peter Connor et al. (Minneapolis: University of Minnesota Press, 1991), 6.
[108] Welsh, *Trainspotting*, 263.

The group of addicts thus enacts the undoing of individuality through their co-belonging in need, through a 'force' – 'whatever force' – that composes a world for which the system of instrumental identification can find no use or viable representation.

This latter aspect is crucial, insofar as the form of life embodied by the junkie, this eminently precarious and insubstantial life founded on intoxication and need, marks the collapse of the representational frameworks on which the political system of capital (that is, the process of absorption or subsumption of the space of the social within the State) is predicated. What this means, in other words, is that the ecstasy, that the *clinamen* through which the non-identified singularity of the junkie emerges, is precisely that which cannot be represented – that form of common being, of common life, that escapes power's representational imperative. Both the defeated, bare life of the traditional working class and the instrumentally driven life of the neoliberal subject (the subject of 'free choice', so to speak) are defined by their representability, by their identifiability, by their availability to the apparatuses of capture mobilized by postmodern capital. In contrast, the junkie is one who, following the ecstatic path of self-abolition (of the abolition of the subject and of the *clinamen* towards common being), manages to resist, and in the last instance break free from, the systemic machinery of control.

When Renton is admitted to the rehab facility at St Monans (where he will write the Orgreave diary that opens the book), he immediately recognizes, in the sanitized appearance of the institution and in the scientific tenor of the staff's discourse, the 'omnipresent vibe ay state control'.[109] The latter is not articulated (as was the case in Kelman) as an abstract, administrative form of control, or (as in the case of Orgreave) as a deployment of sovereign violence; rather, it is presented as a systematic attempt to positivize, to identify, and to *represent* under conditions of control (of 'scientific' control, but also, essentially, of political/State control) the common dimension of being that the ecstatic life of the junkie had first laid bare. As one of the doctors puts it: 'The group is crucial to our philosophy. It's seen as the way to combat the peer structures on the outside that support the substance-dependent client's behaviour.'[110] Two central operations are at work here through which power seeks to re-assert its

---

[109] Welsh, *Skagboys*, 403.
[110] Ibid., 403.

control over the ungovernable junkie. First, the singularity that surfaces in the process of addiction is re-subjectified, re-individualized and re-constructed within the ideological terms of capital: the addict is transformed into a 'client', into a sanctioned partner-in-trade. And second, the unrepresentable group of junkies ('the peer structures on the outside') is disarticulated, domesticated and reinstated as a *representable* and *operative* group. As the doctor informs Renton: 'You'll be part of a group, a *society*, here at St Monans, one that works, rests and plays together, and make no mistake, it *will* be tough, she says, lookin tae ma parents.'[111]

The logic of exodus that Renton rehearses in this novel hinges precisely on the possibility of resisting the institutional drive of power, the attempt to reinscribe singularity as individuality and to – as it were – put it back to work. There is in this sense a proletarian commitment in Renton's determination to overcome this condition of subordination and availability to a system whose ultimate principle is work. By renouncing power's call to re-individualization, to inclusion within an identifiable community, what he undertakes is a radical rethinking of human life beyond the regulative purview of work.

In his exploration of the concept of inoperativeness/worklessness, Giorgio Agamben has suggested that it is precisely in the postulation of man 'as the living being without work' that the coming politics of resistance and transformation may lie.[112] According to Agamben, this possibility can only be thought effectively if the renunciation of work is not conceived of as a mere form of negativity, of passive refusal or inertia (as non-work or 'suspension of labor'),[113] but rather as an ontological opening to pure potentiality.[114] This presupposes thinking beyond the dialectical relationship which ties potentiality to actuality, beyond the aporetic loop which sees the free energy of potential being invariably return as an actualized form, as a constituted fact, or even as an identity:

> [I]f potentiality is to have its own consistency and not always disappear immediately into actuality, it is necessary that potentiality be able *not* to pass

---

[111] Ibid., 404.
[112] Giorgio Agamben, 'What is a Destituent Power?' trans. Stephanie Wakefield, *Environment and Planning D: Society and Space* (2014), 32, 69.
[113] Ibid., 69.
[114] 'The modern epoch ... is constitutively unable to think inoperativity except in the negative form of the suspension of labor', ibid., 69.

over into actuality, that potentiality constitutively be the *potentiality not to* (be or do), or, as Aristotle says, that potentiality be also im-potentiality (*adynamia*).[115]

In the context of the radical re-imagination of the human as an inoperative or workless being, this suggests the necessity of postulating the latter's im-potentiality as a potentiality *not to* work, as an ontological affirmation of abstention from the imperative which makes life available to power. For Agamben, what defines the act of power – or, in his formulation, the 'sovereign act' – is precisely the fact that 'it realizes itself by simply taking away its own potentiality not to be, letting itself be, giving itself to itself'.[116] In this sense, power is always constituted power, actualized power, a fact or an act characterized by its negation of the capacity to abstain from being. Work, insofar as it cannot not be – insofar as its ontology is that of ineluctable actuality/actualization – lies at the heart of power, expressing its basic principle of operativeness.

What the nurses and doctors at St Monans present as a therapeutic remedy for the apparent state of exposure and vulnerability into which the lives of its patients have fallen is rather a sovereign act of neutralization of the potentiality of life itself to *not be* in actuality, to not surrender to the ontological facticity of work or identity. In renouncing the logic of, and the injunction to embrace, constituted society (whether it is the neoliberal society of Thatcherite Britain or the micro-society of the rehab facility), Renton and his friends vindicate a modality of life which, far from marking a nadir of bare or naked life (in Agamben's definition, of that life whose existence is purely conditional on the sovereign act), proclaims the inexhaustibility of potentiality. The life of the junkie, the life of the heroin addict, thus offers a telling – if probably shocking – example of what Agamben calls 'form-of-life': that life which 'can never be separated from its form, a life in which it is never possible to isolate something like a bare life'.[117] This is a life that immediately breaks the capture of actuality which permanently threatens potentiality, affirming living as what cannot be reduced to mere facts or works, as a

---

[115] Giorgio Agamben, *Homo Sacer: Sovereign Power and Bare Life*, trans. Daniel Heller-Roazen (Stanford: Stanford University Press, 1998), 45.
[116] Ibid., 46.
[117] Agamben, 'Destituent', 73.

desire or *cupiditas* for which there is no object, no factual content that may satisfy it.[118] Thus the supposition of positivity, of a functional or operative community through which the life of the junkie may be redeemed or 'cured' is inevitably destined to fail. The medical discourse emerges in this context as no different from the discourse of power, as a system of capture predicated on full control and subsumption, on a full inclusivity which at the same time postulates an excess, an excluded element or exception in the form of bare life (the life of the 'patient' – Wee Davie or the 'medicalized' junkie – or even the defeated worker at Orgreave).

The strategy of rupture and absolute potentiality rehearsed by Renton succeeds at the point where it displays its 'incurability', its irreducibility to any of the captured forms (exceptional or otherwise) through which life is controlled and regulated by power. The latter can only be effectively resisted if the negativity of exodus, if the initial rejection of the terms of integration imposed by capitalism, are affirmatively replaced by an im-potentiality, by a willingness to elude restitution, to avoid going back to 'health'. Only if intoxication is reconsidered as a form-of-life, as a minor mode of being for which no restorative identification, for which no operative incorporation will do, can the ontological truth – which is also the political truth – of Welsh's exercise become apparent:

> Aye, I could go on about addiction as an ailment, absorb myself in the medical model, but now that I've detoxed, I'm officially no longer physically addicted to heroin. Yet at present I crave it more than ever; the whole social thing; copping, banging up and hanging out with other fucked-up ghosts. Shuffling around at night like a vampire, heading for grubby flats in run-down parts of the city, tae talk shite with other deranged, unstable losers.[119]

Addiction – the addict proclaims – cannot be understood or represented as the actuality of a medical 'condition' leading back to operativeness and functionality, but as a mode of being which lacks nothing and yet remains fully inactualized. The evocation of the inoperative – ecstatic – sociality of

---

[118] 'The form-of-life is, in this sense, the revocation of all factual vocations, which deposes and puts in tension from within the same gesture by which it is maintained and dwells in them', ibid., 74.
[119] Welsh, *Skagboys*, 464.

the junkie universe points the way forward in the face of capitalism's 'real subsumption' (or neutralization) of the social. In clear contradistinction to the identifiable, 'factical vocation' of society, the anti-society of the junkie underworld indicates the possibility of thinking and experiencing, of desiring and living, beyond the tutelary reach of the State of advanced capitalism.[120]

---

[120] It is precisely in the revocation of this tutelary role of the State and of constituted, identifiable society, that Agamben sees the rising profile of what he calls 'the coming politics': '*The novelty of the coming politics is that it will no longer be a struggle for the conquest or control of the State, but a struggle between the State and the non-State (humanity), an insurmountable disjunction between whatever singularity and the State organization.* This has nothing to do with the simple affirmation of the social in opposition to the State that has often found expression in the protest movements of recent years. Whatever singularities cannot form a *societas* because they do not possess any identity to vindicate nor any bond of belonging for which to seek recognition. In the final instance the State can recognize any claim for identity – even that of a State identity within the State . . . What the State cannot tolerate in any way, however, is that the singularities form a community without affirming an identity, that human beings co-belong without any representable condition of belonging (even in the form of a simple presupposition)', *Coming*, 85–6.

5

Work in Crisis

Precarious Subversions in Monica Ali and Joanna Kavenna

As we saw in the preceding chapter, the logic of proletarian resistance soon develops, in the context of neoliberal society into a fully-fledged dynamic of subjective transformation and dislocation, which can eventually result in the undoing of subjectivity itself. We could speak of a self-deconstructive trajectory through which the organized social form of the older working-class subject gives way to a number of intensive processes, of corporeal effects exceeding the functional boundaries of the system, or confronting it with an excessive dimension that cannot be accommodated within its utilitarian logic. The process of subsumption of social life within capital is increasingly reliant, in post-Fordism, upon the production of subjectivity as its main support and source of valorization. But this production, as we have seen, must be secured as an internal function of the system, must be regulated and conducted within specific 'governmental' frames. In this context, the outstanding threat to capital's project is no longer the affirmation of a well-defined antagonistic subjectivity, but the proliferation of 'leaky' moments, of uncontrollable fluctuations beneath the level of subjective constitution, beneath the governmental architecture on which capitalist expansion rests.

In this chapter, I will examine the ways in which the precariousness characteristic of post-Fordist labour is constructed as a generalized social – and even ontological – condition that returns to 'haunt' and ultimately dislocate the smooth unfolding of capitalist power relations. By examining two recent novels, Monica Ali's *In the Kitchen* and Joanna Kavenna's *Inglorious*, I will contend that the precarious condition emerges as a profoundly ambivalent dynamic which introduces, in spite of its avowed rationale (namely, to render the subordination of social labour power more complete and inescapable), a constant source of instability and inassimilable excess to the system.

In Monica Ali's 2009 novel *In the Kitchen*, the subsumed complex of work and life is presented through the lens of a generalized precarious condition. I wish to argue here that there is a twofold dimension to the latter, with specific characteristics and pathways in the narrative which nevertheless converge on a unitary sense of fragmentation and dissolution of social bonds and relations. On the one hand, Ali explores the socio-economic aspects of precarious work – that post-Fordist lifeblood of unstable and intermittent labour running in the vessels of the service economy. Job mobility and subjective investment (the rediscovery of the working subject as, essentially, what Foucault described as an 'entrepreneur of the self') appear as staple characteristics of this 'technical' configuration of labour: the novel engages both as it charts the intersecting trajectories of Gabriel Lightfoot, an executive chef at the Imperial Hotel in London with entrepreneurial plans of his own, and those of his underlings, a genuinely global multitude of migrant and refugee workers. Yet beyond this structural, market-driven logic of flexibility – which in varying degrees and forms the novel's entire human universe partakes in – there is a deeper, more diffuse, and radically unsettling dimension of 'precariousness' that threatens to subvert the mobile logic, the systemic coherence on which the neoliberal order is ultimately founded.

Joanna Kavenna's *Inglorious* (2007) makes of this precariousness a psychic limit beyond which life and writing become allied in an uncontrollable – that is, ungovernable – strategy. This novel charts the mental breakdown of 35-year-old journalist Rosa Lane after she decides to quit her job. I will show that, in this character, precariousness becomes synonymous with madness, while the latter is constructed as a last-ditch act of subjective undoing whose ontological premise is the refusal of work qua model, not only of society, but of individual life as well. Rosa's becoming-mad, in a way that finely complements Gabriel's embrace of precariousness towards the end of *In the Kitchen*, illustrates a strategy of unworking and inoperativeness through which neoliberal capitalism is confronted with its own impossibility.

5.1 Untamed bodies, fleeing minds: Monica Ali's *In the Kitchen*

Judith Butler has established a useful terminological distinction between 'precariousness' and 'precarity' that points directly to the multi-layered distribution of this phenomenon.[1] The first term refers to a general characterization of life as ontologically fragile, as constitutively and continuously exposed to finitude. Precarity, on the other hand, alludes to the more contingent and variable realities of the distribution of precarious life within specific socio-political contexts. In other words, the precariousness of life that emerges as an existential given of human beings can – and is – governmentalized and socialized in certain institutional and relational contexts. In this sense, neoliberalism, understood as that particular set of ideological resources and governmental procedures rehearsed and gradually instituted over the last forty years, constitutes a central stake in the transformation of life's inherent precariousness into a hegemonic historical mode of precarity. It is to this particular historical modalization that a vast sociological literature has turned its attention in recent years. Debates about the 'precariat', as the new analytical category promising to finally displace the Marxist concept of the proletariat, offer a paramount instance of this line of critical interpretation.[2]

I would like to suggest, through a reading of Ali's novel, that the 'amplification' of the phenomenological aspects of precariousness that neoliberal precarity fosters entails not only a logic of validation of the latter's ideological and procedural premises, but also a process of ontological transformation that is specific and internal to this historical configuration of capitalism. Precarity supposes in this context a maximization of life's constitutive vulnerability and exposure, as Butler suggests, but also, crucially, a modality of emergence – a transformative sequence that prises open the governmental cages in which precarity is cast and threatens to reimagine life beyond its control. This process of metamorphosis cannot be regarded as exclusively individual, and, as we will see in this chapter, Ali's novel insists on the unmaking of individual subjectivity

---

[1] Judith Butler, *Frames of War: When is Life Grievable?* (London: Verso, 2010).
[2] See, for example: Pierre Bourdieu, 'La précarité est aujourd'hui partout', in *Contre-feux. Propos pour server à la résistance contre l'invasion néo-libérale* (Paris: Liber – Raison d'Agir, 1998); Guy Standing, *The Precariat: The New Dangerous Class* (London: Bloomsbury, 2011); Matthew Johnson (ed.), *Precariat: Labour, Work and Politics* (London: Routledge, 2014); Isabell Lorey, *State of Insecurity: Government of the Precarious* (London: Verso, 2015).

through the latter's encounter with a multitude (with *the* multitude) of bodies that makes up, socially and historically, the constellation of capitalist precarity.[3]

In a recent essay on Ali's *In the Kitchen*, Sarah Brouillette has underlined the continuity between neoliberal practices of labour 'flexibility' and 'therapeutic' discourses of affective and psychological reparation.[4] According to Brouillette, Ali rehearses in this novel a number of subjective strategies through which the creative worker (in this case, Gabriel Lightfoot) overcomes his disabling guilt about the precarious world of labour of which he is both a part and a fundamental proponent. Gabriel is both a self-managing creative professional (with rather inefficient supervisors above him) and a would-be entrepreneur with concrete plans for opening his own business. This ascendant trajectory (ascendant at least in principle and according to the ideological coordinates of neoliberalism) is buttressed on the high levels of job mobility and precarity of the workforce immediately under his control and, more generally, of British society as a whole. But Gabriel is also, as Brouillette suggests, a subject in need of healing the affective wounds inflicted by an all-too-direct experience of that ambient precarity, and by his enduring bonds to an older world of industrial labour, tight communitarianism and general resistance to the social facts of 'flexibility'.

Things start to get complicated for him (i.e. for his project of frictionless transition from waged creative work to entrepreneurship) from the very beginning of the novel, as the dead body of one of the hotel's night porters is discovered in the kitchen's basement, where he had been living clandestinely. There is a central precarious narrative ensuing from this tragic inaugural event: Lena, the porter's lover, immediately enters Gabriel's life – and home – as a surviving remainder/reminder of the existential precariousness that this death announces and as an ineluctable backdrop to his individual project of self-advancement. A Belarussian ex-prostitute with a frightful history of sexual violence and a lingering air of impenetrable mystery about her, Lena punctuates Gabriel's development throughout the novel and ends up triggering an upheaval – a transformation – that goes beyond the limited purview of his entrepreneurial subjectivity. On the other hand, Gabriel is subjected to an

---

[3] The global multitude of precarious, labouring bodies has been described best by Michael Hardt and Antonio Negri in *Multitude* (London: Penguin, 2005).
[4] Sarah Brouillette, 'The Pathology of Flexibility in Monica Ali's *In the Kitchen*', *MFS Modern Fiction Studies*, 58: 3 (2012).

irrepressible inertia of attraction and repulsion towards his family, and the northern, small-town, and essentially industrial universe from which they hail. His sister Jen, his father Ted, and grandmother 'Nana' come to embody yet another block to, and bifurcation from, the subjective highway of postmodern flexibility and self-making that he wishes to travel. This source of otherness concerns, in this case, a residual (yet affectively potent) linkage to a bygone post-war Britain of mines, factories and ethnic homogeneity. It is in the unfolding intersection of these trajectories, of these experiential universes, that the therapeutic needs of the neoliberal subject will eventually give way to what the novel describes as 'denaturing' – a process that I would rather typify as subjective undoing.

Gabriel's projected trajectory of subjective development, of self-making according to the entrepreneurial logic of neoliberalism, is interrupted and dislocated by the discovery of Yuri's dead body in the kitchen's basement. In both a literal and figurative sense, the latter is an *alien* body: an illegal immigrant inhabiting the underbelly of the system, whose uncanny presence qua dead *body* signals a radical disruption of Gabriel's socio-symbolic universe. In psychoanalytically inflected terms, we could argue that the novel's opening approximates a scenario of encounter with what Jacques Lacan called 'the real' – in other words, with that realm of being that is experienced as constitutively traumatic and inassimilable by the subject and his/her inhabiting of the symbolic order.[5] Not surprisingly, the image of Yuri's dead body recurs throughout the novel in a series of nightmares that Gabriel suffers, and that keep reminding him (and us) of the disruptive potential of this body. Yet what is it that makes the latter such a disruptive event? I would like to argue that it is not merely its uncanny deployment according to any conventionally traumatic reading, its figuration as 'Thing' in the Freudo-Lacanian sense,[6] which presents it as a main source of disturbance in the novel (and as a mainspring for subjective unravelling in the case of Gabriel), but, more generally, that its 'haunting' potential resides in the qualitative deviation it signals from the general distribution and functionality of bodies in this social universe. Yuri's death, in what remain unclear circumstances throughout the novel, announces

---

[5] For a recent and rather exhaustive account of this concept, see Tom Eyers, *Lacan and the Concept of the 'Real'* (New York: Palgrave Macmillan, 2012).
[6] Jacques Lacan, *The Ethics of Psychoanalysis*, trans. Dennis Porter (London: Routledge, 1992).

a first (fatal) irruption of the body of the postmodern, global multitude of mobile migrant workers, in a 'capacity' that radically negates its appointed role. In other words, by turning up dead, the worker's body exacerbates the material alienness, the obtrusive otherness, of its sociality, thereby disturbing the smooth process of capitalist expansion.

What this body announces is the presence of a material limit that is also, fundamentally, a social limit to the progress of the neoliberal project of subjective constitution. As we will see, it is not so much that the latter runs into this body as an internal block, as a traumatic obstacle that renders the ideological operation of self-constitution precarious (as a psychoanalytically influenced account would have it), but that the entire process of capitalist socialization is – so to speak – staged upon a slippery ontological surface, premised on a social body that is always in excess of the presumed organization and rationality of the hegemonic social process. In other words, the dead body of the worker marks the point at which the system can suddenly and brutally become disorganized, anarchically confronted with its own incontrollable immanence, and thus exposed to the constitutive vulnerability and precariousness that, under 'normal' circumstances, it unilaterally imposes upon the multitude of workers.[7]

Gabriel Lightfoot's 'therapeutic' project, as Brouillette calls it, is thus primarily predicated on the suppression, or rather the containment, of such vulnerability (precariousness) within its socially appointed forms (precarity). In this sense, Yuri's death can be read – and this is the direction in which Gabriel's first thoughts about the latter go – as an immediate test on the executive chef's managerial skills, on his 'sovereign' ability to decide on the normalized state of exception that this internationally and precariously staffed hotel kitchen effectively is.[8] Thus Gabriel's initial shock is succeeded by an anxiety that his reaction to the discovery might not have been efficient enough: having

---

[7] Brian Massumi refers to this immanent limit, which I am here characterizing through the figure of the migrant worker's body, as the 'dividual' dimension that effectively subtends, and disorganizes, the ideological sphere of individual economic rationality: 'The infra-individual is the regressive – recessive or immanent – endpoint of the economy. The dividual is the noneconomic wonderland of intense and stormy life on the brink of action that lies at the heart of the economy: its absolute immanent limit', *The Power at the End of the Economy* (Durham: Duke University Press, 2015), 10. See also Maurizio Lazzarato, *Gouverner par la dette* (Paris: Les Prairies Ordinaires, 2014), 145–71.
[8] I am once again alluding to Carl Schmitt's definition of sovereignty, as developed in the previous chapter.

failed to check, first-hand and in a necessary display of managerial expertise, that Yuri *is* in fact dead and not, say, merely unconscious, he fears that this event – that this bodily irruption – might directly interfere with his project of entrepreneurial self-making, with his journey to neoliberal success as an independent restaurateur:

> Filling suddenly with impatience, Gabe walked towards the basement door … If Yuri wasn't really dead then the deputy manager would be giving first aid and questioning him closely, doing all the things that Gabriel should have done, before going upstairs to report to Mr Maddox about all the things that Gabriel had failed to do. Gabe was aghast at the enormity of his managerial lapse. He was here not because he wanted to be, but only to prove himself. Show us, said the would-be backers for his own restaurant, manage a kitchen on that scale and we'll put up the money; work there for a year and turn that place around … To report, say, a side of salmon as missing, suspected stolen, only to have it turn up in the wrong storeroom, that would be bad enough, but to report the death of an employee and to have the employee turn up alive if not exactly well, that was ineptitude of an altogether different order.[9]

The (dead? moribund?) body of the worker is not just an obstacle to the smooth progress of the neoliberal entrepreneur of the self, but an internal, immanent limit, an entropic counter, as it were, to the self-organizing possibilities of capitalist subjectivity. What is particularly disturbing for the manager/entrepreneur about this body is not the punctual disruption of the productive system that it may entail, but the undermining of organizational certainty and structure to which it leads. It represents, rather, a problematical actualization of a more general process that is by no means alien to the social constitution – to the social ontology – of this mobile and unruly workforce, of this multitude of bodies that may smoothly cohere under managerial discipline (and thus facilitate and lend impulse to the entrepreneur's career and vital path) or, alternatively, collapse its centripetal lines of productive organization into an uncontrollable inertia of inoperativeness. Thus, the fundamental alternative that is associated with the configuration of precariousness/precarity in the early moments of the novel is one between successful crisis-management

---

[9] Monica Ali, *In the Kitchen* (London: Transworld Publishers, 2009), 15.

involving a disciplinary apportioning of vulnerability (with clear-cut divisions between the dead and the living, the productive and the unproductive, etc.) and the irruption of immanence qua ungovernable, unformed and/or disorganized being.

In this sense, the dead form of the worker's body (its dead appearance, rather than its dead nature, so to speak) offers a first instance of the effect that this immanent subversion can have on the system, on the 'plane of organization' – to use Deleuze and Guattari's phrase – on which the system rests. But the early sections of the novel are full of examples of potential disruption of capitalist continuities through the obtrusive emergence of workers' bodies as essentially inoperative, disorganized, or entropic. Beneath the surface of managerial stringency that is so intimately linked to Gabriel's subjectivity, we find a plethora of potentially or actually disruptive individuals, of tangible bodily presences against which the logic of organization is used and deployed as an always provisional – always precarious – strategy of discipline.

There is the obvious case of Oona, the Jamaican sous-chef who comes to represent not only a paradigm of inefficiency against a background of breakneck productive rhythms, but also an instantiation of affective immediacy (as opposed to the instrumental mediation of the affective that Gabriel's rampant managerialism tends to impose), and thus an intolerable *détournement* of working life's capacities towards grossly unproductive ends:

> There was something about Oona that infuriated him. It wasn't the fact that she was so often late for work, it wasn't the inefficient manner in which she worked, it wasn't that her idea of fine dining was stew and dumplings *with a sprig of parsley on top*, and it wasn't even the fact that she couldn't cook so much as a fish finger without managing to cock it up ... What offended him about Oona was simply this: her domesticity. When she blew into his office and sat down it was as if she had just got home with the shopping, looking forward to a cuppa and a chat. The way she talked, the way she walked, the way she pressed her bosom when she was thinking, all of it, at core, was irreducibly and inescapably domestic.[10]

There is a range of corporeal affects and effects associated with this character that point away from the 'major', hegemonic line of subjectivation represented

---

[10] Ibid., 19.

by Gabriel and that announce an alternative, 'minor', use of the body.[11] Although in the case of Oona this is a use that harks back to a seemingly traditional and organic form of life (as Gabriel's allusion to her domesticity implies), rooted in the 'backward' milieu of her Caribbean origins, it also signals a more general deviation from the organizational injunctions of just-in-time capitalism. Thus the pattern that will be iterated across different characters and personal/cultural backgrounds is one of temporal dislocation, a figuration of the disruptive body as that which hijacks the striated temporality of management and renders it unworkable for its appointed productivist ends. Oona's insistence that Gabriel relax, take a break, and share a 'niii-ce cuppa tea'[12] with her in the manager's office is registered – by him – as a baffling affront to the kitchen's smooth functioning. Similarly, when Nikolai, the Russian commis, suggests that they all keep a minute of silence – that is, that they *stop* working for a minute – to honour the dead porter, Gabriel's reaction is one of uncomprehending surprise: 'Why now, he thought, why in the middle of service, when every minute counts?'[13]

The fundamental opposition here does not lie between the *humanity* of Oona's personal warmth (or Nikolai's care for his dead colleague) and the *inhumanity* of Gabriel's managerialism, but between the divergent temporal logics, between the different 'velocities' that undergird each of these positions.[14] What disturbs Gabriel is the radical – and, for him, impenetrable – slowness that characterizes these alien bodies; a slowness that already stood out in the case of Yuri's immobile (dead or otherwise) body. Thus the basic problem with Oona – Gabriel insists – is all the more visible, all the more disruptive when she does her job properly, for it is then that this slowness, that this immobility that seems to be more ontological than cultural, develops its full potential: 'He had nothing against her personally, and it wasn't like she wasn't willing to do things his way. But even when she was doing exactly what he asked of her there was something so – what? – *static* about her. Even bustling about the kitchen, Oona had a way of seeming to stand stock-still.'[15]

---

[11] My use of the terms 'major' and 'minor' again follows the sense ascribed to them by Deleuze and Guattari.
[12] Ali, *Kitchen*, 62.
[13] Ibid., 83.
[14] For a recent investigation of the differential 'political economy of time' developed by neoliberal capitalism, and, in particular, of 'the processes where bodies are differently valued temporally and made productive for capital', see Sarah Sharma, *In the Meantime: Temporality and Cultural Politics* (Durham: Duke University Press, 2014), 14.
[15] Ali, *Kitchen*, 101–2.

Immobility of a radical, ontological, kind is also what characterizes Yuri's girlfriend, Lena. As Gabriel offers to accommodate her in his flat after he finds her by the hotel entrance, her initial appearance of complete vulnerability is gradually replaced with an enigmatic stasis, with a corporeal opacity that sharply contrasts with his insecure attempts to understand, to explicate, and ultimately resolve her predicament. Lena's name is first mentioned by Oona in a conversation she has with Gabriel shortly after Yuri's body is found. Oona informs him that another temporary agency worker is missing from her post – a young and, she insists, alarmingly *thin* girl: 'The girl. What's her name? You know, washing the pots and all ... Oh, she so skinny that girl she pass under doors, she so thin she hard to see. You want to sit her down with something nice and hot and say, for Lord's sake, child, you eat now. Eat!'[16] It is notable that this remark about her bodily appearance, about Lena's physical fragility (which is characteristically articulated by 'slow' and earthy Oona in her demotic Jamaican voice), transpires, together with her 'flexible' contractual status, as the only solid fact about her (a situation that will effectively persist, despite Gabriel's closer involvement with her later on, throughout the novel).

Lena is thus simultaneously defined by precarity and precariousness in the dual sense suggested above, as both a 'lean' body and a disposable number.[17] And yet the sense of disposability seems to recede, and a resistant, jarring dimension linked to her constitutive leanness, to her impenetrable fragility, to take over as she enters Gabriel's domestic territory. In one of their first conversations, Lena offers him sex, presumably in exchange for her board, although in such a manner that the transactional quality of the offering is distorted, and its libidinal appeal to Gabriel, completely undercut. What surfaces instead, and he does not fail to notice it, is the lean, elusive and insubstantial outline of her frame – a bodily precariousness that not only fails to attract a desire for possession, but effectively confronts the latter with an essential unobtainability, with an elusiveness that reads as hostility, as indomitability: 'The deep slash of her top showed the sharpness of her collar bone and only the faintest suggestion of breasts ... She wasn't in the least bit

---

[16] Ibid., 23.
[17] As Oona punningly suggests, reiterating this fundamental aspect of her description of the girl: 'Lena ... Hoo. She leaner than me, all right', ibid., 23. On the other hand, her being an agency worker implies, as Gabriel points out to Oona, that she is immediately disposable, unlike 'permanent' hotel employees who have to be given three warnings, ibid., 24.

attractive. She was hostile. What was wrong with her? Offering sex like that but not a single word of thanks.'[18]

I would argue that Gabriel's 'discovery' of Lena's meagre body triggers a radical redefinition of desire and subjectivity that inaugurates an alternative trajectory, a bifurcating line of flight from his appointed entrepreneurial path. And it would be correct to note that this process initially takes the paradoxical form of a 'deactivation' of desire provoked by the precarious body itself. At first, Gabriel imposes upon this relationship a phantasmatic structure (an imaginary scenario) that will eventually prove unworkable in the face of such immanence, of such bodily resistance. He attempts to justify his exchanges with Lena – including what soon become sexual exchanges – as a work of 'charity', and thus to contain the inertia unleashed by her impenetrable and inappropriable passivity (or hostility, as he describes it) within the structured path of his self-making. The latter, which at this stage revolves around an increasingly frenzied and dubitative roll-call of goals,[19] including getting married to his girlfriend Charlie, having children, and opening his restaurant, insistently runs aground at the point where the static and hostile body of the precarious migrant worker surfaces, at the limit of an encounter that cannot be pacified or accommodated within his subjective project and which now begins to prompt the unexplored and uncontrollable course of his own transformation, of his own (as he will later put it) 'denaturing':

> When he passed the sitting-room door she was undressing in the lamplight with her back to him. For a few moments he watched her. He focused all his charity on the pathetic ridge of her spine.
>
> In the bathroom he stood before the full-length mirror. His eyes were bloodshot, his hair a mess, stubble on his cheeks and chin. He tried to see what Lena had seen.[20]

Far from managing to reduce her to an object of pity, to find in her the subordinate confirmation of his subjective power, what this 'pathetic' body (or body-part, the ridge of her spine) presents Gabriel with is the inescapable

---

[18] Ibid., 107.
[19] 'He ran over it again. Get Dad to the opening. Get the restaurant on its feet. Move in with Charlie. Have a kid. Dad. Restaurant. Charlie. Kid. Tick them off, cross them out. Tick, cross, tick, cross', ibid., 115.
[20] Ibid., 113.

image of his own precariousness. This is the same logic that underpins those recurrent nightmares that will accompany Gabriel throughout the novel: a static, a barren, a dead bodily surface that manages to deactivate his desire.[21] At the end of this scene, in which he unsuccessfully tries to fixate Lena's body as a fragile object, as an easy target for his dominating 'charity', the horrific dreamscape of the kitchen's basement and Yuri's inert, emptied-out and defaced body returns:

> The body is where he left it. He crouches to look at it carefully, beginning with the toes. Yellowing nails, a bunion, dry skin on the heel. Dense hair on the calves that peters out on chicken-skin thighs, and moving along to the genitals, don't miss anything out, a patch of eczema by the groin. The scrotum is hard and shrivelled, but the penis – he has to look at it – is soft and horribly long. Appendix scar on the stomach, leading to a chest that is, slightly but definitely, concave. He has to look at the face but he cannot. He closes his eyes and – gagging, retching – feels it with his hands.[22]

This evocation of the body as simultaneously a fragmentary multiplicity of apparently disjointed parts and a flat, dead, corporeal surface is reminiscent of Deleuze and Guattari's characterization of the Body without Organs in *Anti-Oedipus*. Although this concept may seem to imply a fundamental contradiction between the body and it organic parts, the real opposition, as these authors point out, lies between the body and the organs (taken as elements of the same multiplicity) *and* the organism understood as the functional integration – as the *organization* – of both: 'The body without organs and the organs-partial objects are opposed conjointly to the organism. The body without organs is in fact produced as a whole, but a whole alongside the parts – a whole that does not unify or totalize them, but that is added to them like a new, really distinct part.'[23]

According to Deleuze and Guattari, this de-totalized and dis-organized multiplicity of body and organs is the proper site of desire's passage, the locus where their transformative concept of desire takes shape. The latter, of course, cannot be understood as the process of satisfaction of a need or lack, but as an immanent dynamic of creation that eschews the structured forms and transcendent logic of the organism/organization. In this sense, desire is

---

[21] Which is now revealed as the driving force behind his subjectivizing process.
[22] Ali, *Kitchen*, 116.
[23] Gilles Deleuze and Félix Guattari, *Anti-Oedipus* (London: Continuum, 2011), 358.

intensive, nothing but a system of relays and passages, of flows and cuts disposed in a molecular or 'inorganized' manner.[24] Looked at from the point of view of intensity, desire has little in common with the expansive will of the entrepreneurial subject, and a lot more with the static model provided by the inert bodies of the dead Yuri and the skeletal Lena.[25] In effect, as Deleuze and Guattari suggest, death itself is closely allied with desire, not only through the psychoanalytic paradigm of the death-drive, but in the sense that it is posited as the immanent cause and horizon of every intensive process, that it furnishes the zero-degree from which intensity-desire flows:

> The experience of death is the most common of occurrences in the unconscious, precisely because it occurs in life and for life, in every passage or becoming, in every intensity as passage or becoming. It is in the very nature of every intensity to invest within itself the zero intensity starting from which it is produced, in one moment, as that which grows or diminishes according to an infinity of degrees ... death is what is felt in every feeling, *what never ceases and never finishes happening in every becoming* ... Every intensity controls within its own life the experience of death, and envelops it. And it is doubtless the case that every intensity is extinguished at the end, that every becoming itself becomes a becoming-death![26]

For Deleuze and Guattari, becoming is the real dimension of desire, while the subject-positions, the formed and organized subjectivities on which the symbolic order is based, are only provisional molar instances from which everything flows and flees. What the encounter with the bodies-without-organs of Yuri and Lena represents for Gabriel is thus the opening up of subjectivity itself, of the capitalist aspiration to success (marriage, kids, business), to the intensive becoming that commences and ends with the absolute zero of death – a death which, only once it is liberated from the compulsions of symbolic transcendence, from the injunctions to organize and succeed, can provide a launch-pad for life itself. Paradoxically, the rebirth of desire that this process announces must necessarily pass through the radical diminution that becoming

---

[24] It is in this sense that Deleuze and Guattari read the Lacanian notion of the real as 'the real inorganization of desire', as a positivity that prises open the symbolic structure and escapes it in a myriad flows, ibid., 361.
[25] As Deleuze and Guattari point out: 'The body without organs is the model of death ... Death is not desired, there is only death that desires, by virtue of the body without organs or the immobile motor, and there is also life that desires, by virtue of the working organs', ibid., 362.
[26] Ibid., 363.

expresses. For indeed, as Deleuze and Guattari argue, the horizon and source of desiring transformation is an immanent space of imperceptibility, a zone of indistinction from which death itself takes its model.[27] I argue that this is the kind of passage, the radical course of subjective undoing that Gabriel undergoes in *In the Kitchen*, a process that is both prompted and sustained by the encounter with the precarious body of the migrant worker.

The history of Gabriel's transformation through his 'non-relationship' with Lena is thus punctuated by a discovery of the intensive diminution, the unearthing of a degree zero of desire, from which a fresh and properly immanent construction of life and selfhood (beyond the organization and transcendence of 'successful' subjectivities) may commence. This trajectory becomes apparent in those passages where Ali narrates their sexual encounters – passages that convey a sense of the unproductiveness and futility of his attempts to appropriate her body, to reassemble it into an organized whole (a lost organic totality that perhaps therapeutic memory, the reconstruction and working-through of her traumatic experiences, may restore). The following passages are particularly revealing:

> Lena had shut her eyes. Close to tears, he sat on the edge of the bed and took hold of her feet. He appraised each toe, the pearly nails, each little knuckle, the delicate articulation of each joint. He slid his fingers around them and down her soles and rubbed gently on the heels, marvelling at how truly she was flesh and bone, his Lena, his ghostly girl. And the anklebones, they were real all right, the shin-bones and the knees, and she raised her hips lightly so he could raise her dress. He worked slowly up her body, connecting every part of her, putting her back together again.[28]
>
> If she didn't go up in a puff of smoke she could vanish simply by walking through the door and never coming back. He died a little death every time he thought of it.
>
> And he pieced her together nightly, assembling all he knew of her with his fingertips, working feverishly up from her toes. Everything that he knew about her and all that he might still learn, examining her heels, her insteps, her calves, her stomach, her arms, as if her body might offer up clues.[29]

---

[27] Gilles Deleuze and Félix Guattari, *A Thousand Plateaus*, trans. Brian Massumi (London: Continuum), 300–41.
[28] Ali, *Kitchen*, 307.
[29] Ibid., 412–13.

We read in these passages about a despair caused by the impossibility of completion, of reconstruction and re-articulation of the organism, which is the unsurpassable limit imposed by the body without organs, the brutal revelation that the real cannot be organically organized, and that the sense of a lost (and hence recoverable *and* re-appropriable) unity is a void mirage: 'the BwO is never yours or mine. It is always *a* body ... The indefinite article is the conductor of desire. It is not at all a question of a fragmented, splintered body, of organs without the body (OwB) ... There are not organs in the sense of fragments in relation to a lost unity, nor is there a return to the undifferentiated in relation to a differentiable totality.'[30] The whole, the totality in this organic/organizational sense, is precisely what cannot be recovered under capitalism. The persistence of the limit, of the impassable barrier of the body without possible reintegration into a structured, functional whole, confronts the presumptively mobile and fluid subject of neoliberalism with its residual dependencies, with its real inability to deal with becoming (i.e. with the kind of intensive mobility expressed by the migrant body).

In this novel, the notion of a lost totality and the melancholic attachments that it can lead to are intimately connected to the old industrial universe of Blantwistle, the northern English town where Gabriel grew up, and where his ailing father, senile grandmother and disgruntled sister still live. What primarily defines this subjective world of unresolved Oedipal bonds and losses is a fundamental ambivalence regarding its protective function, regarding its capacity to sustain the quality Gabriel struggles to accord it as 'a place of safety'.[31] Blantwistle thus appears in the novel as simultaneously the staging of a presumably more wholesome (and hence, far less precarious) version of capitalism rooted in Fordist discipline, and a desiring structure organized around a primordial and fundamental lack. This lack, which at first appears as an all-too-familiar dysfunctional relationship between father and son, is gradually seen as acquiring a more general and social quality, a symptomatic status, as it were, for a broad constellation of failed or deeply flawed relations, of displacements and repressions that only in a deflected manner allow the image of social integration to emerge.

---

[30] Deleuze and Guattari, *Thousand*, 182.
[31] Ali, *Kitchen*, 248.

The *Gemeinschaft* of shared affective continuities evoked by Ted contrasts with Gabriel's perception of this universe as a contradictory and generally backward reality in which a dated and unrecoverable industrial capitalism could smoothly coexist with deeply ingrained racist and conservative feelings. For Gabriel, his senile Nana's xenophobic reflexes only reveal the brutal core, the traumatic underside, as it were, of the ideological mirage of the 'good old days' of solid, productive work and close-knit communities. As he bitterly puts it, questioning Ted's nostalgic faith in the latter: 'The old days when you could start a joke with "an Englishman, an Irishman and a Paki walked into a pub". That what you mean? ... The days when we had the good old National Front and swastikas sprayed on every railway bridge and underpass?'[32]

But this entrenched racism only represents one of the more superficial manifestations of the community's impossibility, of the constitutive precariousness that echoes and replicates its exclusion of the Other, pre-empting both closure and functionality. In the native context of Blantwistle and Gabriel's family, this structure of replication situates the mother as the original weak link, as the source of instability that will condition and determine the ultimate failure of the community. For this communitarian universe that is so deeply rooted in industrial labour and a narrow and hegemonic definition of masculinity[33] is also fundamentally predicated on the exclusion of the mother and of the specific traits of precariousness that made her a threat to the former's smooth functioning.

Gabriel's mother's bipolar disorder encapsulates the form of inappropriability, of indomitability, and of traumatic excess that the bygone world of working-class communitarianism associated with Gabriel's childhood cannot accept/absorb. The organic moment, the successful organization of the social 'organs' is thus pre-empted by the looming figure of the mad woman, by the crazy mother who could manically transform, in an imaginative flash of mental deterritorialization, the drab landscape of working-class domesticity into a Bedouin camp, and who would regularly flee the home on sexual forays with strangers. If the solid basis of community identified by Gabriel's father is work, that is, the material continuity produced by industrial production itself, then the fundamental disturbance introduced into this universe by the mother

[32] Ibid., 217–18.
[33] 'Ted's hands held an entire world, of work, of manliness', ibid., 536.

concerns the radical discontinuity of undisciplined, unexpected and, ultimately, *unproductive* behaviour – behaviour that, not unlike the Bodies without Organs of Yuri and Lena, fails to *produce* a sense of closure and functional integration.

Until the end of the novel, Gabriel continues to fend off memories of this erratic mother, while he strives to advance his understanding and reconstruction of emotional bonds with his father.[34] As Brouillette points out: 'Far from wanting to defeat his father, what Gabriel desires is the restoration of his father's authority as in Gabriel's youth. This longing is itself just a symptom of a deeper yearning for a source of guidance and meaning to anchor him in the world.'[35] On the contrary, any attempt at restoration of maternal memory is called upon to reinscribe itself as pathological knowledge, as rational understanding of the severity of the crazy mother's condition. What this ultimately suggests is not so much that the backward world of solid labour and community has been swept aside by a forward-looking neoliberal ethos that genuinely embraces difference, but that the latter effectively takes up the exclusionary consensus of the former and mobilizes it in the service of its more expansive needs and priorities. Difference remains the inassimilable bone on which the dominant social subjectivity chokes, and, in the primary context of Oedipal relations presented by the novel, this difference is radically embodied in the figure of the mad mother.

I am trying to argue that precariousness, understood as that ontological dimension that serves both as a model for social precarity and as a source of destabilization and resistance to the latter, manifests itself across a range of personal situations and socio-historical contexts in the novel, attaching itself to figures of bodily stasis and psychic flight, and rehearsing, in both, a dynamic of convulsive transformation, of external attraction and irrepressible immanence, through which the safe interiorities of working society are profoundly subverted (whether the latter is defined as Fordist or post-Fordist). As I will further elaborate below, the struggle reveals itself as one between the inside of formed, operative subjectivities and communities, and the boundless outside impersonated by the mad mother, by the corpse, or by the de-eroticized body part.

[34] Ibid., 215.
[35] Brouillette, 'Pathology', 537–8.

In the context of Blantwistle and the bygone universe of job security and 'solid' communitarian bonds, this topological distinction becomes immediately apparent, to the point that even Ted ends up admitting to the oppressive potential of the social structure he had previously idealized: 'Community's good for those what's on the inside, but if there's some inside there's others what's out. I'm thinking of yer mother. Thinking of my Sally Anne.'[36] But this demarcating line is far less appreciable in the context of neoliberal sociality, where the fixity of subject positions and centripetal communitarian dynamics – in other words, where the molar structures underpinning social identification and continuity – have been replaced with molecular lines seeking to simultaneously integrate and abolish difference, to posit it as the degree zero of a potentially infinite production (of affects, subjectivities, semiotic values, etc.). This is not to say that the integrative exercise proposed by neoliberalism is successful (or even honest), but that the pathways it traces offer a more roundabout strategy of confrontation with the destabilizing outside – with that precarious locus that will ultimately question the viability of the attempted subordination of difference to the capitalist machine.[37]

The divide between these two horizons is explicitly formulated by Fairweather, the notoriously named Labour Party politician-turned-speculator who is about to sponsor Gabriel's entrepreneurial venture. As he explains, the unfolding financial crisis, against whose backdrop the novel is set, is no more grounded in hard empirical fact than in the interpretative discourse one wishes to impose upon it. In other words, there is no outstanding, transcendent 'truth' about the contemporary state of the British economy. What it all boils down to is a choice between narratives and the defining question – 'Can you ride it, whatever it is?'[38] Herein lies the fundamental divergence between Ted's symbolic and affective universe and the rhizomatic social ontology to which Gabriel subscribes. Beyond the naïve and dated faith in economic 'substance', in the opposition between the 'real' economy of material production and the

---

[36] Ali, *Kitchen*, 396.
[37] As Félix Guattari puts it: 'Integrated world capitalism does not aim at a systematic and generalized repression of the workers, women, youth, minorities ... The means of production on which it rests will indeed call for a flexibility in relationships of production and in social relations, and a minimal capacity to adapt to the new forms of sensibility and to the new types of human relationships which are "mutating" here and there', 'The Proliferation of Margins', in Sylvère Lotringer and Christian Marazzi (eds), *Autonomia: Post-Political Politics* (Los Angeles: Semiotext(e), 2007), 108.
[38] Ali, *Kitchen*, 321.

'fictitious' one of financial speculation, there lies a semiotic universe in which what counts is the ability to operationalize discontinuity, to construct a field of immanent relations out of heterogeneous elements without any transcendent regard for their truth – what counts is the ability to 'ride it, whatever it is':

> There are two stories you can tell about the economy ... The first story will be the one your father prefers. The economy lacks substance – we've lost our manufacturing base, and the new industries don't compensate ... we're a gigantic casino spinning speculators' money, while asset-stripping vultures shred company pension schemes and turn the few remaining factories into luxury flats and shopping malls.
> But there's another story, a different kind of reality, if you like. Tell it like this. Say the economy is booming because the economy is in good shape. Anyone who says otherwise is a masochist, an idiot, or downright envious. Say that we're into 'sunrise' industries.[39]

The other 'story' makes of immateriality, of the very absence of substance in the old Fordist sense, an inexhaustible raw material. According to Fairweather, the sole mention of the 'knowledge' or the 'creative' economy evokes a universe of possibilities in which what is fundamentally produced is the capacity to 'ride it', that is, the socio-subjective scaffolding of which the economy is merely an appendix or extension. This is, then, the challenge presented by neoliberalism: to produce, yet not to produce objective use-values from pre-defined subject positions, but rather, malleable, porous, molecular or rhizomatic subjectivities that will both embody and narrativize (regardless of any discursive or ontological determination of the 'truth') the immanent logic of production itself.

Maurizio Lazzarato has pointed out that the post-2007 recession should be properly understood as the consequence of neoliberal capitalism's failure to live up to its own subjectivizing programme. It is not that the collapse supervened through the unmasking of financial falsity by solid economic truth, but that the 'work on the self', the subjectivizing tasks imposed by the neoliberal agenda, fell short of their own calculations and projections: '[T]he promise that "work on the self" was supposed to offer "labor" in terms of emancipation (pleasure, a sense of accomplishment, recognition, experimentation with new forms of life, upward mobility, etc.) has been transformed into the imperative

[39] Ibid., 319–20.

to take upon oneself the risks and costs for which neither business nor the State are willing to pay.'[40] What is pointed up here is not so much the falsity or dishonesty of the neoliberal project, but a mismatch between its aspirations and effective practice – a shortcoming that betrays its actual proximity to the governmental, social and economic parameters of its Fordist antecedent. In other words, this suggests that the proposed flexibility of the neoliberal project is ultimately cut short by the confrontation with real heterogeneity, by its exposure to the openness of free and unregulated subjective production that it induces.

The conversation between Fairweather and Gabriel eventually comes up against this mismatch, against a central obstacle to the smooth unfolding of neoliberal subjectivation. After a pause in which Gabriel loses track of Fairweather's argument, and even experiences an anticipation of the cathartic breakdown that will soon take hold of him, Gabriel asks about bonded labour – does it truly exist? What is it exactly?

> 'A form of slavery,' said Fairweather, 'for the twenty-first century. Taking away passports, debt bondage, threats of violence, that sort of thing. The gangmaster stuff you'll have read about in the newspapers. The pressure groups like to call it slavery, sounds more impressive, and we're really world class at that because we've gone so big on deregulation, you see.'[41]

Bonded labour – presumably, the situation in which Yuri had found himself at the time of his death – emerges as the traumatic event, as the real connection flattening the opposition between a rigid capitalism based on stability and continuity and a neoliberal one producing and produced by flexible discontinuities. This twenty-first-century form of slavery delivers the subjectivizing matrix of capital to the paralysing experience of an inassimilable outside. The mere thought of such a combination of precariousness and precarity, of such a bare form of life combining insecurity with uncontainable vulnerability, makes the entire social, ideological and psychological edifice collapse. What will ensue, for Gabriel, is not an intensification of guilt linked to any form of tangible and measurable (and hence, controllable) responsibility,

---

[40] Maurizio Lazzarato, *Signs and Machines: Capitalism and the Production of Subjectivity*, trans. Joshua David Jordan (Los Angeles: Semiotext(e), 2014), 53.
[41] Ali, *Kitchen*, 326–7.

but rather an experience that must break with any such limited apportioning, with any such narrow (for this is all still, under neoliberalism's ideological guise, extremely narrow) definition of subjectivity. As Nikolai, the philosophically inclined Russian commis, later points out to Gabriel as the two discuss the latter's recurring dreams about Yuri's corpse, these conceivably speak of a larger guilt, of a broader sense of responsibility beyond subjectivity: a 'feeling of responsibility – for the world in which we live, for the kind of world in which there will always be more Yuris, struggling to exist'.[42]

The surge, the manifestation of precariousness as a generalized and uncontainable ontological rupture in the midst of the apparently co-ordinated and governmentalized space of precarity brings Gabriel to the end of his development as a neoliberal entrepreneur of the self. The transformation that occurs towards the end of the novel also entails a paradoxical resolution of some of the enigmatic propositions articulated within the neoliberal matrix. Thus, one of the outstanding claims made by Fairweather about the actual content of the idea of Britishness in the contemporary conjuncture (a claim that directly responds to the doubts and hesitations raised by Gabriel's father) is that the latter 'is or has become essentially about a neutral, value-free identity. It's a non-identity, if you like. A vacuum.'[43] And yet the habitation of this vacuum, the real, experiential content of such a non-identity – which is precisely what Gabriel's final crisis will embody – remains excessive and contradictory to the dynamics of subjectivation assumed by neoliberal sociality. In other words, the actualization of Fairweather's prescription is what the actual power relations of capitalist precarity, what its governmental arrangement, cannot accept: bonded labour, Yuri's death, or Lena's mysteries – that is, the sight of the migrant worker incorporating a marginal, multitudinous, transgressive and precarious dimension to the subjective logic of the system, and thus, overflowing it, surpassing and outdoing its functional limits. The final enactment of this vacuum lies outside the scope of neoliberal control, beyond its forms and patterns of subjection and enslavement.[44] Its effective manifestation cannot be but analogous to the part played by the madwoman

---

[42] Ibid., 376.
[43] Ibid., 364.
[44] The two forms, one molar (subjection), the other molecular (enslavement), through which neoliberal domination is exerted. See Lazzarato, *Signs and Machines*, 23–54, and Deleuze and Guattari, *Thousand*, 506.

within the communitarian arrangement – an embodied exteriority without possible internalization; an outside *made body*.

I contend that this is the precise sense of Gabriel's breakdown. A first reading of the final portions of the novel might simply detect here an irruption of the mental malaise that had affected his mother (and this is clearly the suggestion made by his sister, that the bipolar disorder runs in the family). However, it is necessary to insist on the role reserved both to the mother herself – and her madness – within this narrative, and to the effects of Gabriel's iteration of the latter within his own trajectory. The breakdown marks a general existential collapse punctuated by the abrupt end of his relationship with his girlfriend Charlie (after she finds out that Gabriel has been unfaithful with Lena), by his inability to make sense of his incipient and utterly confusing attachment to the girl, and by the insistent deviation from his appointed entrepreneurial path that the cascading series of events following Yuri's death results in. Gabriel's mental breakdown is the effect of contagion, rather than filiation. It is the outcome of his exposure to the constitutive precariousness, to the radical heterogeneity of the migrant body as it breaks loose of its social moorings (of its identity as a migrant, worker, etc).

It would thus be correct to say, following Deleuze and Guattari, that Gabriel 'becomes' mad, if we retain the radical sense that these theorists ascribe to the term, and if we emphasize its essential proximity to the notion of contagion: 'We oppose epidemic to filiation, contagion to heredity, peopling by contagion to sexual reproduction, sexual production.'[45] Rather than inherit it, Gabriel – let us say – 'catches' madness from his traumatic encounter with the unproductive corpse of the dead porter and with the de-eroticized and elusive frame of the prostitute, and, more generally, from the experience of radical, ungovernable exteriority that these command. The productivity implied by becoming, by contagion, is eminently paradoxical and involves an excess that cannot be operationalized or put to work: the desire it expresses – the desire of the recurring nightmares, of the beguilingly 'lean' body, and ultimately of the breakdown of his current self – flows from and through an absolute zero of pure intensity where subjectivity ceases to be, and where the inside becomes confused with the outside.

[45] Deleuze and Guattari, *Thousand*, 266.

The climax arrives after a brief exchange with Charlie in which she describes him as 'the most selfish person' she's ever met.[46] As he leaves her flat, this intimation gives way to its opposite, to a radical unravelling of his selfhood that, for the first time, grounds him in a de-subjectivized experience of the body and its surroundings:

> Buildings, pavement, tarmac and then buildings again. What would it matter if he went on for ever this way? And was he moving or was it the street that moved? It seemed to flow around him. It seemed to pass through him ... For a time he stood there and marvelled at the miracle of his own body, so true to itself, so fully occupied with shivering. The next moment an enormous jolt passed through him, as if he had received an electric shock ... He ran and ran, every muscle, sinew, nerve ending on red alert. He could feel everything ... Only minutes ago he had been nothing, an empty husk, and now this. A million things were happening inside him, a frenzy of activity, dilations and contractions and connections, circuits made and lost, pumping and pounding, absorbing, excreting, reacting, every bit of him living and living from the skin of his fingertips to the very depth of his bowels.[47]

This breakdown is so much more than a breakdown. It rather points to the ontological boundary of the desiring process, to the imperceptible, indiscernible, or even *impossible* space that no subject (only a body, an empty, porous, molecular Body without Organs) can inhabit. This is, again – and this time irrevocably – the embodied outside, the inassimilable heterogeneity for which the neoliberal ethos can find no use, a molecular line of flight, a dynamic of 'denaturing' of the socially and economically organized subject:

> He was in the bloodstream of the city that was in his blood. And he was growing hot, too hot, and he was only a molecule, a protein speck in the city and his bonds were beginning to break. At a certain temperature a globular protein will begin to uncoil. The basic science of cooking. He ran though his legs were shaking now. Heat a molecule and it vibrates more and more, and if the vibrations are strong enough a protein will shake itself free of its internal bonds. He remembered, he still knew this stuff. It was called denaturing.[48]

---

[46] Ali, *Kitchen*, 484.
[47] Ibid., 485.
[48] Ibid., 486.

What follows this un-bonding of the molecular body is a spatial transposition that will erase any remaining oppositions between Fordist stability and post-Fordist dynamism, between inside and outside in these socially determined and historically sequential modes. What follows, then, is nothing but a radical dislocation of the body and its plunging into the precarious outside.

Determined to find Lena's brother Pasha, and thus to make good on his promise to help her by any means possible, Gabriel embarks on a quest along the semi-legal circuits of agricultural sub-employment, following a group of Ukrainian labourers to a farm in Norfolk. It will be there, in a setting and through a form of work that represent the non-internalizable outside of the system of flexibility, that Gabriel will finally envisage the possibility of a life produced whole and irreducible to the forms of power and control that had previously driven him: 'He worked, and while he was absorbed he was surprised to find a new self growing in the space that he had cleared, and it had no voice or thought, and he sensed it rather than knew it, and it didn't ring in his ears, and it did not divide him but made him, for the first time, whole.'[49] By undertaking this final movement in the novel, by following this last line of flight that takes him straight into the heart of what his neoliberal programme of subjectivation had attempted to negate and abject, or at least repress and – almost literally – 'bury' beneath the system of production (in that dark kitchen basement where Yuri's body was found), the novel announces a fresh subjective opening, a tentative reconstruction of selfhood beyond the rehearsed parameters. The final gesture of liberation from his former self – one that flows directly from his immersion within the 'outside' of wage slavery and bonded labour – could be properly described as 'mad'. During a charity auction at the Imperial Hotel, Gabriel physically attacks Fairweather after suddenly imagining him as the violent rapist behind Lena's traumatic stories about her life:

> Fairweather, such a way with the ladies, such a way of making them blush! How did he live with himself? But hadn't he explained to Gabriel the way of dealing with guilt? *Say something often enough, you start to believe it. Let's say you feel guilty about something. Keep telling yourself you don't. It'll do the trick in the end.*[50]

---

[49] Ibid., 518.
[50] Ibid., 531.

As if underscoring the *real*, bodily limit to the elastic discursivity previously proposed by Fairweather as the root of the neoliberal ethos (something akin to the corpse of the Ukrainian porter), Gabriel punctuates his unbridgeable and final distance from the system by, as it were, punching its coded glibness in the face, and thereby forcing himself out of the established conduits and forms of social acceptability within which he had previously functioned:

> Gabriel floated towards Fairweather, he couldn't feel his feet on the ground, couldn't feel anything except the lead in his belly, and the weight in his fists ... In the dim outer circle of his vision, Gabe could see Mr Maddox, he could see Rolly eating a canapé from a stick, but they looked like ghosts to him. Fairweather, flesh and blood, flushed and carnal, spotlit in the centre, raised a hand and smiled ... Gabriel raised his own hand, still shaped into a fist ... He let it fly ... The room imploded into a volley of gasps.[51]

The real effect of this episode, after which Gabriel will return to Blantwistle – with Ted and his nostalgic world already dead, and his own options open – is to inscribe precariousness as a form of life, as a new general horizon of being and belonging extracted from within the brutal power dynamics of social and economic precarity. This is madness (the ultimate figure of subjective precariousness) modulated as liberating agency, as a shift from the still inertial dynamic driving his 'denaturing' to a mobilization of the *outside* as the prompt and foundation of a new sociality.

5.2 'Madness, the absence of work': On Joanna Kavenna's *Inglorious*

In his essay 'La folie, l'absence d'oeuvre', Michel Foucault argues that the technical possibility of eradicating madness, of medically isolating and ultimately removing its pathological content, will not do away with the traces, with the marks of precariousness which it has long embodied within our culture:

> I am contesting something that is ordinarily admitted: that medical progress might one day cause mental illness to disappear, like leprosy and tuberculosis;

---

[51] Ibid., 531–2.

but that one thing will remain, which is the relationship between man and his fantasies, his impossible, his non-corporeal pain, his carcass of night; that once the pathological is nullified, the obscure belonging of man to madness will be the ageless memory of an ill whose form as sickness has been effaced, but which lives on obstinately as unhappiness. Truth be told, such an idea supposes that that which is most precarious, far more precarious than the constancies of the pathological, is in fact unalterable: the relationship of a culture to the very thing that it excludes, and more precisely the relationship between our own culture and that truth about itself which, distant and inverted, it uncovers and covers up in madness.[52]

It is (as we have seen) in the act of this exclusion, in the topological delimiting of this exteriority, that the 'truth' of a social system – of a culture – is uncovered and that the limits to its operativeness become apparent. Madness maintains a privileged relation to this non-place of truth, to this excess that emerges, when confronted with the system, as its point of maximum fragility and non-serviceability.

For Foucault, modern madness represents a fantastic suspension of the forms of meaning through which a given society becomes intelligible and operative. Beyond the primary strategies of subversion and transgression that define the linguistic boundary between the acceptable and the unacceptable, madness points at a formally pure and empty gesture of violence that constructs its own domain of functioning. It is not concerned with the transmission of hidden or intolerable meanings, but with a production of speech that invents its own language (that is, its own system, its own *langue*), and reconstructs the social in its image, rendering it impenetrable to itself:

This is not a question of coded language, but of a language that is structurally esoteric. Which is to say that it does not communicate, while hiding it, a forbidden meaning; it sets itself up from the very first instant in an essential fold of speech. A fold that mines it from the inside, perhaps to infinity. What is said in such a language is of little importance, as are the meanings that are delivered there. It is this obscure and central liberation of speech at the heart of itself, its uncontrollable flight to a region that is always dark, which no

---

[52] Michel Foucault, *History of Madness*, trans. Jonathan Murphy and Jean Khalfa (Abingdon: Routledge, 2006), 542–3.

culture can accept immediately. Such speech is transgressive, not in its meaning, not in its verbal matter, but in its *play*.[53]

What madness creates is the gap or the void left behind by the absence of any recognizable meaning; it creates an 'absence of work', of *oeuvre*, of that which extends, through acceptance or transgression, the functionality of a system, be it linguistic or social. Madness – that which is, as Foucault says, 'far more precarious than the constancies of the pathological' – is that which suspends this cumulative and expansive effect, that which retrieves the blind-spot of a language that says nothing, of a body that is dead, of a life story that cannot be told, and places it at the centre of experience.

We have seen that Monica Ali's *In the Kitchen* was centrally concerned with the fusion of precariousness and precarity into a unitary experiential sequence set in a context of neoliberal crisis, and with the reconstruction of precariousness itself as a paradoxical, last-ditch form of resistance against the internalizing strategies of the system. Madness played in that novel an important role as the form of subjective precariousness that most directly connected the external boundary (the functional limit) of the logics of Fordist labour and social belonging to those fostered by post-Fordism and the neoliberal turn. In particular, the experience of the mental breakdown was singled out as the paramount form of refusal of the internalizing and stabilizing dynamics of power.

In Joanna Kavenna's *Inglorious*, the point of departure is no longer a traumatic encounter with the outer limit of the system, a shock coming straight from the outside, as it were (in the form of a dead body or a horrific story of migration and abuse, for example), but a more gradual unravelling of the void, of the absence that emerges internally as the universe of work is abandoned. In this case, the retreat from work and the ensuing 'discovery' of a precarious condition beyond its limits entails a redefinition of the dynamic of neoliberal internalization, of the process of subjective control that commences with the disavowal of the entrepreneurial will. This novel begins with its protagonist Rosa Lane's decision to quit her job as a journalist, in an 'irrational' gesture of refusal of the ideological parameters which prescribe the conditions of personal fulfilment through professional success. In contrast with Gabriel Lightfoot's entrepreneurial horizon, work for Rosa is nothing but an insistent

[53] Ibid., 545.

reminder of her own finitude, 'an invisible stopwatch tolling her down ... counting the years, the hours spent sitting in offices, staring at the sky, at the flickering screen that was sending her blind'.[54] The post-Fordist promise of creative, flexible labour is once again replaced by an empty temporal carcass of self-justifying purposes and tasks, objectives and aspirations, through which the subject is 'no closer to understanding anything':[55]

> For years she had been productive at work and as idle as anything in the evenings. Time coursed along and she earned money. She stayed firmly in her box. She had been a journalist for years, sliding her way upwards. She wrote on the arts. She understood – it was quite plain to her – that she was meant to be ruled, not to rule.[56]

This scenario of emptiness and repetition, of lack of material content and a prevalent sense of submission to the disciplinary cycle of daytime work and night-time idleness, brings Rosa's initial situation closer to, for example, that of Robert Hines in Kelman's *The Busconductor Hines* than to that of Gabriel Lightfoot. However, there is an element that makes this situation characteristic of the crisis of neoliberalism that the post-2007 recession has brought into sharp relief, and that the still-pioneering post-Fordism of the 1980s could only fail to register. As we have seen above, what characterizes the relationship of the system of neoliberal subjectivation to its outside limit is its radical immanence – that is, the fact that, no matter how apparently external to the nature of the system, what the latter cannot internalize, what it cannot digest, what remains beyond its functional logic, is always already perceived as profoundly and disturbingly *intimate*. In the case of Kelman's bus conductor (and his other characters), the resistant block had to come from a relentless antagonism; it still had to be constructed as struggle, as affirmation of an indomitable subjectivity against which capital and its institutional apparatuses deployed their often violent strategies. In the late-neoliberal universe of *Inglorious* and *In the Kitchen*, by contrast, the true boundary surfaces at the point where the logic of social organization implodes, where it runs into an outside that is now generated and experienced as an internal failure, a collapsing subjectivity, or a

---

[54] Joanna Kavenna, *Inglorious* (London: Faber and Faber, 2007), 3.
[55] Ibid., 3.
[56] Ibid., 4.

gaping void at the heart of the social. This also means that the agential logic that had previously characterized the struggle against work can now be replaced by a paradoxical strategy of vacancy. In other words, what ends up destabilizing the realm of work and its compulsory sociality is the discovery and embrace of the void at its core, of the absence of work (of content, of sense, of meaning, ultimately) that undermines work from within. Needless to say, this is not a victorious and expansive strategy according to the old resistant rationale of the class struggle, but a logic of abeyance founded on negativity and displacement, a paradoxical (and profoundly *ironic*) strategy of immanent separation from the compulsion to succeed that must necessarily engage with new patterns of control and domination whilst seeking to deterritorialize them, to render them inoperative, unserviceable, pointless.[57]

Rosa's primary impulse is a quietly desperate awareness of the impossible realization of the ideology of capitalist success, of the fracture at the heart of her own pale and faithless attempt at embodying the latter. No radical determination or passionate commitment informs her decision to leave, to break with the established perimeter of her socially acceptable life, just the attraction of the gaping void, the radical displacement, that she sees emerging in the midst of this life and sense of belonging: 'Instead of seeing herself as the centre of her own small world, with the city as the backdrop to her life, she began to see everything as a fractured mess, a wild confusion of competing atoms, millions of people struggling to live.'[58] This experience of a central determining absence, of a fundamental disorganization in the place where neoliberalism demands subjective order (the capacity to 'ride it, whatever it is', as Fairweather had put it), is directly connected here to the act of writing on which her job is based. The effects of her rupture with work and its associated life, the unfolding mental breakdown that the novel will chart, is thus intimately related, in a way that echoes Foucault's analysis of modern madness, to the impossibility of writing from the *ordered* centre of a position determined by work. In other words, the axis around which this novel turns is the protagonist's

---

[57] This strategy is in close proximity to Franco Berardi's recent call for 'dystopian irony (dyst-irony)' as an autonomist alternative to political engagement in the more conventional sense: 'We need to correct dystopia with irony, because irony (far from being cynical alliance with power) is the excess of language that opens the door to the infinity of the possible', *Heroes: Mass Murder and Suicide* (London: Verso, 2015), 224.
[58] Kavenna, *Inglorious*, 5.

displacement of the working centre of the system of neoliberal subjectivation (of writing qua work, and of work qua anchoring point of the social), and her substitution, in its place, of an opaque form of expression and behaviour, of an obscure and impenetrable – in the manner of madness itself – *language* that, without aspiring to replace the system (to produce a utopian alternative), challenges it profoundly.

Indeed, Rosa's strategy of refusal commences with the act of linguistic disorganization that affects her professional writing on cultural affairs. The negative inertia that takes hold of her life begins by insinuating itself into her texts, by taking up residence in her articles, thereby 'unworking' them from the inside, rendering them inoperative, unserviceable and meaningless from the point of view of her bosses and the system they stand for:

> With the clock ticking, she was spending her indeterminate span of years on the Underground, holding on tight to a metal pole, sitting at her desk checking her emails, earning money and lining her belly. This sense of the ludicrous crept into her prose. In April she'd written an article on Swedish contemporary dance, which opened: 'Dark, dark, dark we all go into the dark. The dancers have all gone under the hill.' . . . By May she was writing in fragments. It was unfortunate, as her job was to write and explain, to produce quantities of lucid prose. Instead, she stared at the computer, with the bare notes of a story in her hand. Embarrassed, she wrote: 'The Modernist Novel'. After another hour she wrote: 'Rosa Lane reports'. Then it was lunchtime and she wrote: 'If Lunch be the Lunch of Love, Lunch On.' Then later she wrote: 'Shuffle Off' and 'Mortal Coil' on two lines.[59]

This gesture of textual abolition, this slippage from sense and utility through writing, marks the intrusion of the outside into the system – an intrusion that will inevitably acquire the form of madness. For Rosa's first 'symptoms' of madness concern her refusal to produce writing that may be constructed as work, that may be appropriated and organized into what Foucault calls *oeuvre*.[60] For Foucault, what defines the latter is its availability to closure and completion; its functionality and intelligibility as a meaningful product. As we have seen, the immaterial labour of the post-Fordist worker posits itself (ideally, at least)

---

[59] Ibid., 5–6.
[60] Foucault, *History*, 535–8.

as a form that, whilst accepting and even encouraging flexibility, seeks to attain the coherence and positivity of (a) work, of an *oeuvre* in this precise sense. As writing becomes emancipated from coherence, as it projects itself against the various injunctions to 'explain', to mean, and thereby to support the consistency and continuity of the logic of work, it enters a zone of darkness and indistinction in which non-meaning – strictly, nonsense – provides the model for life itself. This is also the nonsensical quality and use of her speech (including her interior monologue), which the novel captures through its highly literate and forcibly ironic narration. Literary quotations, philosophical references and allusions, among other linguistic resources invoked in a highly disorganized and nonsensical manner, provide the mad and *un-worked* grounding of her idiom. This often results in an irresolvable clash of orders of discourse (and by extension, life) leading to no possible understanding, to no possible re-inscription of Rosa's subjectivity under the required parameters.

A good example is the first conversation she has with her father after quitting her job, in which he demands an explanation (and is even willing to volunteer one, the fact that Rosa's mother died recently and this is but a desperate consequence). What he gets by way of an answer, however, is silence; an absence of explanation that her mind rushes to fill in with a stream of language which, strictly, *says* nothing:

> 'It's not a bad thing. I've decided to take stock,' she said.
> 'Take stock, what does that mean?'
> 'I've been feeling a little under the weather. As if I'm suffering from . . .'
> *Malaise. Intellectual disintegration. Epistemological meltdown. A strange rash on my arms that won't be treated. Hypochondria of the undistilled sort. An aversion to conversation. Acedia plain and simple.*[61]

Placing herself beyond the neoliberal injunction to work on her self, beyond the duty of transformation of the subject into a malleable, capacious, but ultimately coherent and closed *oeuvre*, Rosa re-creates herself – through her refusal of work and unfolding mental breakdown – as a linguistic block to working and appropriable sense, as a 'dead body' of words (analogous to the physical dead body of the Ukrainian worker in Ali's novel) gnawing away at

---

[61] Kavenna, *Inglorious*, 10.

the heart of the system.⁶² This will be the primary strategy developed by the novel in its charting of Rosa's breakdown: an essentially linguistic operation whereby the 'coded' function of a possible transgression, of a possible attitude of resistance against what is expected of her (say, in the fragmentary and nonsensical writing of her pieces for the newspaper), is fully replaced by what Foucault called above a properly 'esoteric' one. 'What is said in such a language [Foucault argued] is of little importance, as are the meanings that are delivered there.' The real transgression concerns its 'play', its deployment in a manner that ushers into its own realm of impenetrability, 'its uncontrollable flight to a region that is always dark' and that cannot be stabilized, closed, and assigned the fixed value that pertains to a given *oeuvre* – or, more generally, to work (in the Marxist sense of value).

What this language, what this dark speech is worth is thus nothing but its capacity to accrue impossible meanings and to destabilize the system of references and correspondences (of closure, of *sense*) that they might be forced to assume under 'sane' conditions. This is the effect of the word *TEMP*, which Rosa will recurrently see spray-painted on walls and bridges all over town. Its enigmatic proliferation, combined with the impossibility of assigning it any fixed semantic value, immediately turns it into an attractor of non-sense, into an esoteric node through which meaning passes constantly in a disorganized and disorganizing manner:

> A lonely word, splashed on bridges; she had once seen it on the side of a train, blurred by speed. *TEMP* – a cry from the secretarial classes, or those who worked in the constant peril of a short-term contract, she thought, passing it by. Or an unfinished word: *Tempo, Tempus fugit*, like a warning, or an elegy, *temps perdu*. It seemed to be important, but she wasn't sure.⁶³

The esoteric function revealed by such a word (*SOPH*, with its obscure philosophical and Hellenistic connotations, will be a later addition) results in an abolition of the boundaries, of the limit-effects on which the subjective

---

⁶² Gilles Deleuze provides a suggestive account of the effects of madness on sense, of the irruption, in the midst of a linguistic non-sense that one had thought controlled and playful ('a surface effect'), of devouring monsters made up of words, language turned into a foul, fecal, and terrifying corporeality. In madness, as he puts it, 'Tout mot est physique, affecte immédiatement le corps' (every word is physical, directly affecting the body), *Logique du sens* (Paris: Les Éditions de Minuit, 1969), 107.

⁶³ Kavenna, *Inglorious*, 40–1.

itself was premised. The semantic confusion unleashed by this invading body-word once again produces a topological confusion whereby inside and outside can obscurely co-exist, precipitating every social mandate into an unfathomable depth.[64]

The principal victim of this linguistic erosion of sense will be Rosa's capacity to return to work, to once again embrace a submissive attitude towards the circularity and emptiness demanded by the dominant architecture of sense and meaning, of responsibility and sanity (which her life before quitting her job had effectively embodied). Thus, prompted by the impenetrable pull of 'the *TEMP*', by a compulsion to write open-ended lists of useless tasks, to read philosophy and literature in an inordinate and profoundly senseless quest for understanding, Rosa grows increasingly unable and even *unavailable* to work; unavailable, that is, both for any kind of activity deemed productive by those surrounding her (her father, her ex-boyfriend, her friends and acquaintances, and even her doctor, as we will see below), and for any form of subjective closure, for any possible enactment of herself as *oeuvre*:

> *TEMP*, she thought. *Temper. Temperature.* The tempo of the times. Time's grasping temper. The temperature of the city. Was that what it meant? She couldn't be sure. *Temptation.* The temptation to do nothing. It was heavy upon her ... Work – the sort of work she was fitted for – and thought were, though ideally allied, not necessarily – when thought was excessive – best friends, not strictly speaking teeming with mutual amity. 'Do you understand?' she said to Dr Kamen. Dr Kamen said, 'Not quite yet, but we'll soon get to the bottom of it.'[65]

Of course, the implication of this exchange with Rosa's doctor is that he cannot possibly get to 'the bottom of it', because 'it' – in other words, the impenetrable logic, the 'excessive thought' unleashed by the *TEMP* and all the other nonsensical linguistic enigmas surrounding, engulfing her – is nothing but the 'carcass of night' invoked by Foucault, that mad point of abolition beyond any

---

[64] 'Comme il n'y a pas de surface, l'intérieur et l'extérieur, le contenant et le contenu n'ont plus de limite précise et s'enfoncent dans une universelle profondeur ou tournent dans le cercle d'un présent de plus en plus rétréci à mesure qu'il est davantage bourré' (As there is no surface, the inside and the outside, the container and the content, no longer have a precise boundary and therefore plunge into a universal depth or circle around in a shrinking and increasingly oppressive present), Deleuze, *Logique*, 106–7.
[65] Kavenna, *Inglorious*, 65.

form of definable pathology in which the body holes up, dead and unfathomable. And since work is precisely what stands in opposition to this body, to this carcass, no measure of therapeutic persuading will restore the subject's functionality. Work thus inevitably fails as a strategy of control.

This is not to say that Rosa's journey towards madness, towards that radically unworkable and ungovernable region of being, is 'smooth' and unhindered. There is a fundamental element in the plot that indicates the system's shifting strategy, its determination to abandon work (and its accompanying ethicality) as the primary way of soliciting the subject's compliance – or, more generally, of bringing subjectivity in its defined functional form back into existence. *Debt* emerges as the principal remaining link between Rosa and her working self, as the unbreakable nexus between the realm of uncontrollable exteriority, of madness, of non-sense, of enigmatic and impossible language, and the disciplined, socially useful Rosa of old. Through debt, that is, through the reframing of Rosa's subjection to the system of capitalist utility as an intersubjective relation between a creditor (in this case, her bank, which acquires an increasingly prominent role as the novel unfolds) and a debtor, the fleeing movement of the decomposing subject is arrested and re-inscribed within a form of governable interiority. Thus, her faithless dedication to work will be gradually transformed, as she finds herself in financial straits, into an obsessive dedication to her debt, which at certain moments appears to almost paper over – so to speak – the bottomless depths of her unfolding madness.[66]

According to Maurizio Lazzarato, debt is neoliberalism's primary tool of socialization and subjective production. Beyond the traditional capitalist recourse to the morality of 'effort–reward' embedded in the ideology of work, the creditor–debtor relationship introduces a 'morality of the *promise* (to honor one's debt) and the *fault* (of having entered into it)'.[67] Debt develops a further and more profound aspect of the 'work on the self' promoted by neoliberalism by 'breed[ing], subdu[ing], manufactur[ing], adapt[ing], and shap[ing]' the subject through his capacity to make and keep a promise. This fundamentally 'means constructing a memory for him, endowing him with interiority, a conscience, which provide a bulwark against forgetting. It is

---

[66] As she puts it at one point: '*I am dedicated only to my debt*', ibid., 48.
[67] Maurizio Lazzarato, *The Making of Indebted Man*, trans. Joshua David Jordan (Los Angeles: Semiotext(e), 2011), 30.

within the domain of debt obligations that memory, subjectivity, and conscience begin to be produced.'[68] This retrieval and actualization of an otherwise endangered interiority is further carried out through debt's forcible relation to the future, through its insistence on 'objectivizing time, possessing it in advance ... subordinating all possibility of choice and decision which the future holds to the reproduction of capitalist power relations'.[69]

Through her growing exposure to the pressures of debt, Rosa undertakes an inverted course of re-subjectivation, of re-territorialization within the domain of neoliberal power. It is as if society finds in finance a way of reinstating the antagonism that madness had tentatively undone; a way of re-organizing – or at least provisionally halting the breakup of – Rosa's subjective relation to herself:

> I feel as if the real world, with its laws of time and space, its economics, politics, and even morality, has dissolved. Or I have been detached from it, and have emerged somewhere – I'm not quite sure where. But really it's much better here, on the edge. It affords quite the best view. The only problem is debt, of course. And that's why I need to change a little, sort things out.[70]

Debt emerges as the social structure that reins in, that arrests the dissolution of the subject's self-positing as work, as *oeuvre*, as that which can be measured, profited from and controlled. As Rosa ironically reminds herself, debt is fundamentally pedagogical in nature and must therefore be mobilized against the mad temptation to forget – to forget *oneself*, one's commitments and obligations, and thus one's effective subjection to the system of control. As she puts it after one of her many failed attempts at re-negotiating her debt to the bank:

> She had to tell them that it wasn't a lack of concern for her place in the international system of debit and credit, she was fantastically concerned about it, but she had been prioritising other things, and she had lost her sense of financial basics. She had ignored the rules of supply and demand, and her supply has simply vanished.[71]

---

[68] Ibid., 40.
[69] Ibid., 46.
[70] Kavenna, *Inglorious*, 68.
[71] Ibid., 43.

The debt relation in which Rosa is caught up is incessantly filtered through and mediated by an ironic distance that does not cease to grow, to expand, to bring the dark light of her mad delusions to bear on the social facticity of her subjection, estranging it, rendering it – in the last instance – inoperative. Thus, while gesturally accepting the basic terms, the logic of this phenomenal (and essentially ungraspable) deployment of capitalist power through finance, and while admitting that work – that is, the return to waged labour – is the inevitable corollary of its enactment, there is a fundamental dislocation at the level of discourse; a disruption affecting the articulation of her 'priorities' and the textual staging of her response to the urge to work that will permanently disable her capacity to submit to the system.

Let me insist: it is in and through the act of writing itself that Rosa's madness, that the intimate centre of her exteriority with respect to the universe of social utility and belonging, reaches its peak. There are, on the one hand, her interminable lists of tasks, detailing a fragmentary and illogical – but powerfully de-territorializing, powerfully inoperative – set of 'priorities', of creative detours and bifurcations on the bumpy, and ultimately closed-off, road to subjective stabilization. On the other hand, we encounter Rosa's letters, some of which (in particular, those allegedly written as job-application letters) offer an extreme, and extremely inventive, version of the unworking of work itself, of the depletion of socially consensual meaning towards which her madness keeps pointing.[72] There is in this 'insane' deployment of language, in this *writerly* act of the mad body itself, the implication that only that which remains opaque and irreducible to the discursive value on which the debt relation is founded (that is, the performative value of the 'promise' through which the indebted subject is created) can salvage language itself. What these letters *say* is that only the impenetrable raving of a speech anchored in the unfathomable depths of the body can break free of capitalist work and its

---

[72] These are two revealing examples: '*Dear Sir, I would like a job. Actually that's not true. Without wanting to trouble you with my ambivalence, a job is what I need. Sheer bloody debt has forced me back. I am quite free of many of the more fashionable varieties of hypocrisy, though I suffer from many unfashionable varieties of my own. I have many strengths, most of which I seem for the moment to have forgotten. However, I am a goal-oriented person and so on, und so weiter ... Yours ever, Rosa Lane.*' '*Dear Madam, I am a person of inconstant aims and mild destitution. I find this combination of qualities excludes me from many jobs. But working together, I'm sure we can exploit my talents successfully. I still have a cream suit, a relic from a former life. I am unexceptional in every way, and eager to serve. You can find me in a borrowed room, in west London. Yours faithfully, Rosa Lane*', ibid., 44.

rationality, turning the *real*, impenetrable dimension of this body into the liberated foundation of a new form of life. Writing about Antonin Artaud, Jacques Derrida pointed out that:

> Artaud knew that all speech fallen from the body, offering itself to understanding or reception, offering itself as a spectacle, immediately becomes stolen speech. Becomes a signification which I do not possess because it is a signification. Theft is always the theft of speech or text, of a trace. The theft of a possession does not become a theft unless the thing stolen is a possession, unless it has acquired meaning and value through, at least, the consecration of a vow made in discourse.[73]

The act of disorganization of this vow – of the promise, say, to re-pay one's debt, and of the discursive scenario through which that promise becomes operative – lies, precisely, in the unworking of speech as a possession, as appropriable matter, as *work*. Language qua work, qua organization, is what can be 'blown', 'spirited away', as Derrida says, from the body, what makes the void, the impenetrability at its centre (its 'carcass of night', as Foucault had put it) tidily manageable and exploitable.

In facing what Deleuze calls the 'forces of the outside', the inappropriable language of madness, we attain the nucleus of a strategy that can no longer be described as subjective, as the property of a subject. For indeed, if the logic of capitalist power rests on the possibility of re-enacting subjectivity, of re-articulating it on its own terms (as work on the self, as debt, and so on), only a counter-strategy of dislocation and disarticulation, a decidedly meta-subjective gesture of affirmative precariousness will be able to restore the self-valorizing horizon posited by the old proletarian subject of the refusal of work.

---

[73] Jacques Derrida, *Writing and Difference*, trans. Alan Bass (Chicago: University of Chicago Press, 1978), 175.

6

Conclusion

Rosa Lane's 'fall' into madness amounts to a break with the regime of appropriation and internalization through which capitalism operates. This does not mean that the mad unravelling of the subject, that the unfolding of precariousness and vulnerability at the heart of the latter, situates her/him *beyond* the social logic of capital, in a transcendent location *outside* the ontological boundaries of the power relation. Rather, it indicates that this power relation, that the system's capacity for internalization, for appropriation and subsumption of subjectivity – *through* subjectivity – is permanently threatened and arrested from within. In other words, the outside, far from being a safe exteriority, a vaguely threatening position within a transcendent topology, is what already inhabits the subject, what lurks and haunts it, making its *functional* inscription (even as pathology, or as precarity) within the social system, its full deployment as subjectivity, so to speak, constitutively precarious and ultimately impossible. This means that vulnerability, that the open wound of a given unappropriated life, when it breaks the dynamic of capture that – either exceptionally (in a sovereign gesture) or unexceptionally (through a procedure of control) – the system imposes upon it, can unleash itself as a destabilizing force, as a gesture of refusal that no measure of power can extinguish.

We have seen that the post-war development of capitalism is characterized by a full-scale deployment of its internalizing tendencies, by a logic that, seeking to capitalize on the self-affirming capacities of a reinvigorated working class, turns its antagonistic interaction with the latter into an opportunity for expansion, for growth, for valorization. Capital's socialization, as I have described it in the context of the studied texts and in relation to the basic hypotheses of Operaist Marxism, essentially refers to this opportunity, to this systemic attempt to saturate the field of the social, even while preserving its conflictual possibilities, and to eliminate every discontinuity, every moment of resistance or irruption of the outside. Capitalism appropriates the social, neutralizing the transcendent exteriority represented by traditional working-class struggles (which, in their classic revolutionary version, sought to constitute a beyond – beyond capitalist 'pre-history'), by extending the realm of work, by turning work into an ineluctable social bond. While capitalism remained primarily industrial, organized around the discipline of the Fordist factory, the temptation still existed to identify a space of non-work, an experiential dimension of unbonded life beyond the spatio-temporal regularities of the factory and its productive rhythms. Yet even then, its structural primacy, its overdetermination of the social could be felt – as Sillitoe's fictions attest – in the inward orientation of those peripheral activities, in the overt dependency of non-work upon work, of the pub upon the assembly line, of 'Saturday night and Sunday morning' upon 'black Monday'. However, as the factory loses its centrality, as society becomes an immediate and directly accessible terrain of appropriation and value extraction, the work relation begins to proliferate and expand, however diffusely, however immaterially, over an ever wider range of activities and experiences. The separation between life and work is replaced by a confusion that manifests itself as violent encroachment and savage appropriation. With the displacement of the factory as the primary site of the capitalist extraction of value, work abandons its previous semblance of measure and balance, unveiling its systemic truth in the institutional form of an overtly repressive state apparatus or in the socially pervasive form of a 'precarious' governmentality.

We have seen that Alan Sillitoe and David Storey, writing from the historical vantage point of the late 1950s and early 1960s (that is, from the perspective of post-war capitalism's fully developed socialization), managed to chart the convulsive resurgence of antagonistic class subjectivities as the new primary, even necessary, context of capital's maturation. Shedding the ideological veneer of consensus with which this process had been covered in many areas of public discourse, writers like Sillitoe and Storey were able to reveal the properly subjective profile of capital's penetration of the social. As their fictions show, this implied, on the one hand, that capital ceased to appear as an 'objective' factor of economic development, and emerged instead as an organized and expansive agency, extracting and incorporating, taming and modulating, the vital resources of social life and transforming them into an internal *property* of the system. Consequently, this also implied that the unharnessed matter, that the potential social labour upon which capital subjectively imposed itself, was in turn rediscovered as subjectivity, and as conflicting, resisting subjectivity at that. In contradistinction to previous historical scenarios of class conflict, this subjectivation of living labour by the subjective form of socialized capital announced itself as an irresolvable standoff, as an immanent and interminable struggle. The more the two subjectivities penetrated one another, the more the prospects of transcendence became defeated.

We saw that Sillitoe's young proletarians oscillated between the temporary lucidity granted by the immediacy of capital (embodied in the machine or in the figure of the rate-checker) and the irrepressible instinct to escape the institutionalized compassion of the 'in-laws', of capital's bureaucrats and functionaries. We also saw that the invasiveness of this system of socialized exploitation paradoxically elevated the 'differential' profile of the proletarian subjectivities under siege, propelling them towards an openness, towards an uncontainable exteriority that would soon become an internal quality of their own subjectivity, and would eventually take over and undo the latter. With Storey, we witnessed a fresh development unfold – one that would also punctuate later developments in the antagonistic relationship between capital and the working class. Money, suddenly torn from every form or degree of measure, from every temporal index or connection to the factory, became embodied in a new figure of the professional athlete, uncovering a whole new range of exploitative possibilities. Beyond the disciplinary spaces of the factory and the penal institution, the domain of 'play' offered itself up as a virgin land ready for fresh colonial incursions.

In a similar manner, the fictional explorations of female working-class subjectivity and reproductive labour carried out by Nell Dunn and Pat Barker pointed to the effects of a process of capitalist expansion that increasingly eroded the distinctions between inside and outside, between production and reproduction, work and non-work. In the novels of these authors, we saw the rich subjectivities of the proletarian characters constitute a primary resource, a raw material whose differential quality, whose increasing vital density and autonomy, lent itself to new operations of subsumption, of incorporation and exploitation. Capital no longer appears here as the 'fixed' expression of the machine or as the temporal regularity of a factory shift, but as the possibility of making life – that is, the body and its affects – available for fresh enclosures and appropriations, for fresh valorizations. In the domestic periphery of a declining industrial universe, reproductive labour accrues a new topicality, turning its female protagonists into fully-fledged proletarians, and thus also into the frontline of society's subsumption within capital. Under such circumstances, the old strategy of subjective affirmation, of differential self-valorization à la Arthur Seaton or Smith, proves increasingly inadequate (and unavailable). We begin to encounter forms of conscious and wilful despair, a variety of 'fatal' or suicidal strategies in which subjectivity (let us insist: that fundamental buttress on which the capitalist power relation rests) becomes transfixed, prised open, and eventually left behind.

We have also seen that the experimental narrative forms rehearsed by James Kelman radicalized the experience of subsumption, the erosion of an industrial-proletarian subjectivity that could still by defined by distinction and autonomy, by its effective separation from the technical and institutional forms of capital. With the abolition of the topological and phenomenological boundaries that sustained this possibility, not only the body, but also the 'mind' (the subject's increasingly confused, increasingly anxious psychology) became marked as a primary site of the capitalist process. In the case of the bus conductor, this translated into a sense of insupportable disorientation and suffering, which eventually led to an instinct of flight, to an unprocessed (and ultimately defeated) desire to leave the here-and-now of a life fully immured within the opacity of post-industrial labour. What Robert Hines could not attain, or fully comprehend, due to his structural position within the temporal crisis of the postmodern valorization process, Kelman's cognitive worker – the 'disaffected' Patrick Doyle – manages to enact in a gesture of refusal that will lay the foundations for later strategies.

The problem of subsumption is here understood (by Kelman *and* his protagonist) as a problem of saturation and co-optation of the public sphere, of transformation of the latter into a function or extension of the State apparatus. In a way that Sillitoe's borstal inmate had already intuited, Doyle grasps that the 'truth' about postmodern sociality and the forms of immaterial work on which it is increasingly dependent lies in the confusion between the 'polis' and the 'police', between the social understood as a space of free praxis and its transformation into a punitive institutionality. That the social is recognized as a fresh terrain for capitalist appropriation – in other words, that the process of real subsumption is irreversible in postmodernity – does not imply that the State form decreases in importance. On the contrary, the latter develops a new functionality, a new centrality to the holistic and integrated system of capitalist valorization. As Kelman's crowning achievement, *How Late It Was, How Late*, clearly demonstrates, this new functionality concerns the dismantling of any intermediary role, of any mediating logic, that the State may have retained from its previous Keynesian/Fordist incarnation. The State is thus rediscovered, in those dense and asphyxiating pages depicting Sammy Samuels' interactions with policemen and bureaucrats, as a machine of corporeal and psychological depredation, leaving no option to the subject but to take up the struggle under conditions of intensified immediacy.

I have charted this intensification of the struggle, this brutal expansion of capital's exploitative mechanisms, in the context of Irvine Welsh's writing about the 1980s, especially in his novel *Skagboys*. Here, the relentless process of institutional penetration of the social, the 'militarization' of the public sphere, gives way to a sovereign scenario of exceptionality in which working/working-class life is presented as 'bare life'. Every trace of subjective autonomy has now disappeared, and what remains is nothing but a prostrate figure of the formerly combative proletarian subject. The crucial *turn* occurs precisely at this point – a turn for which everything so far had been preparing us. Indeed, the fact that the machinery of subsumption eradicates the autonomy of the proletarian subject, reducing it to an impotent residue, does not entail that the antagonism disappears. It means, rather, that it undergoes a fundamental displacement; that, having been deprived of the spaces of mediation in which its post-war sociality had been constructed, it is forced to reappear as a dislocated and ex-centric engagement.

Assailed and exploited beyond measure by the apparatuses of capitalist power, the proletarian subject emerges as a non-subject, as an ecstatic singularity that can no longer be accommodated within the social and political forms sustained by industrial capitalism or articulated as the formed subjectivities that made the latter operative. The process of subsumption paradoxically reaches here an impasse. Propelled by its internalizing voraciousness, by its appropriating frenzy, capital meets a limit in the form of an immanent detachment, of an excess which, although generated internally, cannot be assimilated and governmentalized. The social relation depicted by Welsh thus points to those blindspots produced in the interaction between capital and the proletarian subject, those moments where a non-subsumable residue, where a subjective fragment that can no longer be interpellated or rehearsed as a governable subjectivity, breaks through the surface of neoliberal control and/or sovereignty. The *unreformable* junkie emerges in this context as a paradigmatic figure of refusal, as an individual that has already deserted the political logic of engagement rehearsed by his/her working-class forbears and that calls into question the functional logic of subjectivity. In this sense, the 'ecstatic' figure of the junkie pioneers a wholesale process of unworking of the social at a moment when the latter no longer offers any resistant possibility, at a point in capitalism's development where every moment and every space of society has been turned into 'work', into valorizing (that is, capital-generating) activity. The junkie's refusal of work not only challenges the strictly economic dimension of capitalist society – in other words, the forms of production of value it encourages – but also the organization of society as work, as a working and workable – as an operative – mode of collective being. What this figure of the junkie (or any other equivalent version of the inoperative marginal) introduces is the novelty of worklessness; the shocking and subversive novelty of a form of life immune to the injunctions of utilitarian/productive actualization – of the compulsion to *work* in every sense of the term.

We have seen, finally, that this drive towards worklessness grows increasingly prominent as neoliberalism develops. In Monica Ali's and Joanna Kavenna's fiction, the logic of capitalist subsumption is no longer confronted with a subject-based antagonism (nor does it feed off it), but with an implosive possibility of collapse. Thus, while neoliberal governmentality rests on the production of expansive, rhizomatic, and in principle difference-fuelled subjectivities, the lurking menace of an inoperative meta-subjective residue, of a corporeal or psychic trace that could potentially subvert the power regime of capital, puts the entire system at stake. What these writers rehearse is the possibility of a sudden disorganization of a system that, despite its postmodern claims to flexibility, is structurally founded on the exclusion of the outside, on the abjection of any form of life that may not be appropriated and 'put to work' by the system. For indeed the outside represented by the inoperative figure (by the uncontainable psychic crisis, in the examples privileged by Ali and Kavenna) does not constitute a reinstatement of transcendence, but a rediscovery of vulnerability – of precariousness – as a paradoxical new point of departure for resistance. The outside is what lies beyond the functionality of the system of appropriation, what cancels the determinations of capital's operative injunctions – what lacks *work*.

Bibliography

Agamben, Giorgio. *The Coming Community*. Trans. Michael Hardt. Minneapolis: University of Minnesota Press, 1993.
Agamben, Giorgio. *Homo Sacer: Sovereign Power and Bare Life*. Trans. Daniel Heller-Roazen. Stanford: Stanford University Press, 1998.
Agamben, Giorgio. *Means Without End: Notes on Politics*. Trans. Vincenzo Binetti and Cesare Casarino. Minneapolis: University of Minnesota Press, 2000.
Agamben, Giorgio. 'What is a Destituent Power?'. Trans. Stephanie Wakefield. *Environment and Planning D: Society and Space*, 32, 2014, 65–74.
Agamben, Giorgio. *L'uso dei corpi*: Homo Sacer, *IV, 2*. Vicenza: Neri Pozza Editore, 2014.
Ali, Monica. *In the Kitchen*. London: Transworld Publishers, 2009.
Althusser, Louis. *Lenin and Philosophy and Other Essays*. Trans. Ben Brewster. London: New Left Books, 1977.
Arendt, Hannah. *The Human Condition*. Chicago: University of Chicago Press.
Atherton, Stanley S. *Alan Sillitoe: A Critical Assessment*. London: W. H. Allen, 1979.
Barker, Pat. *Union Street*. London: Virago, 1982.
Barker, Pat. *Blow Your House Down*. London: Virago, 1984.
Baudrillard, Jean. *Symbolic Exchange and Death*. Trans. Hamilton Grant. London: Sage, 1993.
Baudrillard, Jean. *Forget Foucault*. Trans. Phil Beitchman et al. Los Angeles: Semiotext(e), 2007.
Baudrillard, Jean. *Fatal Strategies*. Trans. Philippe Beitchman and W. G. J. Niesluchowski. Los Angeles: Semiotext(e), 2008.
Bell, Daniel. *The End of Ideology: On the Exhaustion of Political Ideas in the Fifties*. New York: Free Press, 1965.
Bell, David. *Ardent Propaganda: Miners' Novels and Class Conflict 1929–1939*. Umeå: Umeå University, 1995.
Bell, Kathleen. 'Arthur Seaton and the Machine: A New Reading of Alan Sillitoe's *Saturday Night and Sunday Morning*'. In H. Gustav Klaus and Stephen Knight (eds). *British Industrial Fictions*. Cardiff: University of Wales Press, 2000.
Benjamin, Walter. 'Critique of Violence'. In *Reflections: Essays, Aphorisms, Autobiographical Writings*. Trans. Edmund Jephcott. New York: Shocken Books, 1978.
Bentley, Nick. *Radical Fictions: The English Novel in the 1950s*. Oxford: Peter Lang, 2007.

Berardi, Franco 'Bifo'. *Heroes: Mass Murder and Suicide*. London: Verso, 2015.

Bobbio, Norberto. 'Gramsci and the Conception of Civil Society'. In Chantal Mouffe (ed.). *Gramsci and Marxist Theory*. London: Routledge, 2014.

Bourdieu, Pierre. 'La précarité est aujourd'hui partout'. In *Contre-feux. Propos pour servir à la résistance contre l'invasion néo-libérale*. Paris: Liber – Raison d'Agir, 1998.

Bove, Laurent. *La stratégie du conatus: affirmation et résistance chez Spinoza*. Paris: Vrin, 2012.

Branson, Noreen. *History of the Communist Party of Great Britain 1941–1951*. London: Lawrence and Wishart, 1997.

Brooke, Stephen. '"Slumming" in Swinging London: Class, Gender and the Post-War City in Nell Dunn's *Up the Junction* (1963)'. *Cultural and Social History*, 9: 3, 2012, 429–49.

Brophy, Sarah. 'Working-Class Women, Labor, and the Problem of Community in *Union Street* and *Liza's England*'. In Sharon Monteith et al. (eds). *Critical Perspectives on Pat Barker*. Columbia: South Carolina University Press, 2005, 24–39.

Brouillette, Sarah. 'The Pathology of Flexibility in Monica Ali's *In the Kitchen*'. *MFS Modern Fiction Studies*. 58: 3, 2012, 529–48.

Butler, Judith. *Frames of War: When is Life Grievable?* London: Verso, 2010.

Cleaver, Harry. 'Foreword'. In Ben Carrington and Ian MacDonald (eds). *Marxism, Cultural Studies and Sport*. London: Routledge, 2008.

Craig, Cairns. 'Resisting Arrest'. In Gavin Wallace and Randall Stevenson (eds). *The Scottish Novel Since the Seventies: New Visions, Old Dreams*. Edinburgh: Edinburgh University Press, 1993.

Craig, Cairns. *The Modern Scottish Novel: Narrative and the National Imagination*. Edinburgh: Edinburgh University Press, 1999.

Croft, Andy. *Red Letter Days: British Fiction in the 1930s*. London: Lawrence and Wishart, 1990.

Crosland, Anthony. *The Future of Socialism*. London: Constable, 2006.

Dalla Costa, Mariarosa and Selma James. *The Power of Women and the Subversion of the Community*. Bristol: Falling Wall Press, 1975.

Day, Gary. *Class*. London: Routledge, 2001.

del Valle Alcalá, Roberto. 'Rising with One's Community: Socialist Theory and Bildungsroman in Lewis Jones', *Cultura, Lenguaje y Representación*, 7, 2009, 141–56.

Deleuze, Gilles. *Logique du sens*. Paris: Les Éditions de Minuit, 1969.

Deleuze, Gilles. 'Postscript on the Societies of Control'. *October*, 59, 1992, 3–7.

Deleuze, Gilles. *Essays Critical and Clinical*. Trans. Daniel W. Smith and Michael A. Greco. London: Verso, 1998.

Deleuze, Gilles. *Pure Immanence: Essays on a Life*. Trans. Anne Boyman. New York: Zone Books, 2001.

Deleuze, Gilles. *Foucault.* Trans. Seán Hand. London: Bloomsbury, 2013.

Deleuze, Gilles and Félix Guattari. *Kafka: Toward a Minor Literature*. Trans. Dana Polan. Minneapolis: University of Minnesota Press, 1986.

Deleuze, Gilles and Félix Guattari. *What is Philosophy?* Trans. Hugh Tomlinson and Graham Burchell. New York: Columbia University Press, 1994.

Deleuze, Gilles and Félix Guattari. *Anti-Oedipus.* Trans. Robert Hurley et al. London: Continuum, 2011.

Deleuze, Gilles and Félix Guattari. *A Thousand Plateaus*. Trans. Brian Massumi. London: Continuum, 2011.

Denning, Michael. 'Wageless Life'. *New Left Review*, 66, 2010, 79–97.

Derrida, Jacques. *Writing and Difference*. Trans. Alan Bass. Chicago: University of Chicago Press, 1978.

Drabble, Margaret. 'Introduction', in Nell Dunn. *Poor Cow*. London: Virago, 1988.

Dunn, Nell. *Poor Cow*. London: Virago, 1988.

Dunn, Nell. *Up the Junction.* London: Virago, 1988.

Eyers, Tom. *Lacan and the Concept of the 'Real'*. New York: Palgrave Macmillan, 2012.

Federici, Silvia. *Revolution at Point Zero: Housework, Reproduction, and Feminist Struggle*. New York: PM Press, 2012.

Fordham, John. *James Hanley: Modernism and the Working Class*. Cardiff: University of Wales Press, 2001.

Fortunati, Leopoldina. *The Arcane of Reproduction: Housework, Prostitution, Labor and Capital*. Trans. Hilary Creek. New York: Autonomedia, 1995.

Foucault, Michel. 'The Subject and Power'. *Critical Inquiry*, 8: 4, 1982, 777–95.

Foucault, Michel. *Discipline and Punish: The Birth of the Prison*. Trans. Alan Sheridan. London: Penguin, 1991.

Foucault, Michel. *The Will to Know: The History of Sexuality, vol. 1*. Trans. Robert Hurley. London: Penguin, 1998.

Foucault, Michel. *Society Must Be Defended: Lectures at the Collège de France, 1975–6*. Trans. David Macey. London: Penguin, 2004.

Foucault, Michel. *History of Madness*. Trans. Jonathan Murphy and Jean Khalfa. Abingdon: Routledge, 2006.

Goldthorpe, John H., David Lockwood, Frank Bechhofer and Jennifer Platt. *The Affluent Worker in the Class Structure.* Cambridge: Cambridge University Press, 1969.

Guattari, Félix. 'The Proliferation of Margins'. Trans. Richard Gardner and Sybil Walker. In Sylvère Lotringer and Christian Marazzi (eds). *Autonomia: Post-Political Politics*. Los Angeles, Semiotext(e), 2007.

Guattari, Félix. *Les Anées d'Hiver 1980–1985*. Paris: Les Prairies Ordinaires, 2009.

Hardt, Michael. 'The Global Society of Control'. *Discourse*, 20: 3, 1998, 139–52.
Hardt, Michael and Antonio Negri. *Labor of Dionysus: A Critique of the State-Form*. Minneapolis: University of Minnesota Press, 1994.
Hardt, Michael and Antonio Negri. *Empire*. Cambridge, MA: Harvard University Press, 2000.
Hardt, Michael and Antonio Negri. *Multitude*. London: Penguin, 2005.
Hardt, Michael and Antonio Negri. *Commonwealth*. Cambridge, MA: Harvard University Press, 2009.
Haywood, Ian. *Working-Class Fiction from Chartism to* Trainspotting. Tavistock: Northcote House, 1997.
Head, Dominic. *Cambridge Introduction to Modern British Fiction, 1950–2000*. Cambridge: Cambridge University Press, 2002.
Hegel, G. W. F. *Elements of the Philosophy of Right*. Trans. H. B. Nisbet. Cambridge: Cambridge University Press, 1991.
Hill, Jeffrey. 'Sport Stripped Bare: Deconstructing Working-Class Masculinity in *This Sporting Life*'. *Men and Masculinities*, 7: 4, 2005, 405–23.
Hitchcock, Peter. *Working-Class Fiction in Theory and Practice: A Reading of Alan Sillitoe*. Ann Arbor, Michigan: UMI Press, 1989.
Hoggart, Richard. *The Uses of Literacy*. London: Chatto and Windus, 1957.
Hutchings, William. 'The Work of Play: Anger and the Expropriated Athletes of Alan Sillitoe and David Storey'. *MFS Modern Fiction Studies*, 33: 1, 1987, 35–47.
Hutchings, William. 'Proletarian Byronism: Alan Sillitoe and the Romantic Tradition'. In Allan Chavkin (ed.). *English Romanticism and Modern Fiction*. New York: AMS Press, 1993, 35–47.
Johnson, Matthew (ed.). *Precariat: Labour, Work and Politics*. London: Routledge, 2014.
Kavenna, Joanna. *Inglorious*. London: Faber and Faber, 2007.
Kelly, Aaron. *James Kelman: Politics and Aesthetics*. Oxford and Bern: Peter Lang, 2013.
Kelman, James. *A Disaffection*. London: Secker and Warburg, 1989.
Kelman, James. *How Late It Was, How Late*. London: Vintage, 1998.
Kelman, James. *The Busconductor Hines*. Edinburgh: Polygon, 2007.
Kirk, John. 'Class, Community and "Structures of Feeling" in Working-Class Writing from the 1980s'. *Literature and History*, 8: 2, 1999, 44–63.
Kirk, John. *The British Working Class in the Twentieth Century*. Cardiff: University of Wales Press, 2003.
Kirk, John. *Class, Culture and Social Change: On the Trail of the Working Class*. Basingstoke: Palgrave, 2007.
Klaus, H. Gustav and Stephen Knight (eds). *British Industrial Fictions*. Cardiff: University of Wales Press, 2000.

Kővesi, Simon. *James Kelman*. Manchester: Manchester University Press, 2007.
Kristeva, Julia. *Powers of Horror: An Essay on Abjection*. Trans. Leon S. Roudiez. New York: Columbia University Press, 1984.
Lacan, Jacques. *The Ethics of Psychoanalysis*. Trans. Dennis Porter. London: Routledge, 1992.
Lazzarato, Maurizio. *The Making of Indebted Man*. Trans. Joshua David Jordan. Los Angeles: Semiotext(e), 2011.
Lazzarato, Maurizio. *Signs and Machines: Capitalism and the Production of Subjectivity*. Trans. Joshua David Jordan. Los Angeles: Semiotext(e), 2014.
Lazzarato, Maurizio. *Gouverner par la dette*. Paris: Les Prairies Ordinaires, 2014.
Lorey, Isabell. *State of Insecurity: Government of the Precarious*. Trans. Aileen Derieg. London: Verso, 2015.
Lotringer, Sylvère and Christian Marazzi (eds). *Autonomia: Post-Political Politics*. Los Angeles, Semiotext(e), 2007.
Marazzi, Christian. *Capital and Affects: The Politics of the Language Economy*. Trans. Giuseppina Mecchia. New York: Semiotext(e), 2011.
Marx, Karl. *Capital, volume 1*. Trans. Ben Fowkes. Harmondsworth: Penguin, 1990.
Marx, Karl. *Grundrisse*. Trans. Martin Nicolaus. Harmondsworth: Penguin, 1993.
Massumi, Brian. *The Power at the End of the Economy*. Durham: Duke University Press, 2015.
McCann, Andrew. 'Walter Benjamin's Sex Work: Prostitution and the State of Exception'. *Textual Practice*, 28: 1, 2014.
Mulhern, Francis. *Culture/Metaculture*. London: Routledge, 2000.
Nancy, Jean-Luc. *The Inoperative Community*. Trans. Peter Connor et al. Minneapolis: University of Minnesota Press, 1991.
Nardella, Anna R. 'The Existential Dilemmas of Alan Sillitoe's Working-Class Heroes'. *Studies in the Novel*, 5, 1973, 469–82.
Negri, Antonio. *Revolution Retrieved: Writings on Marx, Keynes, Capitalist Crisis and New Social Subjects (1967–83)*. London: Red Notes, 1988.
Negri, Antonio. *The Politics of Subversion: A Manifesto for the Twenty-First Century*. Trans. James Newell. London: Polity Press, 1989.
Negri, Antonio. *Marx Beyond Marx: Lessons on the* Grundrisse. Trans. Harry Cleaver, Michael Ryan and Maurizio Viano. New York: Autonomedia, 1991.
Negri, Antonio. *The Savage Anomaly: The Power of Spinoza's Metaphysics and Politics*. Trans. Michael Hardt. Minneapolis: University of Minnesota Press, 1999.
Negri, Antonio. *Time for Revolution*. Trans. Matteo Mandarini. London: Continuum, 2003.
Negri, Antonio. *Books for Burning: Between Civil War and Democracy in 1970s Italy*. Trans. Arianna Bove et al. London: Verso, 2005.

Negri, Antonio. *Insurgencies: Constituent Power and the Modern State*. Trans. Maurizia Boscagli. Minneapolis: University of Minnesota Press, 2009.

Negri, Antonio. *The Labor of Job*. Trans. Matteo Mandarini. Durham: Duke University Press, 2009.

Negri, Antonio. *Spinoza for Our Time: Politics and Postmodernity*. Trans. William McCuaig. New York: Columbia University Press, 2013.

Panzieri, Raniero. 'The Capitalist Use of Machinery: Marx Versus the "Objectivists"'. In Phil Slater (ed.). *Outlines of a Critique of Technology*. London: Ink Links, 1980.

Revel, Judith. *Foucault, une pensée du discontinue*. Paris: Mille et Une Nuits, 2010.

Sawkins, John. *The Long Apprenticeship: Alienation in the Early Work of Alan Sillitoe*. Oxford: Peter Lang, 2001.

Schmitt, Carl. *Political Theology: Four Chapters on the Concept of Sovereignty*. Trans. George Schwab. Chicago: Chicago University Press, 1985.

Sharma, Sarah. *In the Meantime: Temporality and Cultural Politics*. Durham: Duke University Press, 2014.

Shiach, Morag. *Modernism, Labour and Selfhood in British Literature and Culture, 1890–1930*. Cambridge: Cambridge University Press, 2004.

Sillitoe, Alan. 'Poor People', *Anarchy*, 38, 1964, 124–8.

Sillitoe, Alan. *Saturday Night and Sunday Morning*. London: Flamingo, 1994.

Sillitoe, Alan. *The Loneliness of the Long Distance Runner*. London: Flamingo, 1994.

Sinclair, Upton. *The Jungle*. New York: Oxford University Press.

Sinfield, Alan. *Literature, Politics and Culture in Postwar Britain*. London: Continuum, 2007.

Smith, Jason. '"I am sure that you are more pessimistic than I am …": An Interview with Giorgio Agamben'. *Rethinking Marxism: A Journal of Economics, Culture and Society*, 16: 2, 2004, 115–24.

Snee, Carole. 'Working-Class Literature or Proletarian Writing?' In Jon Clark, Margot Heinemann, David Margolies and Carole Snee (eds). *Culture and Crisis in Britain in the 30s*. London: Lawrence and Wishart, 1979, 165–91.

Standing, Guy. *The Precariat: The New Dangerous Class*. London: Bloomsbury, 2011.

Taylor, Andrew. *The NUM and British Politics, Volume 1: 1944–1968*. Aldershot: Ashgate, 2003.

Taylor, Andrew. *The NUM and British Politics, Volume 2: 1969–1995*. Aldershot: Ashgate, 2005.

Thoburn, Nicholas. *Deleuze, Marx, and Politics*. London: Routledge, 2003.

Tiratsoo, Nick (ed.). *From Blitz to Blair: A New History of Britain since 1939*. London: Phoenix, 1998.

Tronti, Mario. *Operai e Capitale*. Rome: DeriveApprodi, 2013.

Virno, Paolo. 'Virtuosity and Revolution: The Political Theory of Exodus'. In Paolo Virno and Michael Hardt (eds). *Radical Thought in Italy: A Potential Politics*. Trans. Maurizia Boscagli et al. Minneapolis: University of Minnesota Press, 1996.

Virno, Paolo and Michael Hardt (eds). *Radical Thought in Italy: A Potential Politics*. Trans. Maurizia Boscagli et al. Minneapolis: University of Minnesota Press, 1996.

Von Rosenberg, Ingrid. 'Militancy, Anger and Resignation: Alternative Moods in the Working-Class Novel of the 1950s and Early 1960s'. In H. Gustav Klaus (ed.). *The Socialist Novel in Britain*. Brighton: Harvester Press, 1982.

Waterman, David. *Pat Barker and the Mediation of Social Reality*. Amherst: Cambria, 2009.

Weeks, Kathi. *The Problem with Work: Feminism, Marxism, Antiwork Politics, and Postwork Imaginaries*. Durham: Duke University Press, 2011.

Welsh, Irvine. *Trainspotting*. London: Minerva, 1996.

Welsh, Irvine. *Skagboys*. London: Vintage, 2012.

Westergaard, John. 'The Withering Away of Class: A Contemporary Myth'. In *Towards Socialism*. London: Fontana/New Left Review, 1965, 77–113.

Williams, Raymond. *Culture and Society*. London: Hogarth Press, 1958.

Williams, Raymond. *The Long Revolution*. Harmondsworth: Penguin, 1965.

Williams, Raymond. *Politics and Letters*. London: New Left Books, 1979.

Williams, Raymond. *Writing in Society*. London: Verso, 1983.

Williams, Raymond. *Culture and Materialism*. London: Verso, 2005.

Worpole, Ken. *Dockers and Detectives*. London: Verso, 1983.

Wright, Steven. *Storming Heaven: Class Composition and Struggle in Italian Autonomist Marxism*. London: Pluto Press, 2002.

Index

abjection 75, 77–8, 176
abortion 26, 54
absence of work 157, 159, 161
abstraction 5, 9, 23, 36, 38, 40–1, 45, 53–4, 56, 88, 92, 94–5, 97, 101, 103, 106–7, 112
actuality 129–31
actualization 25, 42, 113, 130, 139, 153, 167, 176
affluence 8, 12 nn.3, 4, 14–16, 18–19, 27–8, 30, 38, 45, 53, 55, 58
Agamben, Giorgio 7 n.7, 112, 114–15, 117, 120 n.90, 127 n.106, 129–30
agency 15, 52, 68, 88, 93, 120, 142, 157, 172
alienation 21–3, 98, 103
Althusser, Louis 96
Angry Young Men 14
antagonism 11, 15–18, 23–4, 28, 31, 34–6, 41, 44, 55, 85, 92–3, 106–7, 113, 160, 167, 175–6
apparatus of capture 102
Arendt, Hannah 2
Artaud, Antonin 169
Aufhebung 5–6, 14
Autonomist Marxism 3, 17 *see also* Operaismo *and* Workerism

bare life 9, 115–16, 118, 128, 130–1, 175
Baudrillard, Jean 74–5, 82 *see also* fatal strategy
Bechhofer, Frank 12 n.3
Bell, Daniel 25 n.35
Bell, David 5 n.5
Bell, Kathleen 21 n.23
Benjamin, Walter 80 115
Bentley, Nick 15, 23, 26 n.40
Berardi, Franco 161 n.57
biopolitics 6, 9, 55, 57, 59, 61, 65, 67, 75, 77–9
biopower 55, 57
Bobbio, Norberto 96 n.29

body 20, 30–1, 60, 64–5, 82, 88, 94–5, 100, 111, 114, 127, 136–47, 149, 154–6, 159, 163–6, 168–9, 174
Body without Organs 144–5, 147, 155
Bonaparte, Louis-Napoléon 122
bonded labour 152–3, 156
Bourdieu, Pierre 135 n.2
bourgeoisie 4 n.4, 122–3
Bove, Laurent 108 n.61
Branson, Noreen 13 n.7
Britain 1, 3, 5, 12–13, 31, 37, 63–5, 85, 113, 130, 137
Brooke, Stephen 51 n.2, 52
Brophy, Sarah 65
Brouillette, Sarah 136
Butler, Judith 135
Butler Education Act 124

camp 115, 117, 148
capital 3, 6–9, 14, 17–25, 27–32, 36–47, 49–56, 62–3, 65, 67, 69–70, 72–6, 78–82, 85, 87, 94, 96–7, 99–105, 108–10, 112–13, 120–1, 123–4, 126, 128–9, 133, 141, 152, 160, 171–7
  fixed capital 21, 24, 52, 99
  socialized capital 173
  variable capital 27, 32
capitalism 1–7, 9, 11, 13, 17, 20–1, 27, 29, 35, 49–50, 57, 62, 65, 68, 78, 85, 90, 92, 96, 99–100, 103, 109–10, 122, 125–6, 131–2, 134–5, 141, 147–8, 150–2, 171–2, 175–6
  industrial capitalism 78, 148, 175
  late capitalism 78, 85, 96, 99–100, 103, 109
  postmodern capitalism 92, 110, 126
catastrophe 82, 84 *see also* fatal strategy
civil society 32, 87, 89, 91, 93, 95–7, 99, 101, 103, 105, 107, 109–11, 113–19, 121, 123, 125, 127, 129, 131
class consciousness 33, 75

class struggle 6, 9, 13, 15, 18, 25, 72, 99, 101, 161
Cleaver, Harry 23 n.30, 38 n.66, 54 n.7
clinamen 127–8
command 6, 14, 21–2, 24, 30–2, 42–3, 45, 51, 53, 54 n.7, 92, 100 n.44, 103–5, 154
commodification 38
commodity 2, 18, 38, 41, 58, 92
common 1 n.1, 71, 74, 79, 128, 145
Communism 15
community 5 n.5, 13, 37 n.63, 65 n.38, 71–3, 83, 98, 127, 129, 131, 132 n.120, 148–50
conatus 108
conduct 55–6, 58
constituent power 100 n.44, 107
constituted power 100 n.44, 107, 109, 130
consumerism 8, 12 n.4, 45
control 13, 17, 19, 21–2, 26 n.40, 64, 67, 69, 85, 88, 92, 96–103, 105–7, 109–10, 114, 122, 126, 128–9, 131–2, 135–6, 153, 156, 159, 161, 166–7, 171, 176
  science as 128
  society of control 97, 110
Craig, Cairns 88, 98
creative work 136
crisis 5 n.5, 7, 9, 26, 29 n.46, 41, 50, 65, 69–70, 76–7, 84–5, 88, 92, 95, 97, 105, 133, 135, 137, 139, 141, 143, 145, 147, 149–51, 153, 155, 157, 159–61, 163, 165, 167, 169, 174, 177
Croft, Andy 5 n.5
Crosland, Anthony 11–12
culture 1 n.1, 5, 12–13, 16, 108 n.63, 112, 115, 121 n.92, 157–9

Dalla Costa, Mariarosa 49 n.1, 77 n.64
Day, Gary 1 n.1
dead labour 18, 25, 37, 39, 49
death 45–6, 70, 74–6, 78–9, 82, 84, 92 nn.16, 19, 107, 114–15, 119–20, 127, 136–9, 145–6, 152–4
debt 152, 166–9
del Valle Alcalá, Roberto 5 n.5
Deleuze, Gilles 83–4, 96–7, 107–10, 112, 117, 125–6, 140–1, 144–6, 153–4
Denning, Michael 123 n.98
Derrida, Jacques 169

desire 8, 49, 51–2, 54–5, 58–60, 63, 76, 93, 98, 131, 142–7, 154, 174
deterritorialization 83, 107, 148
dialectic 5–6, 14, 23, 30, 35, 55, 62, 68, 99, 117
difference 24, 32–5, 42, 50, 78–9, 89, 123, 149–50, 169,176
discipline 31–2, 50, 53–4, 58, 62, 64, 79, 96–9, 114, 123–4, 140, 160, 173

economics 112, 167
ecstasy 82–3, 85, 125–8, 131, 175–6
embourgeoisement 12, 18
employment 8, 20, 37, 66, 77, 121–2, 124, 156
empowerment 8, 57, 68, 73, 101, 105 118
entrepreneur 134, 136, 139, 153
entrepreneur of the self 134, 139, 153
event 61, 68, 75, 79, 81–2, 84–5, 104, 113, 136–7, 139, 152
excess 63, 81, 94, 131, 134, 138, 148, 154, 158, 161 n.57, 176
Existentialism 15
exodus 7, 81, 87, 99–103, 105, 108–12, 120, 124, 126, 129, 131 *see also* flight
experience 1, 3–4, 8–9, 12, 15, 22, 42, 49, 58, 65, 69, 73, 75, 82, 88–91, 94–7, 103, 121, 136, 145, 152–5, 159, 161, 174
exploitation 1, 3–6, 9, 14, 17–19, 21, 27 n.40, 31–2, 36–7, 41–2, 44, 49–50, 53, 55, 57–9, 61, 67–9, 71, 73–6, 78–85, 87, 93–4, 97, 104, 120, 126, 173
expropriation 44, 67–9, 71, 73, 78, 87, 103
exteriority 36, 103–4, 108–9, 117, 154, 158, 166, 168, 171–3 *see also* outside (the)
extraction 31, 50, 53, 62–3, 69, 81, 114, 172
Eyers, Tom 137 n.5

factory 6–9, 14, 17–32, 35–9, 41–6, 49–53, 55, 57–8, 62, 64–7, 75, 77–80, 83, 87, 96, 99, 172–4 *see also* social factory
fatal strategy 82–4
Federici, Silvia 27 n.40, 49 n.1, 69 nn.45, 47, 72
feminism 27 n.40, 49, 65, 72
finance 70, 102, 150–1, 166–8

flexibility 134, 136–7, 150 n.37, 152, 156, 163, 176
flight 7, 58, 88, 90, 99, 100 n.44, 103, 108, 112, 117, 119, 124, 149, 158, 164, 174 *see also* line of flight *and* exodus
Fordham, John 4 n.4
Fordism 7–8, 30 n.47, 64, 78, 87, 99, 133–4, 147, 149, 151–2, 156, 159–60, 162, 172, 175
form of life 3, 85, 120–1, 128, 141, 152, 157, 169, 176
'form-of-life' 130–1
Fortunati, Leopoldina 49 n.1, 65, 76, 80 n.73
Foucault, Michel 55, 56, 59, 62–3, 157–9, 161–2, 164, 169
free indirect style 93
freedom 54–6, 58–61, 71, 78–80, 125

gaze 51–2
Gemeinschaft 148
General Intellect 96, 99–100
Gothic 80–1
Gramsci, Antonio 96 n.29, 110
Guattari, Félix 97 n.32, 107 nn.58, 59, 108–10, 117, 125, 126 n.104, 140, 141 n.11, 144–7, 150 n.37, 153 n.44, 154

Hardt, Michael 55 n.12, 65 n.37, 75, 79 n.69, 96–7, 100 n.44, 101 n.47, 105 n.52, 110, 116 n.80, 127 n.106, 136 n.3
Haywood, Ian 1 n.1
Head, Dominic 59 n.25
Heath, Edward 64, 114
Hegel, G.W.F. 5, 62, 113
hegemony 96 n.29, 110
heterogeneity 108, 123, 152, 154–5
Hill, Jeffrey 37 n. 63
history 3–4, 12, 75, 113 n.75, 136, 146
Hitchcock, Peter 14, 21
Hoggart, Richard 12 n.4, 19 n.16, 89
housework 27 n.40, 49 n.1, 66, 69, 78–80
Hutchings, William 15 n.10, 32 n.51, 37–8

identity 3, 12, 123 nn.96, 97, 125–7, 129–30, 132 n.120, 153–4
ideological state apparatus 96

ideology 2, 25, 64, 93, 161, 166
immanence 5–6, 10, 23, 61, 83–4, 104, 112–13, 138–40, 143–6, 149, 160–1, 173, 176
immeasurability 40, 81–2, 84, 90, 92–5, 97, 99–100, 103, 105–6, 109, 111
imperceptibility 125, 146, 155
impotence 70–1, 98, 118
impotentiality 7
individuality 16 n.12, 19, 54 n.9, 91, 126 n.104, 127–9
inoperativeness 10, 120, 125–7, 129–31, 134, 139, 140, 161–2, 168, 176 *see also* worklessness
institution 30, 32, 97, 107, 128, 173
institutionality 15, 96, 110–11, 113, 115, 118, 120–1, 124–5, 175
intensification 7, 63–4, 152, 175
intensity 58, 60, 64, 68, 125, 127, 145, 154
irony 98, 161

James, Selma 49 n.1, 77 n.64
Johnson, Matthew 135 n.2

Kelly, Aaron 93
Keynesianism 14, 175
Kirk, John 1 n.1, 16 n.12, 92
Knight, Stephen 1 n.1, 21 n.23
Kővesi, Simon 88
Kristeva, Julia 78 *see also* abjection

labour movement 117
Labour Party 150
labour power 2, 4, 23, 28, 38–9, 42, 46, 54, 56, 63, 65, 67, 72, 76, 79, 134
Lacan, Jacques 137, 145 n.24
language 67, 83, 96, 99, 104–7, 158–9, 161 n.57, 162–6, 168–9
langue 158
law of value 41, 80–1, 91, 95
Lazzarato, Maurizio 138 n.7, 151, 152 n.40, 153 n.44, 166
line of flight 7, 63, 87, 109, 110 n.67, 112, 143, 155–6 *see also* flight
literary history 4
living labour 18, 21, 24–5, 32–3, 36–9, 42–4, 50, 53, 59, 62, 67, 70, 99–100, 173
Lockwood, David 12

Lorey, Isabell 135 n.2
Lotringer, Sylvère 18 n.15, 150 n.37
Lumpenproletariat 122–3

McCann, Andrew 80
machine 18, 20–4, 32, 51–2, 62–3, 96 n.27, 99, 103, 108–9, 126, 150, 152 n.40, 173–5
madness 9, 74, 134, 154, 157–9, 161–2, 164 n.62, 166–9, 171
management 11, 18, 27 n.40, 55, 94, 141
managerialism 20, 32, 138–41
Marazzi, Christian 18 n.15, 96 n.27, 150 n. 37
marginality 9, 30–2, 111, 119, 120, 122–3, 176
Marx, Karl 17, 21, 23–5, 29, 36–7, 41–2, 45, 54, 62, 96 n.27, 122–3
Marxism 1–3, 5, 17, 21 29, 38, 49, 96, 112, 122, 123, 135, 164, 171
masculinity 37 n.63, 38, 148
massification (of labour) 29, 50, 52–4, 87
Massumi, Brian 97 n.32, 138 n.7, 146 n.27
measure 22–4, 34, 39–41, 45, 72, 79, 81–2, 88–90, 92, 94, 97, 104, 114, 166, 171–3, 175
 measure of value 81, 92
memory 146, 149, 158, 166–7
minor literature 107 n.59
modernism 1, 4, 23, 93, 162
modernity 2 n.2, 4, 6, 15, 32, 53, 59, 88, 96–7, 99, 100, 106, 110, 113, 115, 129 n.114, 136, 158, 161
molar 145, 150, 153 n.44
molecular 51, 109, 124–5, 145, 150–1, 153 n.44, 155–6
monetarism 91
money 8–9, 16, 32, 36–8, 40–6, 50–1, 53, 61, 70, 80–1, 91–2, 95, 139, 151, 160, 162, 173
monster 81, 83, 164 n.62

Nancy, Jean-Luc 127
nation 12, 125–6
negativity 7, 129, 131, 161
Negri, Antonio 3, 22–3, 25, 29, 35, 36, 41–2, 45, 53 n.7, 54–6, 62, 65, 71, 73, 75, 79, 81, 87, 90–2, 94, 96, 97, 100–1, 105 n.52, 110, 113, 116, 136 n.3

neoliberalism 9, 64, 85, 96, 113, 115, 121–2, 126, 128, 130, 133–9,141, 147, 149–53, 155–7, 159–63, 166–7, 176
nomad 108–11, 113, 117
nomadism 109–12

objectification 21, 42, 62
oeuvre 157, 159, 162–5, 167
ontology 3, 5–7, 24, 33, 58, 71, 85, 87, 92, 98, 104, 106–7, 109, 118, 120–1, 124–6, 129–31, 133–5, 138–9, 141–2, 149, 150–1, 153, 155, 171
Operaismo 21, 29, 49 *see also* Autonomist Marxism *and* Workerism
operativeness 130–1, 158 *see also* inoperativeness
organism 144, 147
Orwell, George 89
otherness 33, 79, 81, 84, 109, 137–8
outside (the) 75, 117, 128–9, 154, 157, 159, 162, 165 n.64, 169, 171–2, 176–7

plane of organization 125, 140
Platt, Jennifer 12 n.3
police 32, 79, 98, 100, 102–6, 108, 112–17, 119, 174
police State 105 n.52, 112
post-Fordism 133, 159–60
post-Fordist 99, 133–4, 149, 160, 162
postmodernity 4, 6–7, 50, 67, 81, 85, 88–9, 91–6, 98–106, 108–13, 117, 120, 124,126, 128, 137–8, 174–6
potentia 73, 100 n.44, 107, 120
potentiality 7, 99, 129–31
potestas 100 n.44
poverty 16, 55, 70, 122
power 2, 5, 8, 11–12, 16, 20, 21 n.24, 22–3, 27, 33, 35–7, 40, 42, 44–5, 47, 54–63, 68, 71, 74–5, 94, 96–102, 106–10, 112–17, 120–1, 128–34, 143, 153, 156–7, 159, 161 n.57, 167–9, 171, 174–6 *see also* constituent power, constituted power *and* empowerment
precariousness 24, 71, 77, 122, 128, 133–6, 138–9, 140, 142–3, 144, 146–50, 152–4, 156–9, 169, 171–2, 177
precarity 135–6, 138–9, 142, 149, 152–3, 157, 159, 171

primitive accumulation 67
profit 25, 28
proletarian autonomy 6, 64
proletariat 4 n.5, 19, 62, 123, 126, 135
prostitution 49, 61, 67, 76–80, 83
psychoanalysis 137
public sphere 99–101, 103, 110, 174–5

race 35
racism 56, 148
rape 59, 67–9, 81, 84
Realism 4–5
reformism 15, 17–18
refusal 9, 14, 16–19, 23, 28–30, 35, 47, 63, 72–4, 78, 83–4, 93–4, 100–2, 109, 119–22, 124, 126, 129, 134, 159, 162–3, 169, 171, 174, 176
reproduction 9, 18, 26–31, 37, 44–5, 49, 63, 65–6, 70, 72–4, 76–8, 81, 84, 90, 96, 99, 154, 167, 173
Revel, Judith 62 n.33
revisionism 20
revolution 3–5, 9–10, 13, 15, 22, 27, 29, 72, 96 n.29, 99, 110 n.67

sabotage 35, 123
Sawkins, John 21 n.23
Schmitt, Carl 106 n.56, 114–15, 138 n.8
Scotland 125
security 57–8, 61, 71, 105, 150
serial killer 81
sex 45, 67–9, 76, 79–80, 82, 123–4, 142–3
sexual violence 74–5, 136
sexuality 49, 59–60, 62–3, 67–9, 80–1
Sharma, Sarah 141 n.14
Shiach, Morag 1 n.1
Sinclair, Upton 77
Sinfield, Alan 1 n.1
singularity 16, 83–5, 126–9, 132 n.120, 175
slowness 141
Smith, Jason 112 n.73
smooth 96–7, 99, 111, 117, 120–1, 124, 133, 138–9, 141, 148, 152, 166
Snee, Carole 5 n.5
social factory 30, 35, 77 n.64
socialism 11–13, 15
sovereignty 106, 109, 113–15, 117, 121, 128, 130, 138, 171, 175–6
speech 34, 52, 106–7, 158–9, 163–4, 168–9

Spinoza, Baruch 73, 100 n.44, 108 n.61
sport 36–8, 41–2, 46
Standing, Guy 135 n.2
State (the) 9, 11–12, 30–2, 35–6, 51, 69, 96–8, 100–6, 108–10, 113–18, 128, 132, 152, 174–5
state of exception 75, 80 n.74, 114–15, 138
stream of consciousness 89, 93
striated 96–7, 111, 141
strike 72, 94 n.23, 112–14
subalternity 68, 70–2, 75, 76, 80–2, 97, 120–1
subjective undoing 134, 137, 146
subjectivity 6–9, 11, 18–19, 21–3, 27, 31, 33, 35–6, 43–7, 49–54, 56, 58, 60, 62–3, 65, 71, 73–4, 84, 87, 92–3, 107, 110 n.67, 118, 127, 133, 135–6, 139–40, 143, 145, 149, 152–4, 160, 163, 166–7, 169, 171, 173–4, 176
subsumption 11, 13, 15, 17–19, 21, 23–5, 27–31, 33, 35–7, 39, 41, 43, 45–7, 49–50, 60–2, 65, 67, 69–70, 74, 87, 90, 92, 94, 96–7, 99–100, 102–5, 108–9, 112, 117, 128, 131–3, 171, 173–6
  formal subsumption 17
  real subsumption 17, 37, 46, 49–50, 87, 92, 94, 97, 99–100, 104, 108–9, 132, 175
subversion 5, 9, 25, 49, 76–7, 79, 109, 124, 140, 158
suffering 4 n.4, 42, 71–2, 74, 76, 92, 118, 163, 174
suicide 74–5, 161

Taylor, Andrew 113 n.75
Taylorism 30 n.47, 78
teleology 5, 33, 47, 76
temporality 7, 18, 22, 40–1, 45, 62, 65, 85, 87–90, 93, 95, 104, 107 n. 58, 118, 141, 160, 172–4
Thatcher, Margaret 64
Thatcherism 87, 113, 130
Thoburn, Nicholas 122 n.94, 123 n.96
time *see* temporality
Tiratsoo, Nick 63–4
totality 5, 21 n.24, 33, 112, 146–7
trade unions 63–4, 113, 117–18
transcendence 5, 60, 83, 126, 145–6, 173, 177

transgression 80, 153, 158–9, 164
trauma 7, 9, 68, 73, 75, 137–8 146, 148, 152, 154, 156, 159
Tronti, Mario 3, 17, 18 n.15, 27–9, 31, 36

uncanny 80, 137
unemployment 4, 69,103, 121, 122, 124

valorization 7–8, 16–18, 25, 27–8, 30–1, 35–8, 40, 46–7, 49, 53, 56, 64–5, 67, 70, 72, 75, 81, 87, 94, 103–4, 126, 133, 171, 174–5
value 2, 9, 24–5, 27–8, 31, 35, 40–1, 43, 45–6, 50, 53, 62–3, 67, 72, 74, 76, 80–5, 87, 91–3, 95, 97, 101, 104, 126, 153, 164, 168–9, 172, 176
  exchange value 24, 41, 46
  surplus value 27–8, 31
victim 57, 68, 72–3, 75 165
Virno, Paolo 96 n.27, 99, 103
virtuosity 99–100
vulnerability 18–19, 25, 54, 57, 63, 67, 69, 74, 85, 94, 118, 120, 124, 130, 135, 138, 140, 142, 152, 171, 177

wage 2, 23–5, 27–31, 35–6, 38–45, 54, 64–5, 67, 69–72, 76, 78–9, 81, 100, 123–4, 156
war machine 108–9
Waterman, David 68–9
Weeks, Kathi 49 n.1
Welfare State 14, 124
Westergaard, John 12 n.2
Williams, Raymond 1, 12–13, 64, 121
women 8, 26–7, 39, 44, 49–54, 57, 63, 65–7, 69–75, 77, 79, 83, 150
Workerism 17, 21 n.24 *see also* Operaismo *and* Autonomist Marxism
working class 1, 4, 7, 11, 17–18, 28–9, 64, 100, 112–13, 118–19, 121, 124–5, 128, 171, 173
working-class literature 1 n.1, 4 n.4, 5
worklessness 121, 126, 129, 176 *see also* inoperativeness
Worpole, Ken 4 n.4
Wright, Steven 17 n.13

zone of indistinction 117, 127, 146